Tablet PCs For Dum

Common Speech Commands

Command	Result
All caps <phrase>	Changes specified phrase to all caps
All caps that	Changes selected phrase to all caps
Backspace	Inserts backspace
Clip Art	Opens Insert Clip Art task pane
Copy that	Copies selected item
Correct <word or phrase>	Opens up smart tag for specified word with alternatives for correction
Delete <phrase>	Deletes spoken word or phrase
Enter	Moves insertion point to next line
Go to bottom	Moves insertion point to bottom of document
Go to top	Moves insertion point to top of document
Launch <application>	Opens the specified application
New line	Moves insertion point to next line
New paragraph	Creates new paragraph
Open Input Panel	Opens Input Panel
Page down	Moves down one half page in document
Paste that	Pastes current clipboard item
Select <phrase>	Selects specified word or phrase
Sent text	Sends text entered in Input Panel Writing Pad to a document
Spell it	Starts Spelling feature
Switch to <application>	Switches to another specified open application
Tab	Tabs insertion point to next tab stop
Undo that	Undoes most recent action

Tablet PC Functions

Function	How to Do It
Calibrate pen	Control Panel⇨Tablet and Pen Settings, click Calibrate
Display Input Panel	Click Tablet PC Input Panel button in Windows system tray
Turn on Speech	In Input Panel choose Tools⇨Speech
Customize tablet buttons	Control Panel⇨Tablet and Pen Settings, Tablet Buttons tab
Train Speech	In Input Panel choose Speech Tools⇨Voice Training
Set up microphone	In Input Panel choose Speech Tools⇨Microphone Adjustment
Dock/undock Input Panel	In Input Panel choose Tools⇨Dock or Undock

For Dummies: Bestselling Book Series for Beginners

Tablet PCs For Dummies®

Cheat Sheet

Tablet Computing Web Sites

URL	Description
www.infocater.com	Distributor of Tablet PCs that offers a Tablet PC newsletter and links
www.tabletnews.com	News about Tablet PC and links to manufacturer sites
www.tabletpctalk.com	Pictures, links, FAQs, and news about Tablet PC
www.microsoft.com/tabletpc	Windows XP for Tablet PC home page
www.microsoft.com/windowsxp/ tabletpc/downloads/powertoys.asp	PowerToys download page
www.tabletpcbuzz.com	Discussion areas, FAQs, and Tablet PC hardware comparison
www.pencomputing.com	*Pen Computing* magazine featuring reviews and hardware comparisons
www.franklincovey.com	Web site for Franklin Covey Tablet Planner software
www.corel.com	Web site for Corel Grafigo, Tablet PC graphics software
www.zinio.com/tabletpc.html	Download electronic magazines to read on Tablet PC
www.webex.com	Web site for WebEx Mobile Meetings online meeting software

Note: In the following table, dots on lines indicate the starting point for drawing the line.

Tablet PC Gestures

Gesture	Result	Example
Hover pen over screen and wave back and forth rapidly	Starts Input Panel	N/A
Rub pen back and forth over screen	Scratches out handwriting	N/A
Line from right to left	Inserts Backspace	
Line from left to right	Inserts Space	
Short line down and long line going to the left	Enter	
Short line up and long line going to the right	Insert Tab	

Tablet PC Mouse Action Equivalents

Mouse Action	Pen Action
Click	Tap
Double-click	Double-tap
Right-click	Press and hold
Click and drag	Tap and drag

For Dummies: Bestselling Book Series for Beginners

Tablet PCs

FOR

DUMMIES®

by Nancy Stevenson

WILEY

Wiley Publishing, Inc.

Tablet PCs For Dummies®
Published by
Wiley Publishing, Inc.
909 Third Avenue
New York, NY 10022
www.wiley.com

Copyright © 2003 by Wiley Publishing, Inc., Indianapolis, Indiana

Published by Wiley Publishing, Inc., Indianapolis, Indiana

Published simultaneously in Canada

No part of this publication may be reproduced, stored in a retrieval system or transmitted in any form or by any means, electronic, mechanical, photocopying, recording, scanning or otherwise, except as permitted under Sections 107 or 108 of the 1976 United States Copyright Act, without either the prior written permission of the Publisher, or authorization through payment of the appropriate per-copy fee to the Copyright Clearance Center, 222 Rosewood Drive, Danvers, MA 01923, (978) 750-8400, fax (978) 646-8700. Requests to the Publisher for permission should be addressed to the Legal Department, Wiley Publishing, Inc., 10475 Crosspoint Blvd., Indianapolis, IN 46256, (317) 572-3447, fax (317) 572-4447, e-mail: permcoordinator@ wiley.com.

Trademarks: Wiley, the Wiley Publishing logo, For Dummies, the Dummies Man logo, A Reference for the Rest of Us!, The Dummies Way, Dummies Daily, The Fun and Easy Way, Dummies.com and related trade dress are trademarks or registered trademarks of Wiley Publishing, Inc., in the United States and other countries, and may not be used without written permission. All other trademarks are the property of their respective owners. Wiley Publishing, Inc., is not associated with any product or vendor mentioned in this book.

LIMIT OF LIABILITY/DISCLAIMER OF WARRANTY: WHILE THE PUBLISHER AND AUTHOR HAVE USED THEIR BEST EFFORTS IN PREPARING THIS BOOK, THEY MAKE NO REPRESENTATIONS OR WARRANTIES WITH RESPECT TO THE ACCURACY OR COMPLETENESS OF THE CONTENTS OF THIS BOOK AND SPECIFICALLY DISCLAIM ANY IMPLIED WARRANTIES OF MERCHANTABILITY OR FITNESS FOR A PARTICULAR PURPOSE. NO WARRANTY MAY BE CREATED OR EXTENDED BY SALES REPRESENTATIVES OR WRITTEN SALES MATERIALS. THE ADVICE AND STRATEGIES CONTAINED HEREIN MAY NOT BE SUITABLE FOR YOUR SITUATION. YOU SHOULD CONSULT WITH A PROFESSIONAL WHERE APPROPRIATE. NEITHER THE PUBLISHER NOR AUTHOR SHALL BE LIABLE FOR ANY LOSS OF PROFIT OR ANY OTHER COMMERCIAL DAMAGES, INCLUDING BUT NOT LIMITED TO SPECIAL, INCIDENTAL, CONSEQUENTIAL, OR OTHER DAMAGES.

For general information on our other products and services or to obtain technical support, please contact our Customer Care Department within the U.S. at 800-762-2974, outside the U.S. at 317-572-3993, or fax 317-572-4002.

Wiley also publishes its books in a variety of electronic formats. Some content that appears in print may not be available in electronic books.

Library of Congress Control Number: 2003101834

ISBN: 0-7645-2647-2

Manufactured in the United States of America

10 9 8 7 6 5 4 3 2 1

1B/RS/QT/QT/IN

WILEY   is a trademark of Wiley Publishing, Inc.

About the Author

Nancy Stevenson is the author of over 30 business and technology books on topics ranging from project management to e-commerce, distance learning to hardware, and software products. She has been quoted on technology topics in publications such *US News and World Report* and *Modern Maturity,* and has appeared on the television show "The Computer Chronicles." Nancy makes her home in Washington state, where she runs a yearly playwriting festival and writes novels in her spare time.

Dedication

To world peace. Seriously.

Acknowledgments

I'd like to thank Greg Croy, a seasoned acquisitions editor, for giving me the chance to write this book; Nicole Haims for managing the process and providing valuable editorial feedback; and Susan Stenger-Meyer for her able technical review. And, as always, to all the folks at Wiley who make working with their organization a real pleasure.

Thanks to Geoff Palmer of Infocater (www.infocater.com) for hooking me into the Tablet PC manufacturing community. And special thanks to Debbie Crosek of Motion Computing, Jay Buckner of Acer America, Trevor Bratton and Dan Coffman at Viewsonic, Mike Beirne and Megan O'Neil of Fujitsu PC Corporation, and Angela Griffo of The Benjamin Group/Toshiba for providing me with evaluation models and product photos for use in this book. Finally, thanks to Courtney Brigham at Pen&Internet for providing information about its very neat software, RiteMail.

Publisher's Acknowledgments

We're proud of this book; please send us your comments through our online registration form located at www.dummies.com/register/.

Some of the people who helped bring this book to market include the following:

Acquisitions, Editorial, and Media Development

Senior Project Editor: Nicole Haims

Acquisitions Editor: Greg Croy

Senior Copy Editor: Barry Childs-Helton

Technical Editor: Susan Stenger-Meyer

Editorial Manager: Leah Cameron

Senior Permissions Editor: Carmen Krikorian

Media Development Manager: Laura VanWinkle

Media Development Supervisor: Richard Graves

Editorial Assistant: Amanda Foxworth

Cartoons: Rich Tennant (www.the5thwave.com)

Production

Project Coordinator: Nancee Reeves

Layout and Graphics: Michael Kruzil, Jacque Schneider, Jeremey Unger, Mary Virgin

Proofreaders: Laura Albert, John Greenough, TECHBOOKS Production Services,

Indexer: TECHBOOKS Production Services

Special Help: Rebekah Mancilla

Publishing and Editorial for Technology Dummies

Richard Swadley, Vice President and Executive Group Publisher

Andy Cummings, Vice President and Publisher

Mary C. Corder, Editorial Director

Publishing for Consumer Dummies

Diane Graves Steele, Vice President and Publisher

Joyce Pepple, Acquisitions Director

Composition Services

Gerry Fahey, Vice President of Production Services

Debbie Stailey, Director of Composition Services

Contents at a Glance

Table of Contents

Introduction

*T*ablet PC is a revolution in computing that represents the way people and computers will come together in the future — or a big yawn, depending on who you talk to. The promise of pen computing has been around for a long while, and many computer pundits (you know, those folks who write those self-important columns for geek magazines) are not impressed by yet another effort.

But blasé pundits aside, Tablet PC *is* a leap forward for the way people compute. It combines several ways to interact with data — through handwriting, voice, or keyboard. Its portable design makes it ideal for workers on the job — from census takers to nurses, insurance inspectors to shipping agents.

And (let's not forget the important stuff) it's cool.

About This Book

Obviously, I'm in the camp of people who think Tablet PC has a role to play in the future of computing — and I think you're going to love your Tablet PC. But I didn't write this book to gloss over its shortcomings. It's a brand new computing device, and like any brand new machine, it has its glitches. So my first goal in writing this book was to give you an honest picture of the strengths and weaknesses of your Tablet PC and provide tips on how to be the most productive with all its features.

My second goal was to not make this a PCs for Dummies book. You know how to use a PC — I assume that you want to read about what's unique to using a Tablet PC. So I focused on what's different and special, while pointing out where you can just fall back on the standard Windows knowledge you already have.

Computer Savvy, 1 Presume?

Frankly, not just any computer novice is likely to run out and spend something like $2,200 on a brand new type of computer, so I've made some assumptions about you. I assume you are computer literate — that is, you have made the acquaintance of one or two mice (mouses?) in your life, and know that Windows isn't something you use a squeegee on. You know your way around a keyboard and have probably worked with a handful of computer software programs in your time. You may not be an expert, but you're no novice, either.

I figure you have worked with a version of Windows at least as recent as Windows 2000, but possibly you've already worked with Windows XP. Because Windows XP for Tablet PC is a close cousin of Windows XP, you should be fairly at home in the Tablet PC environment. I'm also guessing you use the Internet and understand the basics of browsing and e-mail, so I don't have to waste your time with a table of emoticons.

Was I right?

Conventions Used in This Book

I want to get a few more ground rules out of the way so you can get going with your Tablet PC.

First off, Tablet PC technology is still new, and I suspect that its lingo hasn't quite gelled yet. You may see the terms *click* and *right-click* for performing actions with a pen that emulate mouse operations — even though what you're really doing is tapping or double-tapping with the pen.

Web site addresses, also known as URLs, are highlighted by setting them in a special computer font, which looks like this:

```
www.microsoft.com
```

Menu commands are shown with arrows that lead from one to the next in the order that you choose them, for example, "Choose View➪Toolbars➪Reviewing."

Options in dialog boxes use initial caps, even though they are lowercase on your screen. The idea is to make the names of the fields that appear in dialog boxes easier to identify if you're scanning the book. (For example, the field named "Provide feedback with sound" in a dialog box will appear as "Provide Feedback with Sound" in this book.)

Oh, one more thing. Some Tablet PCs come with keyboards, and some don't. But all Tablet PCs have an Input Panel that simulates a keyboard. When I use the word Keyboard, I'm talking about the electronic simulation of a computer or laptop keyboard.

Icons Used in This Book

In case you wonder what those icons to the left of the text are for, here's a rundown:

When you see this icon, it's pointing out a handy bit of information you're likely to need later on, or something to keep in mind while you're following a particular instruction.

When you see this icon, watch out — there's a shark lurking around in the water. Okay, not literally. But you get my point, don't you? You'd be advised to take a look at the information here, lest you end up having a Really Bad Day instead of enjoying your Tablet PC computing experience.

This icon gives you a peek behind the glamorous exterior of your Tablet PC, to see why it does what it does. (Those of you who prefer to think of computers as the equivalent of Aladdin's lamp — "I give it input, I get output, who cares what happens in-between?" — can skip ahead.)

This icon calls your attention to handy shortcuts, practical advice, and nuggets of wisdom to enhance your Tablet PC experience.

How the Book Is Organized

Understanding something new often depends on how logically it's presented to you so your brain can grab it and run with it. For that reason (and because my editor told me to) I've organized this book into Parts.

Part 1: Getting Up to Speed with Tablet PC

In this section, you meet the hero of this book — Tablet PC — find out about the various models available, turn the computer on, put pen to screen for the first time, and learn how to take advantage of built-in help and tutorials. You check out the features of your device, rotating the Tablet PC screen and figuring out what the buttons are likely to control (depending on the model you own). Finally, this section helps you get your Tablet PC connected to handy things like a printer, wireless network, or docking station — while imparting sage advice about power management so your portable wonder won't run out of juice far from an outlet.

Part II: Tablet PC Basics

Part II is where you discover the intricacies of getting content into software documents with Tablet PC's various input modes: the onscreen keyboard, the pen, and speech. These ways of communicating with your computer are perhaps the most revolutionary thing about Tablet PC and, as you'll find out in this part, practice with them makes (almost) perfect.

Part III: Exploring Tablet PC's Unique Apps

Tablet PCs get their functionality from Windows XP for Tablet PC. Besides the pen and speech functionality you read about in Part II, the Tablet PC operating system has a few unique programs built in that aren't in plain old Windows XP. This Part takes the time to introduce you to them: Windows Journal, Sticky Notes, and InkBall. I also throw in some information about Microsoft Reader for reading eBooks (which has been around for a while, but is just so perfect an application for a Tablet PC user, I couldn't resist).

Part IV: Office XP, Tablet PC Style

Right out of the gate, Tablet PC has been set up to work with Microsoft Office XP (through a Tablet PC Office Pack you can download for free). The interaction is pretty much limited to the use of ink and speech through the Tablet PC Input Panel (more about that later) — but that's an impressive start. This part shows how you can take advantage of Tablet PC's features in Word, Excel, PowerPoint, and Outlook.

Part V: The Part of Tens

Quick . . . list ten things you can write on with a pen . . .

Because everybody from talk show hosts to your Aunt Maisie makes lists, and those lists often contain ten items, why shouldn't I? This part of the book introduces several lists-by-ten — ten neat things you can do with Tablet PC just for the fun of it, ten software products that take advantage of the Tablet PC computing environment, and ten interesting ways that various industries are making use of tablet computing.

Part I

Getting Up to Speed with Tablet PC

The 5th Wave   By Rich Tennant

"OK — ANTIDOTE, ANTIDOTE, WHAT WOULD AN ANTIDOTE ICON LOOK LIKE? YOU KNOW, I STILL HAVEN'T GOT THIS DESKTOP THE WAY I WANT IT."

In this part . . .

If you're old enough, you remember when the world switched from rotary phones to touch tone, from records to CDs, or from board games to video games. Changes like this can prove to be revolutionary or just small steps on the technological highway. But whatever effect they have, they mean a shift in the way people do things.

Tablet PC is a shift in the way people use computers. In this part of the book, you'll be introduced to Tablet PC's hardware and input methods, including writing on your screen with a pen and speaking your commands or content into a built-in microphone. You'll take a look at Tablet PC's buttons and screen, learn about rotating the display to look at things from different angles, and connect your Tablet PC to peripheral devices, such as printers. You'll also explore some power management settings that will help you when you take Tablet PC out on the road.

Chapter 1

The World of Tablet PC

*T*ablet PC is a neat new style of portable computer that Microsoft has invested big bucks in helping to develop. It's lightweight, sleek, and offers an interesting variety of ways to input information that Microsoft is betting will appeal to you.

Now, we can't all come from royalty — and frankly, Tablet PC has a less-than-impressive family tree. In fact, Tablet PC comes from a long line of less-than-successful ancestors, including Apple's Newton, Go Corporation's Eo (I haven't a clue what that stands for), and Sony Vaio's Pen Tablet. These were all early entries in the world of *pen computing,* technology that enables you to write your input with a pen-like device instead of typing (as you would on most other computers).

Tablet PC adds voice-recognition capability to the pen technology. Twenty-odd manufacturers have brought out their versions in various portable, easy-to-hold designs that weigh around three pounds. But what really sets Tablet PC apart from its ancestors — and gives it a crack at finally making pen technology work — is its operating system. Tablet PC is driven by Microsoft Windows XP for Tablet PC — a full version of Windows on which you can run *any program written for Windows.*

Will this difference be enough to make Tablet PC the big success story its relatives aspired to be? Only time will tell, but I predict it will.

Introducing the Tablet-Style PC

Tablet-style PCs have been used by various businesses for several years now. You've probably seen them in action — perhaps being carried around a store by a clerk to update the inventory of canned peas in grocery stores — or you may have actually used one yourself when signing your signature electronically after you received a package from an overnight shipping company.

The main features of a tablet-style PC are that you can write your input, and it's portable (as the Motion M1200 Tablet PC demonstrates in Figure 1-1), so it works well for those who run from meeting to meeting, make the rounds in the plant, or spend most of the workday "in the field" in various industries.

Figure 1-1:
The Motion
M1200
Tablet PC
comes
with a
detachable
keyboard.

The Marriage of Windows XP and Tablet PC

Tablet PC in its current form (to which this book is devoted) came about when Microsoft partnered with manufacturers such as Toshiba, Fujitsu, Compaq, and Acer to produce *actual computer hardware* while Microsoft developed the operating system — Windows XP for Tablet PC. This program is actually a superset of Windows XP that can run any standard Windows program and adds pen and voice technology on top of that — a far cry from Windows CE (a version that ran cramped little no-frills programs on "palm-top" computers in the '90s). Make no mistake: Tablet PC is no handheld computer and it doesn't run on a pale imitation of an operating system. It's a very robust computer in a very convenient package.

Windows XP for Tablet PC has some surprises all its own:

- **Handwriting recognition:** The operating system includes what may be the most sophisticated handwriting-recognition technology yet devised.
- **Speech recognition:** It also has a speech-recognition program.

  Handwriting recognition lets you turn handwritten input into standard text with minimum hassle; you can even *speak* input and commands to your computer *and it does what you say.*

Being able to write handwritten notes into your computer, save them, and search them later is a seriously handy feature. Of course, it's a less than ideal way to input data for longer documents, so the Tablet PC hardware doesn't limit you to handwritten input. In fact, it offers you several options.

And what does the package that all these handwriting and speech features come in look like? All models sport an on-screen Keyboard that you can tap away at with your pen. Some models are designed like a laptop with a built-in keyboard that swivels and folds flat to convert the unit into a tablet-like format. Others offer a detachable keyboard.

Who Needs a Tablet PC?

Not sure whether you have a use for a Tablet PC — or how to get the most from it if you buy one? Well, take a moment to see how this style of computer fits most working lifestyles.

The Tablet PC is being promoted as the perfect tool for somebody called the *corridor warrior*. Cousin to the road warrior who travels frequently on business, the corridor warrior spends his or her time running from meeting to meeting, apparently with no life beyond the conference room. This creature has the following needs:

✔ To take quick notes on the run in hallways and elevators.

✔ To take more extended notes in meetings where tapping away on a keyboard might be annoying.

✔ To store (and even search) handwritten notes for gems of information, without having to convert all of his or her notes to type.

✔ To have a portable, lightweight computer that he or she can connect to peripherals or a docking station back at that old-fashioned desktop.

Tablet PC may or may not be your perfect solution if you're a road warrior — depending on the model, you may have to carry with you a detachable keyboard, external CD drive, and other peripherals that may prove more weighty in the end than a standard laptop. But some Tablet PC models are designed more like a laptop (some have a built-in keyboard), and all are wireless devices, allowing you to connect to the Internet through your cell phone (for example), something your laptop may not allow you to do. Tablet PCs are also more comfortable to work on when you have no work surface available. (Remember what fun it is to juggle a laptop on your knees and type while waiting to board your plane? Writing on a Tablet PC is much less of a juggling act.)

If you write a lot of lengthy documents, don't travel or leave your office much, or think the idea of writing on a computer screen is about as useful as being able to write on your cat, you might consider returning your Tablet PC and giving this book to a more mobile friend.

Choosing Your Tablet PC

Knowing that a Tablet PC is right for you is just the first step. Choosing one can be challenging because there are actually about 23 different models of Tablet PC, and each offers slightly different design and hardware features. If you've already bought your Tablet PC, skip this section. But if one of your reasons for buying this book is to figure out which Tablet PC to buy, read on . . .

All the models use the same operating system, so most activities covered in this book work exactly the same with whatever Tablet PC you buy.

Something to write home about?

The big debate about Tablet PC is whether people even want to enter information into a computer with a pen. Well, handwriting is easier than typing for some — and a convenient method of input in cramped spaces certainly has its appeal. Imagine writing happily away at 30,000 feet with your pad-like Tablet PC resting on your meal tray, avoiding the fool who slams his seat back into your knees without warning. Just imagine the disaster that would ensue with a clamshell-style laptop.

Of course, handwriting *is* harder to read than typed text — and handwriting-recognition programs still make mistakes, so converting your handwriting to text can be cumbersome. Still, consider the possibilities: Delivery people and

salespeople can capture actual signatures while visiting customers. Hospital staff can jot notes about treatments in settings where a keyboard would be difficult to come by. Market research can be done by having people in a shopping mall fill out any one of several versions of survey forms stored on a Tablet PC, and through wireless technology, the results can be sent to the home office in minutes, instead of taking weeks to compile paper forms.

The debate about the viability of handwritten input will probably continue until pen technology and handwriting-recognition software become user-friendly enough to end the uproar once and for all.

Slate versus convertible

The first choice to make is between a *slate* model, such as the ViewSonic Tablet PC (illustrated in Figure 1-2), which has no attached keyboard, and a *convertible* model, such as the Acer TravelMate C100, which sports the clamshell design of a traditional laptop — with a twist. The twist is that you can spin the monitor panel around and flatten it to turn the laptop-style unit into a tablet form.

Here are a few things to consider when choosing between convertible and slate models.

Slate models:

   ✔ **Pro — Detachable keyboard:** You can attach a keyboard to any slate model, so none of them is totally keyboardless. Some come with detachable keyboards; others offer this as an option.

   ✔ **Con — No protective cover:** Most slate units (the Motion M1200 Tablet PC is an exception) have no protective cover over their screens, as a convertible does when it's closed up. You can buy screen protectors, but if you treat your portable computer roughly, you may be better off with a convertible model.

Figure 1-2:
The
ViewSonic
model offers
a good-size
screen and
rubber
edging to
help you
grip the unit.

Convertible models:

- ✔ **Pro — Size:** Convertible model keyboards tend to be somewhat smaller than traditional laptop keyboards.

- ✔ **Con — Weight:** Convertible units can be a half-pound to a pound heavier than slate units.

- ✔ **Con (sometimes) — Price:** Convertible models tend to be a bit pricier than slate models (but not always and not by much — maybe $100 or so).

Deciding which model makes sense for you

There are six models offered by mainstream computer manufactures such as Compaq and Toshiba. The rest are made by either regional manufacturers (for example, Taiwanese Tantung's Tangy is pretty much available only in Asia) or manufacturers such as PaceBlade Technology (which sells its PaceBook Tablet PC mainly through value-added resellers).

If you want to buy several units for your business or want any kind of consulting about how to roll out your Tablet PCs into your workforce, a less-well-known manufacturer may offer you better value and support. Also, some distributors, such as InfoCater (www.infocater.com), provide consulting services to help you fit Tablet PC into your business needs.

In essence, about six models are available to you as an everyday consumer. Being a fan of handy tables, I've created Table 1-1 to help you make the Tablet PC choice from among these models. Try ranking your own computing priorities to make a choice from among these models. For example, is a lightweight model more important than speed? Or is price the most important thing to you?

Table 1-1		Tablet PC Models					
Model	*Price*	*Design*	*Memory*	*Processor*	*Hard Drive*	*Weight*	*Screen Size*
Acer Travel Mate C100	$2,200	Convertible	256MB	800 MHz	20GB	3.2 Pounds	10.4 inches
Compaq TC 1000	$1,700	Slate/ Convertible	256MB	1 GHz	30GB	3 Pounds	10.4 inches
Fujitsu Stylistic ST 4000	$2,200	Slate	256MB	800 MHz	20GB	3.2 Pounds	10.4 inches
Motion M1 2000	$2,200	Slate	128MB	866 MHz	20GB	3 Pounds	12.1 inches
Toshiba Portage	$2,300	Convertible	256MB	1.33 GHz	40GB	4.1 Pounds	12.1 inches
View Sonic V1100	$1,999	Slate	256 MB	866 MHz	20GB	3.4 Pounds	10.4 inches

One comparison

What do all these numbers and initials mean? Here's a quick-and-dirty rule that can help you understand which numbers are good. The better value would have higher numbers for processor speed, memory, hard drive capacity, and screen size, and lower numbers for weight and price.

Try comparing a couple of these models to determine which would offer the best value. The Toshiba Portege, which retails at $2,300, is a convertible model. It has 256MB of memory, a 1.33 GHz Pentium III processor, 40GB hard drive, 12.1-inch monitor, and it weighs 4.1 pounds. Compare that to the Fujitsu Stylistic ST4000, which is cheaper (at $2,200). This model is a slate with 256MB, a slower 800 MHz Pentium III, half the space on a 20GB hard drive, a smaller 10.4-inch screen, and a weight of 3.2 pounds. Bottom line: You may save $100 and one pound of weight, but you lose speed, memory, and screen size.

Making the Tablet PC choice for your business

If you've been put on the spot to recommend a Tablet PC purchase for your business, you may have different considerations than you would if you were buying one for yourself, so I'll take a moment to look at this choice from a business perspective.

First, you have to determine if the Tablet PC is going to replace another form of computer or be used in addition to a desktop or laptop computer. Replacing older computing devices may be perfectly cost effective, but if you find that your workers will need both their desktop computers and Tablet PCs, that can carry a pretty hefty price tag. Tablet PCs may replace laptops, but seldom replace desktops for those already using one.

If you want to provide portable computing for members of your workforce who don't currently use computers (such as inventory checkers in your warehouse), Tablet PCs may provide increases in speed and productivity that can help you justify their cost.

If you have a specialized use for Tablet PCs (beyond standard word processing or spreadsheets, for example), consider whether you'll also need to have proprietary software written for your business. A commercial application already written for your industry may do the trick.

Although any software that runs on Windows will run on Tablet PC, not all such software is designed to work with handwritten or spoken input — which might defeat the purpose of your purchase.

If you have workers who deal with product or packaging design, they may find that pen input is a useful addition to their existing computing capabilities. Programs such as Corel Grafigo (shown in Figure 1-3) make drawing on the screen a natural way to input line art into a computer.

Taking Tablet PC for a Spin

If you haven't already futzed around with your Tablet PC, now is the time to start playing with your newest high-tech toy. In the following sections, I take you through a quick tour to get your Tablet PC turned on, play a bit with the touch screen interface, and see how you can reorient your screen to make holding your Tablet PC comfortable for you.

Figure 1-3: Corel Grafigo offers artistic types a more natural input approach for drawing.

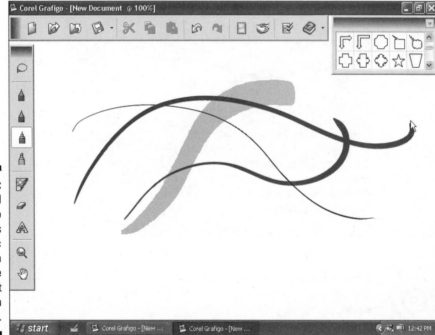

Turning it on

Different models put that all-important power switch in different places. For example, the Acer model has a slider button on its right edge — you push the slider forward to turn the power on. The ViewSonic model has a small button on its face. Your user manual shows you the exact configuration and location of your power button.

The first time you turn your Tablet PC on, make sure you have either charged its battery or plugged it into a power outlet. If your unit uses a docking station, then you already have a handy way to charge your battery and provide power as you work.

When your system has booted up, you'll be presented with the Windows XP for Tablet PC desktop, with a window open for accessing Tablet PC tutorials (as shown in Figure 1-4).

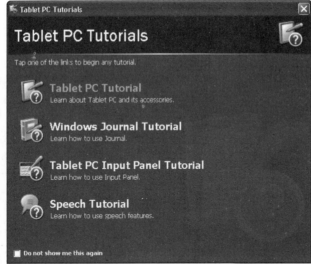

Figure 1-4:
If you don't want to see this window every time you reboot, tap in the Do Not Show Me This Again check box.

If the window of tutorials doesn't appear, it probably means you've turned the computer on before and checked the option to not show the window again.

Meet your Tablet PC pen

Your Tablet PC came with a special *EMR* (electric-magnetic resonance) pen, designed to input handwriting and commands into your computer.

Don't use any other kind of pen to touch your screen — in fact, put your regular old pen well out of reach so you don't grab it and begin scratching away at your screen by mistake. You would do serious and expensive damage to your Tablet PC.

You'll find that other objects, including your hand or finger, won't input anything into Tablet PC. That means that you can rest your wrist on the screen as you write, safe in the knowledge that you won't be making stray entries. But it also means that without the pen, you're stuck. Don't lose it, or you've basically lost your ability to write on your screen until you get another one from the manufacturer.

Jewelry alert: Because I wear a watch on my right wrist and I'm right-handed, I take my watch off when writing on the Tablet PC screen. Although your watch won't write any input, it could scratch the screen. Be sure to prevent your jewelry (rings, watches, and bracelets) from doing any damage when you write on-screen.

You use your pen to tap things on your screen just as you click things with a mouse button. Start by tapping the close button to close the Tutorial window if it appeared when you turned on the computer.

Tap the Input Panel icon (it's just to the right of the Start menu on the Windows taskbar). The Input Panel appears. If the Writing Pad tab isn't displayed, tap on it with your pen to view it (as shown in Figure 1-5).

Putting pen to tablet

Although you'll learn much more about writing with your pen in Chapter 4, you won't want to wait till then to try out this neat feature.

You use the Input Panel Writing Pad to write text with your pen that you then insert into an open document in an application such as Word or Excel.

For now, practice writing your first sentences with WordPad by following these steps:

1. **Choose Start➪All Programs➪Accessories➪WordPad.**

   The WordPad program opens.

2. **With your insertion point in the blank WordPad document, write the following text on the writing line in the Writing Pad (press your Tablet PC pen firmly but gently):**

   Welcome to Tablet PC.

   After a moment, your handwritten entry appears in the WordPad document. Depending on how neat your handwriting is, you should see the words you wrote turned into text.

3. **Tap the arrow on the Send button in the Writing Panel and select Send as Ink.**

4. **Tap the Enter button on the Writing Pad keypad.**

5. **Write the following text in the Writing Panel:**

   Enjoy writing with your pen.

   After a moment, your handwriting appears in the document (as Figure 1-6 shows).

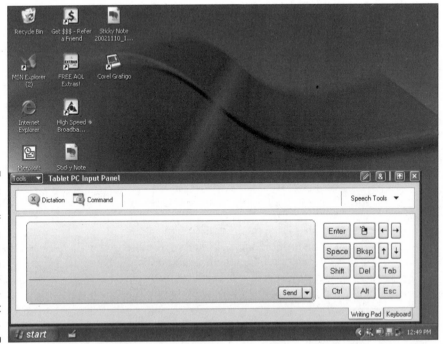

Figure 1-5:
This screen is typical of what you see on a combination keyboard- and-writing- pad input device.

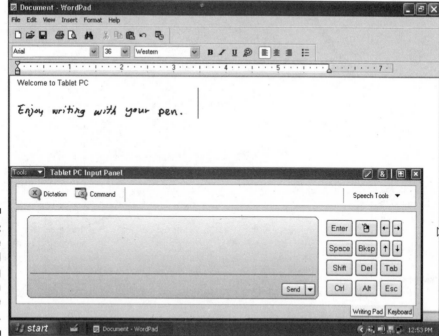

Figure 1-6:
You can use
text and
handwriting
entries in a
single
document.

Spinning your display

Besides being able to write on your screen, one of the coolest features of
Tablet PC is the ability to change the orientation of the computer's display.
This enables you to hold the unit differently depending on the setting. For
example, you may prefer a landscape orientation when you have a writing
surface and want a more PC-like screen appearance; or, you may prefer a portrait orientation if you have to hold the tablet to work on it — for example, if
you're working in an airport waiting area. Holding the tablet in portrait orientation enables you to hold it easily with one arm, which is generally more
comfortable for longer periods of time — more like holding a legal pad.

Some Tablet PCs allow you to spin your orientation in any of four ways, 90
degrees at a time. Others allow only one landscape and one portrait orientation. The method of changing orientation also differs from model to model.
The Motion M1200 Tablet PC, for example, provides a button on its face; you
rotate the screen 90 degrees with each press (as in Figure 1-7). The Acer
TravelMate 100, on the other hand, requires that you press a function key on
the unit, as well as an arrow key, to move between landscape and portrait
orientation.

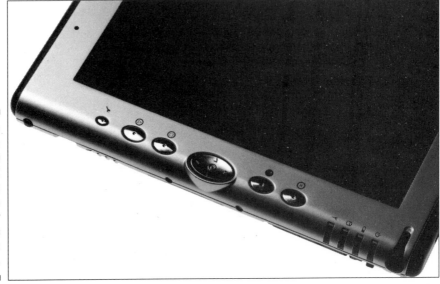

Figure 1-7:
The Motion
M1200
Tablet PC
enables you
to adjust to
any of four
orientations
with a touch
a button.

This is one of the ways you can enter handwritten input into documents. For more about this process (and the other writing tools and features), sneak a peek at Chapter 4.

If you have applied a lower screen-resolution setting, such as 800 x 680, most models don't allow you to use the display-orientation feature. Simply choose Control Panel⇨Display and change the resolution.

To try this, you'll have to refer to your user manual for display orientation. When you've found the method to use, try it out to change from the default landscape to the portrait orientation.

The Motion M1200 Tablet PC automatically changes its screen orientation if you rotate the tablet while it's in its docking cradle. Cool!

You Are Not Alone

I have been very grateful to computer help systems over the years — because they have kept me in business writing computer books for people who find most Help less than helpful. Well, even I have to admit that Help is getting more sophisticated these days, what with interactive tutorials, connections to online help resources, and more. So the help system may actually provide something you need in your quest to master your Tablet PC. It's worth a look . . .

. . . but I won't quit my day job.

Welcome to the Tablet PC

I admit that some of the information built into Windows XP for Tablet PC Help is useful to the first-time user. In the Help and Support Center, for example, there's a Welcome to Tablet PC link that provides information about Tablet PC features, tools to do things like calibrating your pen to work optimally on your screen, and demos and tutorials (as shown in Figure 1-8). You can display the Help and Support Center by tapping the Start button on the Windows taskbar with your pen, and then tapping on the Help and Support link on the Start menu.

Note that there is also a list of Help and Support Resources on the Help and Support Center screen. Here's what they offer:

✔ **Remote Assistance** is a feature that enables you to invite a friend to access your computer online to see whether he or she can help solve your problem. You can also use this feature to allow a tech-support person to fix your problem for you, rather than walking you through the steps while you juggle a phone and try to figure out what they're talking about when they say "Now just defrag the hard drive while repeatedly pressing F2 and whistling Dixie."

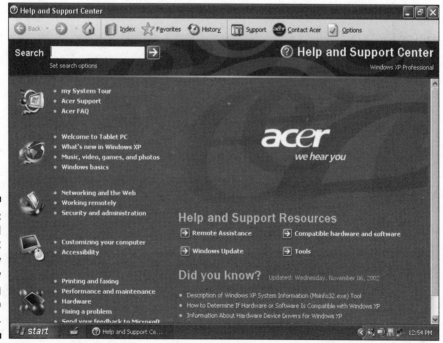

Figure 1-8:
Find
Tablet PC
functionality
help by
clicking
Welcome to
Tablet PC.

✔ **Windows Update** takes you to the Microsoft site for downloading any updates to the operating system that might help solve the problem you're having.

✔ **Compatible Hardware and Software** connects you to the Microsoft list of products compatible with Windows XP. If you have a hardware or software incompatibility problem, downloading an updated driver from this site may resolve things for you.

✔ **Tools** is a link to features such as Network Diagnostics and System Restore that you can use to scan your system for problems or restore earlier settings.

Check out the option for customizing how your computer buttons function (tap Welcome to Tablet PC, then Customizing Your Tablet Computer). Though the buttons on each tablet model differ somewhat depending on the computer's design, this portion of the Help system has been customized to your specific unit's tablet buttons.

Get going with Tablet PC tutorials

The Tablet PC tutorial for working with the Input Panel and speech are perhaps most useful to new users because these features are most likely new to you. You can use simple controls to play, stop, and pause the narrated tutorials (illustrated in Figure 1-9).

You can select Tablet PC Tutorials from the Welcome to Tablet PC area of the Help and Support Center.

Getting help on the Web

The Help and Support Center offers a few options for online help. First, you can tap the Support button and choose Go to a Windows Web Site Forum to visit Windows newsgroups. These are forums where you can chat with other Windows users about what works — and what doesn't — in Windows XP. You may pick up some useful tips from somebody who has gone boldly before you into this territory and found some answers.

The Did You Know? feature in the Help and Support Center offers links to recently released help documents or updates to Windows XP. You can often access live WebCasts that offer information about computing from here as well.

You have to be connected to the Internet for links to the latest news and support information to be available.

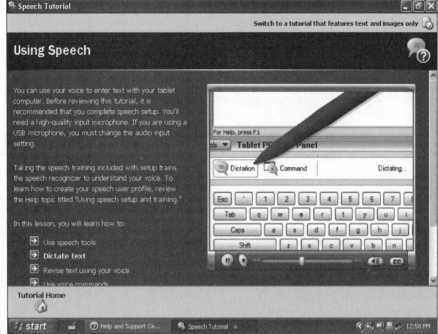

Figure 1-9:
You get
audio
narration as
well as
on-screen
instructions
in these
tutorials.

Turning Off Tablet PC

Turning the Tablet PC off is no different from turning off your desktop computer, except you should be kind to your battery and get in the habit of not leaving your Tablet PC on when you don't need it. In addition, a hibernation mode provides a way to conserve battery life.

Putting it into hibernation

Hibernation is defined as spending the winter in a torpid state. Interestingly, it turns out that hibernation is good for both bears and Tablet PCs.

Hibernation is a feature that's available in regular old Windows XP for every season of the year, but it's especially useful for your Tablet PC because it helps you manage your battery power. Windows Help and Support Center defines hibernation a la Tablet PC as "a state in which your computer shuts down to save power but first saves everything in memory on your hard disk." The perk here is that you save power, and when you restart the computer, everything comes back just the way it was when you left — with the programs and documents you were working in open and ready to go and no nasty little rebooting sequence to wait for.

See Chapter 3 for more about power management and power schemes.

You can set up Tablet PC to go into hibernation automatically. Follow these steps to set up automatic hibernation:

1. **Use your pen and tap to choose Start➪Control Panel➪Power Options.**

2. **Tap the Hibernate tab (shown in Figure 1-10).**

Figure 1-10:
This screen
tells you
how much
disk
space is
required to
hibernate —
and whether
you have
that much
available.

3. **Make sure the Enable Hibernation check box is selected.**

4. **Tap the Power Schemes tab.**

5. **In the System Hibernates area of this tab, tap the drop-down arrows on the fields labeled Plugged In and Running on Batteries.**

6. **Select the amount of time you want to pass before the system automatically goes into hibernation (as shown in Figure 1-11).**

7. **Tap OK to save the new settings.**

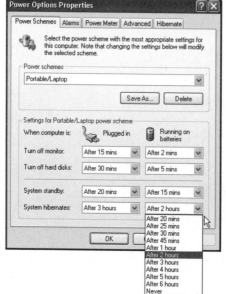

Figure 1-11:
You may
want to go
into
hibernation
mode more
frequently if
you're
working off
of battery
power.

Standing by or saying sayonara!

If you've ever turned a Windows computer off, this one will be like shooting ducks in a barrel (something I discourage you from trying, by the way). When you choose Start➪Turn Off Computer, you have three simple options:

- ✔ **Stand By** puts the computer in a sort of sleep mode — it isn't actually turned off as it is with hibernation, and it will come back to life when you tap the screen. But it does save your battery power somewhat.

  Some models snooze for a set length of time in sleep mode, and then they automatically shut down — you'll have to hit the power button to start up again.

- ✔ **Restart** reboots your computer. This is sometimes necessary if your system has a serious problem and crashes, or after installing some software or changing some system settings to make the changes take effect.

- ✔ **Turn Off** does just what it says. The power goes off, and when you next turn the computer on you'll have to wait those excruciating seconds for Windows to reboot. But you can always browse the cartoons in this book while you're waiting, so it's really not so bad.

Chapter 2

Redefining the PC Experience

· ·

· ·

*O*kay, 'fess up: You keep pulling your Tablet PC out of its case and looking at it, don't you? It's neat, it's slick, and it's like no other computer you've ever used. Even the convertible models, which bear a striking resemblance to garden-variety laptops, are special. There are buttons you've never seen before, that touchable screen, perhaps a little slot for your pen to slip into. How could you not want to haul it out and show it off?

That's why I decided it's worth a chapter to let you linger over that hardware, and discover a bit more about the pen, the display, and the Tablet buttons surrounding your computer screen. In addition, I even throw in some advice about how to keep your new baby safe from damage and itchy-fingered Tablet PC stalkers.

Taking a Good Look at That Pen

They're called cordless pens, styluses, digital pens, pen styluses, virtual pens, or EMR styli (styluses?). They are the size of regular ballpoint pens or smaller. Most sport a button you can use to initiate a right-click action that displays shortcut menus, some even have a virtual eraser. Whatever you call them, they are the one and only way for you to write or perform mouse-like clicks on your Tablet PC screen.

Not your father's fountain pen

Your EMR (electromagnetic resonance) pen stylus (see Figure 2-1) has electronics instead of ink inside. This technology enables the active digitizer screen to sense the pen when it hovers nearby, activating the on-screen cursor; it's also what enables your Tablet PC to respond to the touch of the pen on-screen to perform the following actions:

✔ Dragging and dropping

✔ Clicking tool buttons

✔ Opening menus

✔ Accepting double-clicks to open files and applications

Some pens even have an eraser on the top end to erase text and handwritten entries in your documents.

Figure 2-1:
A pen like this comes with the Motion M1200 Tablet PC. The pen fits into a slot for safekeeping.

Although pens for one Tablet PC should work with other Tablet PC models, other types of devices (say a ballpoint pen or your fingernail) will have no effect. Some manufacturers advise that you use only their approved pens.

Nope, not even your PDA pen will work with the Tablet PC; it has no fancy electronic brain.

Taking care of your pen

Most Tablet PCs have a slot on the unit for you to tuck the pen out of harm's way. The Tablet PC made by Acer actually provides two pens: a smaller one that fits in the unit and a larger one that slips into a slot on the side of the computer case. Whether you have one or two pens, don't lose them because you'll have to buy a replacement. Replacement pens are not cheap: You'll pay anywhere from $30 up to $100 to get one from your Tablet PC manufacturer.

One model of Tablet PC, the Compaq, requires an AAAA battery in the pen itself.

Replacing a pen tip

Eventually, pen tips do wear out and need to be replaced. This is not as traumatic an occurrence as you may think, because your Tablet PC comes with replacement tips. When you originally unpacked your pen, you may have noticed a small metal ring and packet of small white plastic rods. These plastic thingies are replacement pen tips.

You can use the metal ring, called a *pen tip puller,* to pull the tip out. Simply place the open part of the ring on the pen tip, squeeze it closed to grab the tip (you'll know when you've got it when you try this yourself), and pull gently.

To insert a new tip, you can simply hold the tip between your fingers, and slide it into the opening until it won't go any farther (it protrudes almost a quarter of an inch from the pen).

Looking at Things from a Different Angle

Your Tablet PC display is special for a couple of reasons. Unlike other computer screens, the display is sensitive to the touch of a pen stylus. You can also choose to view your display in either landscape or portrait orientation. In this section I fill you in on how this feature works, and how you can modify your screen's appearance.

Sometimes you may want to write notes just as you do on a legal pad. If so, the *portrait* orientation is the one for you. Most people find portrait orientation, shown in Figure 2-2, to be the most comfortable for writing on the screen. This view also enables you to write down the length of a page with typical, document-length lines of text.

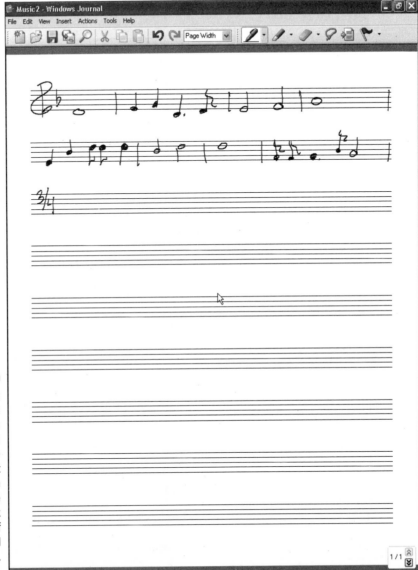

Figure 2-2:
Working in
Windows
Journal, you
can use
portrait
orientation
to emulate
the look
and feel of
a typical
legal pad.

You may want to have a wider *landscape* orientation — perhaps to draw in a graphics program (see Figure 2-3) or work with a wide spreadsheet in a program such as Excel. In this case, you might stick with the default landscape orientation.

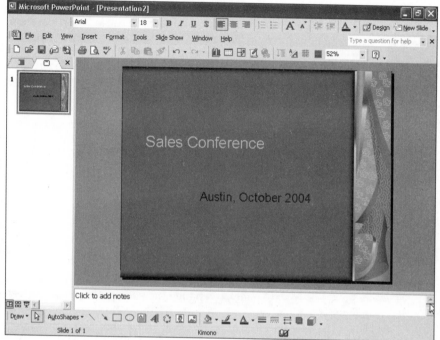

Figure 2-3:
Graphics
programs
such as
PowerPoint
are
sometimes
a better fit
with a wider
orientation.

Rotating the screen

Depending on your Tablet PC model, you may be able to rotate your screen in all four directions by changing the orientation setting. Some models have a single button that turns the display by 90-degree increments, providing two portrait and two landscape settings. Others, such as ViewSonic, only allow one portrait and one landscape setting. For example, you can display content in portrait orientation or turn the screen 90 degrees in a clockwise direction so that the screen (and the content) is sideways. With a model that allows four settings, you can rotate another 90 degrees and be in portrait, only upside down from the first portrait setting. Then you can shift another 90 degrees and be in landscape again, but reversed from the primary landscape orientation. (See "Understanding primary and secondary orientation," later in this chapter.)

To rotate the screen, you can use one (or sometimes two) of the tablet buttons that surround the screen on your computer.

Regardless of which Tablet PC model you're using, you can click the Change Tablet and Pen Settings icon that appears in the Windows System Tray, and choose Change Screen Orientation to change the orientations one at a time in a preset sequence (from landscape to portrait, for example, or from primary landscape to primary portrait to secondary landscape to secondary portrait, depending on whether you have a two- or four-orientation model).

You may have connections such as a phone line or power cord plugged into the side of your unit. If you do and you spin the screen so the bottom of the screen rests on the edge that a plug is poking out of, it may be difficult to avoid the cords as you work. For this reason, the units that enable four differ-ent orientation directions are most practical.

Understanding primary and secondary orientation

You can use the Tablet and Pen Settings dialog box, which you'll find in your computer's control panel, to change the sequence for your screen orientation changes.

All Tablet PCs are set up to use a primary landscape setting and a primary portrait setting. If you have a unit that turns the screen in four directions, you also have secondary landscape and secondary portrait orientations.

Think of your Tablet PC screen (as shown in Figure 2-4) as a clock. Your orien-tation settings appear in the following order when you press your orientation tablet button:

- ✔ 12:00 is the top of the primary portrait orientation.
- ✔ 9:00 is the top of the primary landscape orientation.
- ✔ 6:00 is the top of the secondary portrait orientation.
- ✔ 3:00 is the top of the secondary landscape orientation.

If you have your screen resolution set to 800 x 640, you won't be able to rotate your display orientation at all. Change this setting on the Setting tab of the Display dialog box, accessed through the control panel.

Primary portrait top

Secondary portrait top   Secondary landscape top

Primary landscape top

Figure 2-4:
Starting
with the
primary
portrait
setting, the
orientations
move in this
sequence.

Changing default orientation settings

You can modify the order in which the primary and secondary orientations appear when you initiate an orientation change with your tablet button. For example, you can set secondary landscape as the first orientation, primary landscape as the second orientation to appear, and so on. Follow these steps to make this change:

1. **Choose Start➪Control Panel➪Tablet and Pen Settings.**

2. **Tap the Display tab.**

   The Display tab is shown in Figure 2-5.

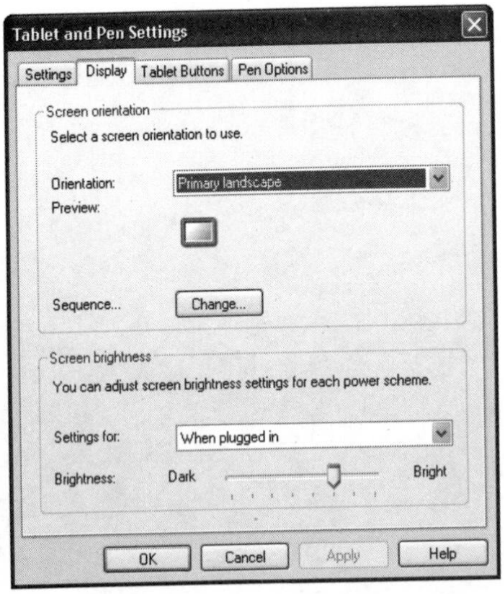

Figure 2-5:
You can change your screen orientation by selecting an orientation from the Orientation drop-down list and tapping Apply.

3. **To change the sequence in which your orientations appear, tap Change.**

   The Orientation Sequence Settings dialog box (shown in Figure 2-6) appears.

4. **Select one of the four possible orientations from the four drop-down lists.**

   These orientations, numbered 1 through 4, appear in just that sequence (1 first, 4 last).

5. **Tap OK twice to save the changes.**

Figure 2-6:
After you change these settings, various orientations will appear in the order that you selected each time you tap your tablet button.

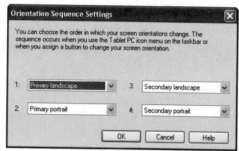

Adjusting Screen Brightness

Your Tablet PC comes with a Liquid Crystal Display (LCD) screen, though the exact specifications may differ depending on your model. The *Microsoft Computer Dictionary* defines an LCD display as, well, never mind. Something about liquid compounds and molecular structures. Oh yeah, and electrodes. This is all you need to know, and actually, you don't even need to know this much.

If you own a laptop computer, you've probably dealt with an LCD screen before. They are kind of squishy if you press your finger (gently) against them.

Suffice it to say that your screen is unique, and the brightness may differ from your desktop computer. LCD screens are known for providing nice, sharp color; however, depending on the light you're working in, you may have to adjust the brightness so you can see content more clearly.

Tablet PC screens are not that easy to read outdoors in bright sunlight. In the Tablet world, some models can be ordered with an outdoor screen or indoor screen, and even a hybrid screen, which is supposed to work in either locale. Alas, the outdoor screens aren't that hot — and the hybrids may work in both places, but not very well in either one. Except for overcast days, you'll probably stick to indoor uses of your Tablet PC if you want to see what you're doing.

To adjust screen brightness, follow these steps:

1. **Tap the Change Tablet and Pen Settings icon on the Windows taskbar system tray, then choose Properties from the menu that appears.**

2. **Tap the Display tab to display it (you can see this panel in Figure 2-5).**

3. **For most situations, leave the default setting (When Plugged In) unchanged.**

   You can set separate brightness levels for AC-powered or battery-powered operation. If you want to save power by dimming the setting when the Tablet PC is running on batteries, tap the arrow in the Settings For field and select Powered by Batteries.

4. **Tap the Slider on the Brightness scale and drag it to the right to make it brighter or to the left to make it darker.**

5. **Tap OK to save your settings.**

Most Tablet PC models also offer tablet buttons or keyboard Function key combinations (with convertible models) to adjust screen brightness. See your user manual to see how your model handles this.

A screen is a screen is a screen — isn't it?

Though all Tablet PCs have LCD screens, you'll see other display specifications for the different models (such XGA, XVGA, high luminance, and transmissive). Of course, the best way to know whether one model's screen will work better for you than another is to examine them all before you buy. But if you buy online, and at least initially that's where most Tablet PCs are sold, you may need some guidance to these features.

✓ *Pixels* are individual cells on your computer screen. The more pixels, the higher the resolution (quality of the image). For example, an 800 x 600 pixel resolution is lower quality than 1,024 x 768.

✓ XGA stands for eXtended Graphics Array. It's a standard for graphics display from IBM that supports either 640 x 480 resolution or 1,024 x 768.

✓ XVGA is a sort of a higher-level XGA. With an XVGA you can display anywhere from 800 x 600 pixels to 1,600 x 1,200 pixels.

✓ TFT is the acronym for *thin film transistor.* It means the machine has one thin transistor for each cell (pixel) on your screen. TFT is used in what's called an active-matrix display. Most Tablet PCs use a TFT screen.

✓ *Luminance* is a measurement of how much light is available to light up your screen. A high-luminance (or high-brightness) screen seems to make colors brighter.

Now that you know what all these are, I have no doubt that somebody will come along and change all the display technology out there next week, so don't worry — enjoy the screen you have because it is a pretty darn good one, no matter which Tablet PC model you bought.

Fringe Benefits: Getting to Know What Surrounds the Screen

You may have noticed that Tablet PCs are lightweight. To make them that way, manufacturers made economical use of every square inch of screen real estate — and some even ditched the Keyboard to drop a few more ounces.

With no keyboard available when you're working with a Tablet PC (even a convertible model when it's in tablet form), the manufacturers had to make even the tiniest bit of space that surrounds the screen count.

What they used this space for are tablet buttons that you can use to quickly perform various common functions, and LED readouts to clue you into the power usage of your system.

What's flashing?

LED lights on your Tablet PC unit show power-management information, such as whether your battery is charged or charging, as well as usage of external media or your hard drive. For example, when the computer is reading data from your hard drive, a light may flash.

Here's what a couple of manufacturers have done with their LED lights to give you the idea of the kind of functions the lights on your unit represent. Of course, your Tablet PC may signal additional or different information.

The ViewSonic model has three lights (see Figure 2-7):

- **Power LED:** This light is green when the unit is turned on and it blinks when the computer is placed in Standby mode.

- **Hard Drive LED:** This light blinks green when your computer is reading data from the hard drive or when data is being written into memory.

- **Battery Charge LED:** This light is red when the battery is charging and doesn't light at all when it's fully charged.

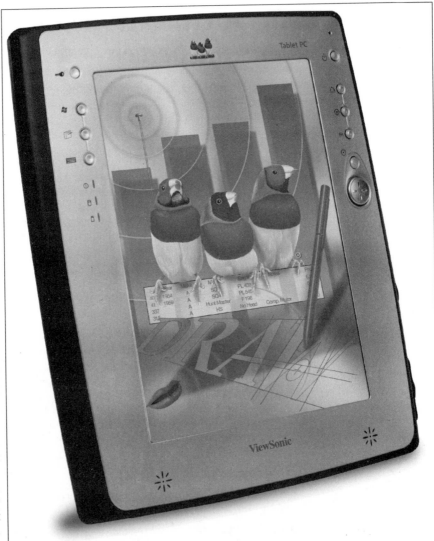

Figure 2-7:
The
ViewSonic
LED lights
are lined up
on the left
side of the
screen in
primary
portrait
orientation.

Acer has seven — count 'em, *seven* — LED displays:

✔ **Num Lock:** Displays a light when the Num Lock feature is turned on.

✔ **Caps Lock:** Displays a light when Caps Lock is activated.

✔ **Battery Charge:** Displays a light when the battery is charging.

 ✔ **Media Activity:** Displays a light when a floppy drive, hard drive, or optical drive is reading a file or performing some other task.

 ✔ **Sleep:** Displays a light when the computer is in Sleep mode.

 ✔ **Power:** Displays a green light when the Tablet PC is turned on.

 ✔ **Wireless Communication:** Glows red if you've enabled Wireless LAN.

The Motion M1200 Tablet PC has four LED indicators (see Figure 2-8) showing Wireless Activity, Hard Drive Access, Battery Status, and Power Standby.

Button, button, who's got the Tablet PC button?

Buttons on the face of Tablet PCs replace many of the functions you're used to performing on a typical keyboard. For example, you're missing the Enter, Function, and directional arrow keys from a keyboard. Never fear — you're likely to find these keys recreated as buttons on your Tablet PC hardware.

Figure 2-8:
Motion puts four lights on the face of its M1200 Tablet PC.

Wireless activity

Hard drive access

Power standby

Battery status

The buttons available to you vary from model to model. They may run along the bottom or sides of the unit. Some, such as the directional arrows button shown in Figure 2-9, may be a single large button that you press on one side or another to move your cursor in a particular direction.

Typical buttons include some old friends and some new kids:

- **Power On/Off:** Does just what it says. (Refreshing, isn't it?)
- **Rotation:** May be used alone or with a Function key to rotate the screen 90 degrees at a time.
- **Escape:** Works like the Escape button on a regular keyboard to back you out of actions you wish you hadn't done — but (alas) only on the computer.
- **Function:** Works like the Function key on a standard keyboard; when pressed with other buttons or keys on a keyboard, it calls up alternate functionality such as pressing Function+F1 to display help or Function+F4 to put a unit into Sleep mode.
- **Enter:** Functions like the Enter key on your keyboard to accept an entry in a field or cell or to move your cursor to the next line of a document.
- **Directional keys:** Emulates the right, left, up, and down keys on a keyboard to move your on-screen cursor around a document.
- **Security:** Mimics the "three-finger salute," Ctrl+Alt+Del (a function you may have used on a standard keyboard to call up Windows Task Manager or shut down your system in case of a crash).
- **Start Menu:** Displays the Windows Start menu.
- **Journal:** Opens Windows Journal.
- **Input Panel:** Opens the Input Panel.

Some of these buttons, when used with the Function key, can perform alternate functions. For example, press the Fn key with the Escape key on the Motion M1200 Tablet PC and it is the equivalent of the standard keyboard Alt+Tab function that switches you among open applications.

Resetting button functions

If you're one of those people who considers *have it your way* a personal mantra, put aside that burger and read on.

Figure 2-9:
Press the
larger
button in
any of four
directions to
use the four
directional
arrows.

All Tablet PC models enable you to reset some button functions. Some, such as ViewSonic, only enable you to change functionality that you get when you press the Function key with a button.

Others let you reset the primary button functions. For example, you can change the key that is set to the Enter function on an Acer to an alternate function such as opening your e-mail program or turning the speaker on and off. These are known as programmable buttons.

No matter what changes your unit's manufacturer enables you to make, you can make those changes by following these steps:

1. **Tap the Input Panel icon to display the on-screen Keyboard.**

2. **Tap the Windows key on the Input Panel to display the Windows taskbar.**

3. **Tap the Change Tablet and Pen Settings icon in your system tray (that is, the taskbar), and choose Properties from the menu that appears.**

4. **Tap the Tablet Buttons tab (see Figure 2-10).**

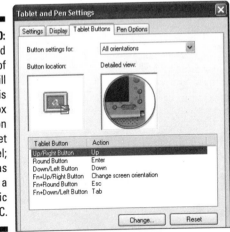

Figure 2-10:
The detailed
view of
buttons will
differ in this
dialog box
based on
your Tablet
PC model;
this was
taken on a
ViewSonic
Tablet PC.

5. **To change button settings for only a single orientation, tap the arrow in the Button Settings For drop-down list and select the orientation you want.**

6. **Select a Tablet Button name from the list, then tap Change.**

   The Change Tablet Button Actions dialog box appears.

7. **Select an action from the Action list (see Figure 2-11).**

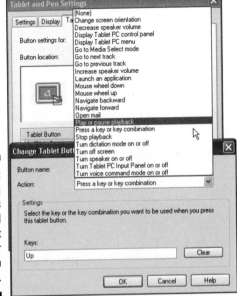

Figure 2-11:
This dialog
box offers
several
preset
options for
tablet button
functions.

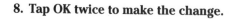

8. **Tap OK twice to make the change.**

To reset buttons to the original settings, tap the Reset button on the Tablet Buttons tab of the Tablet and Pen Settings dialog box.

Care and Feeding, Tablet PC Style

You have a $2,000-plus baby on your hands and the last thing you want to do is abuse it or lose it (or drop it on its head). Tablet PCs typically have one-year warranties, but those often don't cover certain components such as the all-important touch screen. So the best solution is to stop stuff from happening to your Tablet PC in the first place.

Tablet PCs are pretty neat little things, and some people (not the nice ones) may want to steal yours. I include a few ways to prevent that — or at least make the thing useless to others if they do make off with yours.

Keeping your Tablet PC in good condition

Deep, deep inside your user's guide is a section telling you what you should and shouldn't do to keep your Tablet PC in good condition — but if you're like everybody else in the world, you never read that stuff. So I've slaved over most of the advice the manufacturers give to make it pithy, amusing, and readable. Here's how to take care of your model:

- **Don't use a pen stylus that's not approved by your manufacturer.** Doing so could hurt your screen and void your warranty. In addition, don't use a non-Tablet PC type of pen on your screen — ever.

- **Use only recommended screen-cleaning cloths.** Most units come with one. If yours didn't (or you lose it), go for a 3M Scotch-Brite High-Performance Cloth, which you'll find in your office or computer supply store. Also, because you may use a slightly damp cleaning cloth to clean your screen, it's a good idea to turn the power off and disconnect the power source if you don't want to become toast.

- **Keep water away from your Tablet PC.** Think of it as a cat that would get really, really mad if you put it in a bathtub. Also, you might get yourself electrocuted if you drop the Tablet PC into that same bathtub with the power cord plugged in, and you don't want that to happen.

- **Don't use a power cord that didn't come with your unit.** Again, this could void your warranty — besides blowing up your computer.

✔ **Be careful about the computer screen.** You can buy screen protectors, a carrying case, or wrap your screen in a blanket, but don't just leave it lying around with no protection.

✔ **Don't leave the computer in direct sunlight, or put it near something really hot like a radiator or heat vent.** Don't ask what happens, just don't do it — it's not a pretty picture!

Conversely (there's always a "conversely"), don't leave your computer in the Artic Circle or your refrigerator. Temperatures below 32 degrees Fahrenheit can also do damage. If you do expose your computer to extreme changes in temperature or humidity — and condensation forms on or inside the screen — let it evaporate before you turn the computer on.

✔ **Here's a two-parter: a) Don't rest your Tablet PC on an uneven surface, and b) don't drop it.** I know you knew this one, but I had to include it. When you're working, keep the Tablet PC on a flat surface so you don't end up dealing with a or b. Also, don't place anything heavy on it (like the dog or a Hyundai).

✔ **Don't put it somewhere really dusty or dirty.**

So what about that trek down the Grand Canyon? Carry your Tablet PC in a case or leave it home (unless your home is really dusty or dirty).

Keeping thieves at bay

Everybody is going to want your Tablet PC. Unfortunately, some people will act on the impulse (or at least try to). You can, of course, set up your Windows user password to keep information on the Tablet PC safe if someone manages to walk away with it.

Of course, I'd rather not have anyone take my Tablet PC in the first place. Certainly, if someone does manage to take it, I'd be pleased to keep Mr. or Ms. Sticky Fingers from getting anywhere near the Windows operating system. (Accessing the operating system brings a criminally minded individual one step closer to cracking your password.)

To stop theft from happening, follow this ridiculously obvious rule: Don't leave your Tablet PC unguarded.

But wait, there's more:

✔ **Consider getting a computer security lock.** One end of this lock fits into a slot in your computer, with the other end wrapped around a table leg or your wrist to keep it secure. Only the key that you have can unlock the cable from your computer and enable you to walk away with your computer.

> ✔ **Use a Smart Card.** Your Tablet PC may have come with a Smart Card, or you can buy one that fits into a card slot. Smart Card technology ensures that if somebody tries to turn on your Tablet PC and doesn't insert the card, the Tablet PC won't complete the boot sequence. The downside is that you're not likely to get back the data you lost (and you can forget about seeing the Tablet PC again), but the good news is that no one else will be able to use information stored on it.

If you just can't get comfortable with the idea of having your Tablet PC stolen and taking the financial hit of that loss, get insurance so you can buy another one (and sleep nights).

On the road . . . again

Basically this whole section consists of warnings, so here are some special ones for travelers:

✔ **Don't check your Tablet PC as baggage and don't let it go through the now ubiquitous metal detector.** Security scans are fine, but metal detectors do weird and wonderful magnetic tricks that — well, let's just say your Tablet PC wouldn't like it.

✔ **Protect your pen when you travel.** If your unit provides a slot for your pen, keep it in the slot while you travel.

✔ **Have a charged battery with you in case the airport security folks ask you to start up your Tablet PC.** If you can't start it up, they may dump it in a bucket of water to defuse it, and I already told you that's a really bad thing.

✔ **Don't use the wireless operation while on a plane.** It makes pilots really mad.

✔ **If you're going out of the country, bring adapters with you.**

Chapter 3

Connecting to Your Office . . . and Beyond

In This Chapter

▶ Checking out connection ports

▶ Adding Plug and Play peripherals to your Tablet PC

▶ Using docking stations

▶ Working with power schemes and battery settings

Someday, perhaps, Tablet PCs will contain in their slim, lightweight packages everything a computer user ever needs. But for now, Tablet PC is more like a baby that survives on accessories. Whenever you see a baby, it's bound to be accompanied by parents carrying a car seat, diapers, a bag of crackers and fruit, a rattle, and a pacifier. Well, like a baby, Tablet PC has to be connected to other stuff in order to have a complete computing experience.

For example, it has to be connected to an electrical outlet for its battery to be charged periodically (think feeding time), and it needs to have connections to other hardware to print, store files on media such as a CD-ROM, and so on. And there's something to be said for putting Tablet PC into its cradle — called a *docking station* — when it's tired of traveling roads and corridors.

Plug and Play, Tablet PC Style

Plug and Play is a technology that enables you to plug hardware such as a printer into a computer and have your computer recognize and communicate with that hardware somewhat seamlessly. The first step in Plug and Play is "plug," and that's what you'll learn about in this section.

Any port in a storm

A piece of additional hardware that you connect to your computer, such as a printer or external modem, which is called a *peripheral,* connects to your computer through ports. This connection enables the transfer of data between the two pieces of hardware.

On older computers (not that old — say computers manufactured before 2001) there were different kinds of ports, such as serial ports and parallel ports. Not every peripheral could work with every kind of port — which was, quite frankly, annoying — and techies stockpiled boxes of different kinds of cables in their closets.

Enter USB, or Universal Serial Bus. USB is a kind of all-purpose port that you can use to connect any number of things, from a printer to a mouse, CD-ROM drive (see Figure 3-1), or digital camera. Tablet PCs use USB ports to connect most peripherals.

If you have a piece of hardware (such as a keyboard) that doesn't have a USB connector, you can buy a USB adapter at any computer store.

Figure 3-1:
You can use various cable adapters to connect peripherals such as this CD-ROM drive through a USB port.

But you'll also find a few other kinds of ports on Tablet PCs. Though Tablet PC models will vary slightly in their configurations, here are some typical ports and jacks to look for in addition to the USB ports:

✓ **Modem ports** are for connecting to external modems.

✓ **LAN ports** enable you to connect to a network.

🖊 **VGA Monitor ports** are there to connect to a monitor or LCD device used to display presentations.

🖊 **IEEE 1394 ports** are for electronics, such as optical disc drives or video cameras.

🖊 **Input and output jacks** are for microphones, headphones, and speakers.

These ports and jacks are located somewhere around the edges of your Tablet PC (see Figure 3-2), and your user guide identifies each one for you.

Generally, peripherals come with their own connection wires, but if they don't or you've lost yours, you can usually purchase a cord of that type from an office supply or computer store.

Figure 3-2:
Various kinds of ports are tucked away around your Tablet PC; some ports are in cases behind protective plastic flaps.

If your Tablet PC was designed to fit into a docking station, it also has a pin connector (a male plug that typically has 28 pins that fits into a corresponding female plug) for hooking it up to the dock.

Just send a card

As you scan the edges of your Tablet PC, you see some card slots. These are little doorways into which you can plug cards into slots. The cards themselves are about the size of a playing card, only thicker. These cards, called PCMCIA or, simply, PC cards, are typically used to add memory to a portable device, but can also add functionality such as a modem, wireless network connection (see Figure 3-3), or fax.

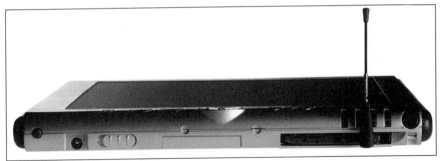

Figure 3-3: This wireless card sports an antenna and fits right into a PC card slot.

You can purchase PC cards at computer stores or through your Tablet PC manufacturer. Cards provide a lightweight way to add memory or functionality to your Tablet PC.

Some manufacturers provide plastic spaceholders to protect the card slot from invading dirt or debris when there's no card in it. You have to remove these spaceholders in order to insert a card, but be sure to keep the space-holders in a safe place.

Connecting things

Connecting through plugs and ports is pretty much a matter of matching up (yep) the connectors. It's generally pretty easy to tell which oddly shaped plug fits into which kind of receptacle. But here's a rundown anyway to help you out.

The first thing you may want to connect to your Tablet PC is the power cord. (Gee, ya think? See Figure 3-4.) This cord has two parts:

- **An AC power cable** with a standard, grounded, three-prong plug on one end to attach to a wall outlet

- **An AC adapter** to convert the power to direct current, and a single pin connector that plugs into the Tablet PC

Figure 3-5 shows you connectors for an additional monitor, and USB ports where you can connect devices such as a keyboard or mouse.

Figure 3-6 shows two jacks: one for a phone line to connect to the internal modem, the other for an Ethernet connection, used to plug a computer into a network.

Figure 3-4:
You can use the AC power cable and adapter that you get with all Tablet PCs to provide power and charge your battery.

Figure 3-5:
The plug on the far left is for a monitor, and the small ports on the right take connectors such as the one shown for a keyboard.

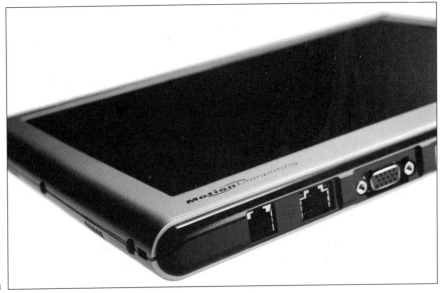

Figure 3-6:
These two jacks look similar to any regular phone jack, though the one on the right is for a network connection and doesn't accept a standard phone line.

In Figure 3-7, on the far right, you see two jacks to connect speakers and a microphone or headphone, and just to their left a FireWire (IEEE 1394) port for connecting electronics, such as video cameras.

Figure 3-7:
This Motion M1200 Tablet PC places the audio/micro phone jacks next to the FireWire port.

Hooking Up with Docking Stations

You know how sometimes you want to be something you're not, like a millionaire or a femme fatale or a superspy? Well, Tablet PC wants to be a desktop computer, and it tries very hard. Even as a pretender, the Tablet PC does a pretty good job, too, by means of a docking station.

If you're a fan of science fiction, you've seen those fancy space stations where spaceships dock to share the air and power of the station while making repairs or just having shore leave among alien species.

A computer docking station is a unit that not only holds your Tablet PC upright on your desk, but provides more user-friendly connections for peripheral devices.

Figure 3-8 shows you how desktop-computer-like a Tablet PC can get when you put it into a docking station. You can use plugs and jacks located on a docking station to connect a regular keyboard, speakers, and more, putting all the functionality of a regular desktop PC at your fingertips.

Figure 3-8:
The Motion M1200 provides a nice setup for using a Tablet PC on a desktop with its FlexDock.

Most docking stations include a CD-ROM drive, and usually a few extra USB ports for connecting more peripherals than you're likely to use with your standalone tablet. Connecting your Tablet PC to a docking station is usually as easy as resting it in a stand which contains a docking port connection that lines up with the connection on your Tablet PC automatically when you position it correctly.

Docking stations are usually designed for a specific Tablet PC model, so you should buy the one that your manufacturer offers.

You can use your Tablet PC in either landscape or portrait orientation on a docking station. (See Chapter 2 for details.) In addition, some docking stations have adjustable positions so you can easily write on-screen while the unit is docked.

The Motion M1200 docking station enables you to turn the Tablet PC around and the screen orientation adjusts automatically.

Surprising Surprise Undocking

Call it grab-and-go, hot-docking, or surprise undocking. Whatever you call it, it's cool.

With laptop computers that use docking stations, you typically have to close all your software applications and shut the computer down before removing it. When you have your Tablet PC connected to a dock, you don't have to unplug anything or even turn off the computer to remove it from all the connections the docking station makes. Just pick up your Tablet PC and head out to a meeting, solve a sudden problem with your manufacturing plant, or close a hot sale.

Power to the Tablet PC

Even though docking stations may make a Tablet PC act like a desktop computer, these PCs are really all about portability. They were designed to be lightweight and manage battery power efficiently for those times when you can't be tethered to a wall socket.

I'll be frank: Most Tablet PCs advertise battery life (that is, how long you can run the computer on a battery before it needs recharging) of 3.5 to 4.5 hours, with Standby battery life (battery life when you have the unit in Standby mode) of about three days, but in reality, they usually fall short of that. You want to take best advantage of your battery's potential, but first you have to understand a little bit about power-management and Tablet PC.

A AAA battery this ain't

Like their cousins, laptop computers, Tablet PCs come with a lithium-ion battery (see Figure 3-9), which is the best type of battery for holding a charge the maximum amount of time. The more cells these batteries have (for example six cells versus three cells) the longer they'll hold a charge, but the higher cell models are also a bit heavier to cart around.

Figure 3-9:
A battery will slide right into the body of your Tablet PC.

These batteries aren't cheap (a six-cell battery can cost about $180), so if you buy a second one to carry more charge around with you, be prepared to spend some money.

If you travel a lot, a second battery is worth the price. With two charged batteries, you may get as much as six or seven hours of battery life, which should get you through most plane flights.

Where you're supposed to insert the batteries varies depending on the model of Tablet PC you own. The ViewSonic battery is about 11 inches long and actually runs all along one side of the unit. Many other manufacturers fit their batteries into the body of the Tablet PC on the underside of the unit.

There's often a sliding latch you have to push to release a battery to remove it. See your user manual for specific instructions on how to install and remove the battery.

Charging the battery

Some manufacturers recommend that you charge the battery with the Tablet PC turned off for a few hours (usually two to three) when you first get it out of the box. Others say the battery that comes with the unit is already fully charged and requires no start-up charge at all. Be sure to read your manual for manufacturer recommendations.

You charge the battery with it installed in your Tablet PC by connecting the Tablet PC power cord into a standard electrical outlet. It's always best to plug the AC adapter into the wall and then into the Tablet PC with the Tablet PC turned off. Then turn it on and say, "Charge this battery." (Just kidding; it will ignore you and charge the battery anyway.) You can do this whole operation while you're working on the Tablet PC, if you like.

Some manufacturers warn that if you don't fully charge the battery before using it the first time, you could affect the battery's overall life. It's important that you read your manual regarding charging when you first buy your Tablet PC.

If you leave your Tablet PC turned off or remove a charged battery from it, the battery will keep its charge for anywhere from one to two months.

You can check your power level by following these steps:

1. **Choose Start⇨Control Panel.**

   The control panel is displayed.

2. **Double-tap the Power Options icon.**

   The Power Options Properties dialog box is displayed.

3. **Tap the Power Meter tab (shown in Figure 3-10).**

   The current power source and the current percent of remaining battery power are shown here.

4. **Tap OK to close the dialog box.**

You can also hover your pen over the Battery icon on the Windows system tray to get a look at how much battery power you have left.

Choosing a power scheme

Windows XP for Tablet PC includes *power schemes*. No, they aren't plans for world domination; they're instructions to the computer on how to save electricity. Several power-management settings are saved into schemes that fit your use of the Tablet PC, such as Home/Office Desk, Presentation, and Always On.

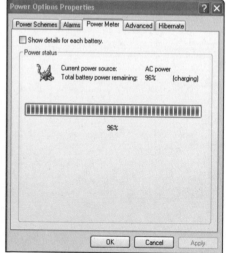

Figure 3-10:
Get the
exact
percentage
of charge
and current
power
source here.

You can even make settings manually and save new power schemes that fit the way you use your computer.

To set a power scheme, follow these steps:

1. **Choose Start⇨Control Panel.**

   The control panel is displayed.

2. **Double-tap the Power Options icon.**

   The Power Options Properties dialog box is displayed.

3. **Tap the Power Schemes tab (as shown in Figure 3-11).**

4. **Tap the arrow on the Power Schemes drop-down list box and select a power scheme.**

   The individual settings are shown.

5. **When you locate a scheme that fits your needs, tap Apply, and then OK to close the dialog box.**

Want a shortcut? You can also tap the Battery icon on the Windows system tray and the saved schemes will be displayed. Just tap another scheme to apply it.

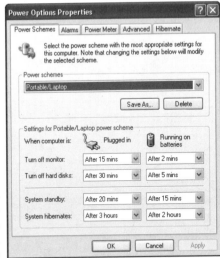

Setting a lower battery warning

Windows XP for Tablet PC displays a battery power indicator in the task tray on the taskbar when you are running off of a battery charge. Check it to see if you're running low.

Windows XP also provides a low battery warning to alert you when a battery is about to be completely drained so you can save your work and attach to a power source if one is available. An LED low battery light on the front of your Tablet PC begins blinking to let you know that the battery is low. You also hear a beep every 15 seconds or so. By default, the Tablet PC is set to alert you when it's got 6 percent of its charge remaining, which translates to about ten minutes of battery life before your power goes *phffft*.

There's also a *very low battery* warning that occurs when you have only 3 percent of your charge left. This warning, quite annoyingly, beeps at you about every four seconds.

You can change this setting to give you more or less notice by following these steps:

1. **Choose Start⇨Control Panel.**

   The control panel is displayed.

2. **Double-tap the Power Options icon.**

   The Power Options Properties dialog box appears. If it's not already displayed, tap the Alarms tab and get the dialog box shown in Figure 3-12.

3. **Tap the slider for the Low Battery Alarm and drag it left or right to set the first level of battery warning.**

4. **Tap the slider for the Critical Battery Alarm and set the second-level alarm — the one that sounds when the battery is almost drained.**

You can also set the alarms to function in specific ways; for example, to display a message instead of sounding an alarm. Follow these steps:

1. **From the Alarms tab of the Power Options Properties dialog box (shown in Figure 3-12), tap the Alarm Action button for either the Low Battery Alarm or Critical Battery Alarm.**

   The Low Battery Alarm Actions dialog box (see Figure 3-13) appears.

2. **Choose how you want the alarm to notify you by tapping in the Sound Alarm and Display Message check boxes.**

   You can choose sounding an alarm, displaying a message, or doing both.

3. **If you want the computer to take an action when the alarm sounds, tap the When the Alarm Goes Off, the Computer Will check box; then select an action from the drop-down list.**

   To run a program (for example, an executable file that saves an open document and then shuts down the computer), tap in the When the Alarm Occurs, Run This Program check box, and tap Configure Program to select the program to run.

4. **When you've completed your settings, tap OK twice to save them.**

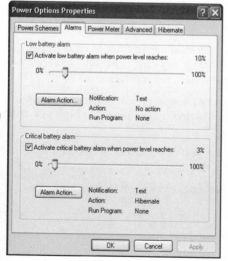

Figure 3-12:
You can
make
settings for
two battery
alarms
in this
dialog box.

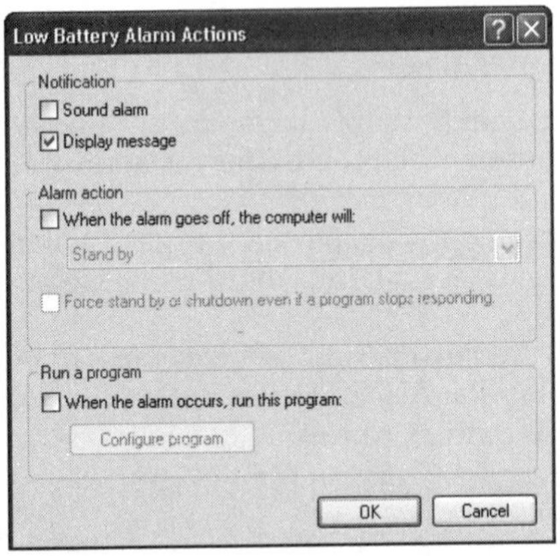

Figure 3-13:
Choose how
an alarm
will function
by choosing
settings
in this
dialog box.

Battery pointers and power-saving tips

Tips are free, so I've got a few for you that can help you become a powerful power manager:

- If you're installing software or writing files to a CD-ROM, use the power cord to save battery drain.

- Put the system in Standby or Hibernate mode if you're not using it for a few minutes (for example, while you take a phone call).

- Lower display brightness settings can save battery power.

- Don't touch the ends of the battery where they connect with the Tablet PC.

- Don't put batteries in very cold or very hot temperatures. Lithium-ion batteries work by converting dry chemicals into electricity and those chemicals don't like extreme temperatures.

- Before a trip, plan battery charging time. Don't just get up in the morning to dash for a plane when you may need two hours or so to get your battery up to speed.

- Don't keep PC cards that you're not using in the unit. Even if they're not active, they can drain a tiny bit of power from your battery.

- Use the Max Battery Power Scheme, which saves the most power of any of the schemes.

Part II
Tablet PC Basics

The 5th Wave   By Rich Tennant

"Okay, have we all signed in on our Tablet PC's?
Good. I see we have Barge, Teabag, Dink, and
Boob with us today.

In this part . . .

When you learned to drive, you didn't jump in a car and start driving around the neighborhood willy-nilly. Somebody had to tell you what those switches were for and how you pump one pedal to get gas into the engine and another pedal to stop the car. Discovering how to use a new computer is kind of like that.

In this part, you find out all about how Tablet PC works, including using the on-screen keyboard, wielding a pen to perform mouse functions and write on-screen, and controlling spoken commands. This is the part where you explore different ways to enter ink content (stuff that you write or draw with your pen), to edit ink entries, and to set up your pen and speech features to match your input style. With the skills you learn here, you'll be able to drive any application that you encounter on Tablet PC.

Chapter 4

Discovering Pen Basics

*W*ho would have imagined that the most cutting-edge way to enter stuff in your computer today would be . . . with a pen? But this is no ordinary pen — it has sophisticated electronic stuff inside that allows it to interact with the Tablet PC's digitized screen.

When you think about it, communicating with your computer by using a pen makes sense. Writing with a pen is much more natural than hunting and pecking at a mechanical keyboard. It's pretty much the same way cave people wrote things down by scratching in the dirt with sticks. (How much more natural can you get than that?)

A Tablet PC solves the legibility issue by converting your handwriting to legible text. You get the benefit of a natural input method *and* writing that people can actually read. If you want to leave your notes in their original handwritten form for your own use, but still be able to store, organize, and search them, Tablet PC can do that, too.

The Tap Is Mightier than the Click

If you're like me, you spent a few days (or weeks) learning how to control a mouse to get things done on your computer. Now you can forget all that — because Tablet PC uses a pen (also referred to as a *pen stylus* or cordless Motion pen) to do everything you do with a mouse.

With your pen you can

- ✔ Select things (text or objects)
- ✔ Open and close programs and windows
- ✔ Drag and drop things
- ✔ Rotate and resize objects
- ✔ Display shortcut menus
- ✔ Reactivate your computer when it's in Stand By mode
- ✔ Follow hyperlinks

. . . and even more . . . all by tapping the pen that came with your Tablet PC on the computer screen — firmly but gently — in a variety of ways.

Don't use just any old pen on your Tablet PC screen. The pen that came with your unit is a specially designed pen made to work with the LCD touch screen. In fact, Tablet PC input is so specific to this style of pen that pressing on the screen with any other implement (even your finger) won't have any effect. Sharp implements, of course, could damage the screen surface.

In general, however, don't worry — learning to use a pen is much easier than learning to use a mouse for the first time!

Tablet PC documentation varies in how it refers to taps and clicks. As a general rule, if you run across a direction to *click* or *double-click,* consider it the equivalent of tapping and double-tapping. This book sticks to tapping.

First, pick it up

Pens vary in size; some are the size of a traditional ballpoint pen, others are like those mini-pencils you get as free gifts in envelopes from groups asking for donations to save iguanas in Borneo.

No matter the size, essentially you hold a pen stylus just as you hold any pen.

If there is a button on your pen (about which you'll hear more in a moment), always position the pen so you can press the button easily with your thumb or forefinger.

Confidential to lefties

If you're left-handed, follow these steps to change the Handedness setting in the Tablet and Pen Settings dialog box:

1. **Choose Start⇨Control Panel⇨Tablet and Pen Settings.**

2. **With the Settings tab displayed (as shown in Figure 4-1), tap the Left-handed button to select it.**

3. **Tap OK to save the setting.**

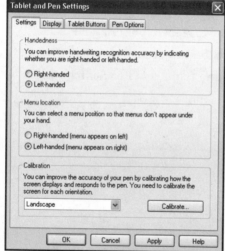

Figure 4-1:
You can tap more accurately if you choose the appropriate Handedness setting in this dialog box.

Calibrating your pen

To ensure that your pen and screen see eye to eye, you should calibrate your pen. Calibrating sounds awfully scientific, but it just means showing Tablet PC how you perceive the center of a set of crosshairs, so it can accommodate your on-screen taps more accurately.

In fact, some manufacturers of Tablet PCs recommend that you calibrate every time you change your screen orientation. Tedious? Yes. But it only takes a few seconds — and as pen technology improves, we can hope this chore goes away entirely.

Follow these steps to calibrate your pen:

1. **Choose Start⇨Control Panel and double-tap Tablet and Pen Settings.**

   Your screen may show a Change Tablet and Pen Settings icon in the Windows icon tray that you can double-tap instead.

   The Tablet and Pen Settings dialog box appears.

2. **On the Settings tab, tap Calibrate.**

   A dialog box appears, instructing you to tap in the middle of a set of crosshairs in a corner of the screen (as in Figure 4-2).

3. **Tap in the center of the crosshairs.**

   Another set of crosshairs appears.

4. **Repeat Step 3 until you've tapped four crosshair sets.**

5. **Tap OK to close the Calibrate screen.**

6. **Tap OK again to close the Tablet and Pen Settings dialog box.**

That's all there is to calibration. Now you're free to start using that pen.

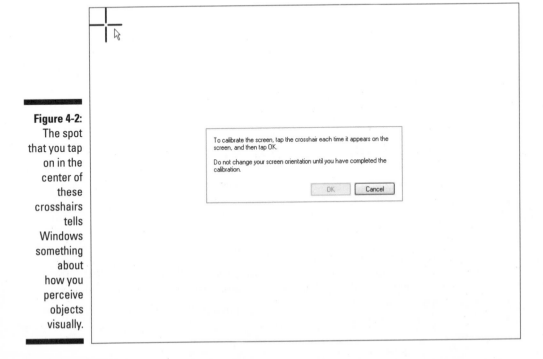

Figure 4-2:
The spot that you tap on in the center of these crosshairs tells Windows something about how you perceive objects visually.

To calibrate the screen, tap the crosshair each time it appears on the screen, and then tap OK.

Do not change your screen orientation until you have completed the calibration.

OK   Cancel

Lining Up the Pen and Screen

The first thing you might notice when you move your pen near your Tablet PC screen — say within an eighth of an inch or so — is that you don't even have to touch the screen to get a cursor to appear.

That's because the screen senses the pen as it hovers nearby, enabling you to move the cursor anyplace on the screen and take an action. This feature saves you from having to drag the pen stylus around the surface any more than necessary.

 When you're trying to judge whether you're in a position to take an action with the pen (such as tapping), use the *position of the on-screen cursor* — not the pen tip — as your guide.

Accessing the Windows Start Menu for the First Time

It's a good idea to practice lining up the pen with on-screen elements. For example, when you hold the pen over one of the Start menu choices, the pen tip and arrow cursor are in close alignment. From some other positions, however, the alignment can vary.

In fact, as you move toward the outer edges of a Tablet PC screen, the pen tip and cursor tip move slightly apart. You think you're pointing at, say, a Close button — but when you tap, nothing happens. So here's a hot tip about pen tips. . . .

To access the Start menu, follow these steps:

1. **Place the pen so it rests over the screen but isn't touching it.**

   A selection cursor (a white arrow) appears.

2. **Move the cursor until it is over the Windows Start menu button.**

3. **Tap the Start button with the pen tip.**

4. **Move the pointer around the Start menu (still without touching the screen).**

   Different items on the menu are highlighted as the pointer passes over them (as shown in Figure 4-3).

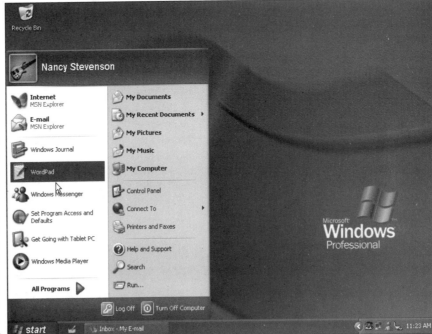

Figure 4-3:
Even if the
pen isn't
touching the
screen,
selections
are
highlighted
and the
selection
cursor
appears.

The submenus don't open when you move the cursor over them — but if you keep the cursor on the selection for a short time, they appear after a few moments.

Tapping = Clicking

Think a moment about all the things you get accomplished on a desktop computer with a simple mouse click. With a click, you place an insertion bar within a paragraph of text or in a text box in a dialog box, ready to begin typing. Clicking selects objects, opens menus, activates tool buttons, and closes windows, dialog boxes, and software applications.

On your Tablet PC, that single mouse click (the one you use the left button for on a mouse) is replaced by a single tap of your pen tip. With a single tap, you do all these things:

- Use the Close button to close dialog boxes, windows, and programs
- Activate tool buttons

✔ Select an object

✔ Open drop-down lists and palettes

✔ Place your insertion point in a document

✔ Open menus and choose commands

✔ Reactivate your computer if it's in Stand By mode

✔ Follow hyperlinks

Using single taps to access Windows Journal

The pen tap becomes an old friend after you've used the Start menu button or opened the Input Panel a few times. But it's time to use a pen in a Tablet PC application, and I've got just the ticket. Though you'll explore Windows Journal in detail in Chapter 7, for now you can start to get some pen practice in Journal by follow these steps:

1. **Choose Start⇨Windows Journal.**

2. **Tap the View Recent Notes tool button.**

   The View Notes panel appears.

3. **Tap on the arrow on the right of the View Notes field.**

   A drop-down list appears.

4. **Tap anywhere outside the list to close it.**

5. **Tap the Close button (in the top-right corner of the View Notes panel).**

   The panel closes.

6. **Choose Tools⇨Options.**

7. **Tap Pen Settings (depicted in Figure 4-4).**

8. **Tap Medium Point on the Pen Settings tab.**

9. **Tap OK twice — once to close the Pen and Highlighter Settings dialog box and again to close the Options dialog box.**

   The new setting takes effect.

10. **Tap the Close button in the top-right corner of Windows Journal.**

Figure 4-4:
You make
selections,
enter text,
and display
drop-down
lists and
color
palettes in
dialog boxes
by tapping
them with
your pen.

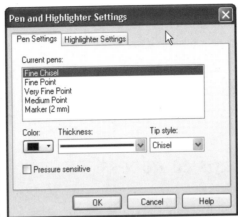

Pen and Highlighter Settings

Pen Settings | Highlighter Settings

Current pens:

Fine Chisel
Fine Point
Very Fine Point
Medium Point
Marker (2 mm)

Color: Thickness: Tip style:

[ ] Chisel

[ ] Pressure sensitive

OK   Cancel   Help

Though I'm not usually a big fan of the tutorials and demos that come with software, I can highly recommend going through the Tablet PC welcome tutorial called "Get Going with Tablet PC" (just choose Start⇨Get Going with Tablet PC). As shown in Figure 4-5, you can use this interactive tutorial to practice moving the cursor and tapping on the screen.

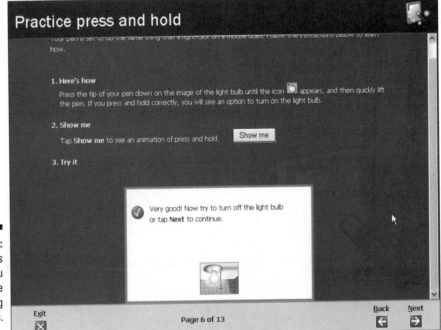

Practice press and hold

Your pen is set to do the same thing that a right-click on a mouse does. Follow the instructions below to learn how.

1. Here's how

Press the tip of your pen down on the image of the light bulb until the icon appears, and then quickly lift the pen. If you press and hold correctly, you will see an option to turn on the light bulb.

2. Show me

Tap **Show me** to see an animation of press and hold.   Show me

3. Try it

Very good! Now try to turn off the light bulb or tap **Next** to continue.

Exit   Page 6 of 13   Back   Next

Figure 4-5:
In this
tutorial, you
practice
your tapping
skills.

Getting out of your own way

One of the things I found disconcerting when I began to use a Tablet PC was working with menus. When you tap a menu to open it and move your pen down the list of commands, your hand — and the pen itself — block your line of vision, making viewing the commands (and, in some cases, the submenus that pop up) difficult.

I did find some ways to help overcome this inherent awkwardness:

✔ First, try holding the pen between your thumb and forefinger, rather than in traditional writing fashion with your entire hand wrapped around the pen. This minimizes the area of your hand that will obscure the menu.

✔ You can move the pen straight down the line of commands (as if you were moving down

a ladder rung by rung), with the pen tip below each command as you move down the menu, rather than to the side of it. This keeps your hand beneath the command line you are reading at the moment.

✔ You can modify the Menu Location setting in the Tablet and Pen Settings dialog box, which you can display from the control panel. Doing so moves submenus to the left of the main menu (for right-handed users) or to the right of the main menu (for left-handed users) and makes it easier to select commands with your pen.

As with everything new, practicing these new input methods makes them come more naturally.

If you want to change your pen setting back to its default, go back through these steps to change the Pen Settings back to Fine Chisel.

Double-tapping to access My Pictures

You know that a single pen tap is the equivalent of a single mouse click, and I bet by now you've figured out that a double-tap equals a double-click.

Using a double-tap, you can

✔ Open folders and files in Windows Explorer

✔ Open program icons on the Windows desktop

✔ Select a word in Microsoft Office-type applications

✔ Open dialog boxes for objects

✔ Open applications associated with embedded objects

Well, okay, you've probably been double-clicking with your mouse for years — but I bet that sometimes you double-click and nothing happens. That's usually because you didn't click quickly enough.

Double-tapping is no different — if you don't tap that second tap quickly enough, it won't work. Also, with a pen, you have to be careful not to move the pen tip on the screen between taps. So a bit of practice with double-tapping is in order. Follow these steps:

1. **Choose Start⇨My Computer.**

2. **Double-tap the Owner's Document folder.**

   This folder may have your name on it.

3. **Double-tap the My Pictures folder.**

4. **Double-tap one of the images in the folder to open it.**

5. **Tap the Close button on all open windows, one at a time, to close them.**

Adjusting double-tapping speed

Not happy with your double-tapping response? That's okay. You can adjust the speed required for a double-tap by following these steps:

1. **Choose Start⇨Control Panel.**

2. **Double-tap Tablet and Pen Settings.**

   The Tablet and Pen Settings dialog box appears.

3. **Tap the Pen Options tab to display it.**

4. **Tap Double-Tap Settings.**

   The Double-Tap Settings dialog box (shown in Figure 4-6) appears.

5. **Tap the slider in the Double-tap Speed setting and move it.**

   Move the slider to the left to specify a longer interval between taps; move it to the right for a shorter interval.

6. **To test the new setting, double-tap on the picture of the door at the bottom of the dialog box.**

7. **When you're happy with your setting, tap OK to save the new setting.**

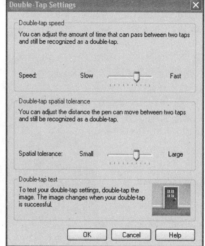

Figure 4-6:
Change
both the
speed and
spatial
settings for
your pen
stylus in this
dialog box.

Pressing and Holding (The Right-Click)

From the heading, you may have the impression that this is the section where you get warm and snuggly with your pen, but you'd be wrong. Pressing and holding is how you right-click with a pen.

Right-clicking with a mouse displays shortcut menus (called context menus) that offer commands related to whatever you right-clicked on. For example, if you right-click text in a Microsoft Word document, you get a shortcut menu with commands such as Cut, Paste, and Font.

To do the same with a Tablet PC pen, you simply press the pen close to the object of your desire; to get the equivalent of a right-click, keep holding your pen on the screen, and then release it after a few moments.

Instead of using the press-and-hold feature, you can use the Right-click button on the Writing Pad (it looks like a little mouse) to perform a right-click.

Here's how it works: Press on the Windows desktop with your pen right now. (Be patient, this may take a couple of seconds.) After a moment, a little mouse icon appears. Lift your pen tip and the shortcut menu appears (see Figure 4-7).

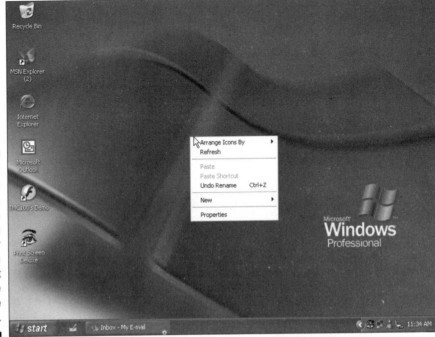

Figure 4-7:
The little
mouse icon
disappears
as soon as
you lift your
pen; then a
shortcut
menu like
this one
appears.

You can adjust how long it takes for a shortcut menu to appear in the Tablet
& Pen Settings dialog box accessed through the control panel.

Putting Pen to Tablet

When you've discovered how to perform mouse actions with your pen,
you're ready to explore how you use your pen to write in a Tablet PC. You can
write directly in some applications, such as Windows Journal and Sticky
Notes, which I discuss more in Chapters 7 and 8 in Part III of this book. In
other applications, such as a Word or Excel, you'll do your writing in the
Writing Pad on the Input Panel.

Displaying the Input Panel

The Writing Pad is a part of the Input Panel. Tap on the Writing Pad tab (the
other tab displays the on-screen Keyboard). To enter text, you first display a

document in an application such as Word, then write your input in the Input Panel, then send it to the document as either text or handwriting (called, appropriately, *ink*).

To display the Writing Pad, follow these steps:

1. **Tap the Tablet PC Input Panel icon on the Windows taskbar (just to the right of the Start button).**

   Alternatively, you can wave your pen over the screen rapidly (a technique called a *gesture*).

   The Input Panel appears, and whatever input mode you used last is displayed.

2. **Tap the Writing Pad tab to display it, if it's not already displayed (see Figure 4-8).**

The Writing Pad displays a line on which you write your text, a Send button to manually send your text to a document as either text or ink, as well as buttons for common functions such as Enter, Space, Backspace, Delete, and so on.

You can modify the number of writing lines on the Writing Pad by opening the Input Panel Tools menu, choosing Options, and then selecting the Two Lines setting on the Writing Pad tab. With the two lines displayed, you should alternate writing on the lines. If you write on only one line, it may cause some lag time while the text is converting — or even result in missing text.

The Right-click button

Die-hard mouse user? You may have noticed a little button located just about where your thumb rests when you hold your Tablet PC pen. Many pen styluses come with this little button, but not all — it's used to right-click. You simply hold the point just above the screen, press the Right-click button, and then tap the screen once. Be sure you don't move the pen when performing this action.

You can control whether this Right-click button works in this way in the Tablet & Pen Settings in the control panel. Just make sure the Use Pen Button to Right-Click option is selected there. Note, however, that turning on this option doesn't turn off the press-and-hold functionality.

Figure 4-8:
The Input
Panel
replaces
your
standard
keyboard —
and it
accepts
handwriting!

Writing in WordPad for the first time

Okay, this is what you've been waiting for. Time to put pen to screen and see what Tablet PC can make of your own, unique scrawl.

You can send your entry as handwriting (Tablet PC calls this ink), or as text. You should first select the format you want to send your entry in, then write the entry. The Input Panel will send your entry after a short delay, or you can send it manually by tapping on the Send button.

If you want a shorter delay before sending text to preview, you can adjust the Automatic Text Insertion setting in the Input Panel Options dialog box.

Try entering some text in WordPad now. First be sure the Input Panel with Writing Pad is displayed, then follow these steps:

1. **Choose Start⇨All Programs⇨Accessories⇨WordPad.**

   The WordPad application opens with a blank document. If you need to, you can tap and drag on the corners of the WordPad application window and the Input Panel to resize them to fit on-screen together.

2. **Write whatever text suits your fancy in the Writing Pad in either print-ing or script style.**

   For example, type **To be, or not to be**.

   After a few seconds, the text appears in the document.

3. **Tap the Enter button on the Writing Pad to go down to the next line in the document.**

4. **Tap the arrow to the right of the Send button and tap Send as Ink from the options displayed.**

5. **Write some more text in the Writing Pad:**

   For example, **That is the question**.

6. **Tap Send. The line appears (with apologies to Shakespeare) as script, as shown in Figure 4-9.**

You can also use your pen to draw within certain applications such as Journal, PowerPoint, and drawing programs like Corel Grafigo. You can get the lowdown on drawing with a Tablet PC in Part III.

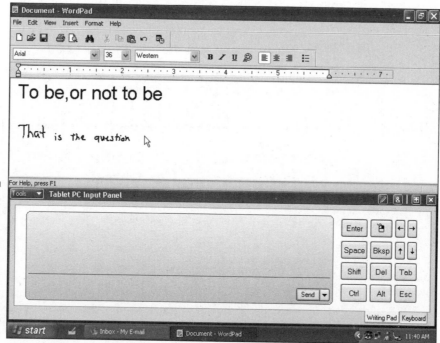

Figure 4-9:
I've enlarged the font size here so you can see the two entries more clearly.

Making Corrections

When you use handwriting as an input method in your Tablet PC, if you want that handwriting converted to text when it's inserted in a document, there's room for error. Though the handwriting recognition program built into Tablet PC is remarkable — one of the best to ever come down the road — it isn't perfect.

Making corrections by using the Text Preview pane

One way to check your input before it goes to a document is to use the Text Preview pane of the Input Panel. With the Text Preview pane displayed, when you write in the Writing Pad and tap Send, you can see the writing, in its converted type format, in the Text Preview pane. If what you read in this window is what you wrote, you're good to go and can send the text to the document. If your Tablet PC doesn't quite read your handwriting right, you can make corrections to the text before it ever appears in your document.

You can, of course, correct text after it's been inserted in a document by using the editing tools within that application.

Follow these steps to display the Text Preview pane, review preview text in it, make corrections, and then send it to a document:

Writing advice from someone who learned the hard way

It takes a bit of time to get the hang of writing on-screen. Here's some advice to get you over your learning curve faster.

First, whenever you pick the pen up off the screen, Windows XP reads that as the end of one character. When you're writing letters that have several lines in them — for example, *w* or *M* — avoid taking your pen from the screen at any point while you're writing the letter. As much as possible, practice writing all letters with a single stroke.

If you're writing letters that have sets of lines, for example *F* or *T*, be sure that the lines touch at some point. Although you may not be able to write a letter like *T* with a single stroke when you're using print, if you can do so with script, then consider using the script style (***T***) for that letter. Tablet PC will read a combination of script and print, even within the same word, with no problem.

1. **From within the Input Panel, choose Tools⇨Text Preview.**

   The Text Preview panel appears (as shown in Figure 4-10).

2. **Tap Enter to move down one line in the document.**

3. **Write some text:**

   For example, write **from Hamlet, by William Shakespeare.**

4. **Tap Send.**

   You can tap Enter in the Writing Pad (instead of Send) to achieve the same results.

   The text appears in the Text Preview window (as shown in Figure 4-11).

5. **Tap in the Text Preview pane to place your cursor at the end of the line that appears there.**

6. **Tap the on-screen Backspace key to delete the last letter on the line.**

7. **To send the corrected text to the document, tap Send.**

Do not display the Text Preview if you want to insert handwritten content into a document in its original handwritten form. With Text Preview displayed, handwriting is automatically converted to type, which means the option to Send as Ink is unavailable to you.

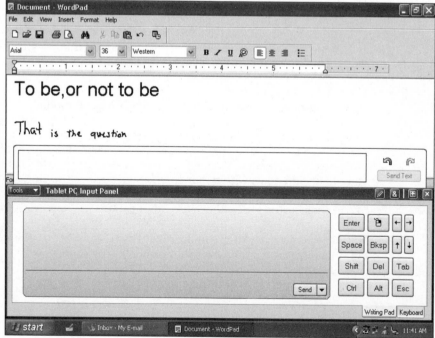

Figure 4-10: This little window at the top of the Input Panel displays your handwritten entry so you can check it for accuracy.

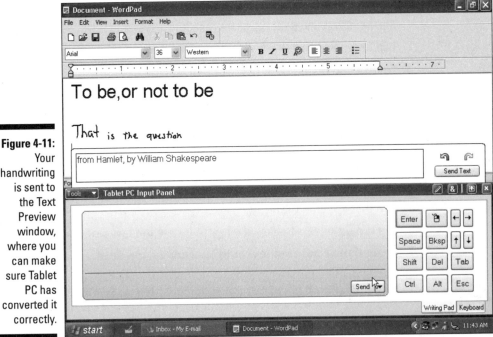

Figure 4-11:
Your
handwriting
is sent to
the Text
Preview
window,
where you
can make
sure Tablet
PC has
converted it
correctly.

Make corrections after you send text to a document? I won't kid you: When you use Ink input you will have to correct the handwriting conversion now and then (or all the time, depending on your handwriting — those who received a *D* in penmanship, take special note).

The more you use Ink, the more efficient you'll become at it, and if handwriting entry is of use to you, you probably won't mind it too much after awhile.

If you slip up now and then, don't panic. You do have a couple of methods you can use to correct errors, whether they come from a slip of the pen or problems in conversion. First, if the text has already gone to your document, you can use the tools within that application, such as the editing tools in Word, to make changes. Be sure to look for specific editing steps you can use to correct inserted text within Office applications in Chapters 10, 11, and 12.

You can also use Quick Keys in the Input Panel, and a Smart Tag feature to put things right.

Using Quick Keys to make corrections

You can use Quick Keys on the Writing Pad, or the pen eraser to delete text you've entered. The keys to the right of the entry line in Writing Pad, such as the Enter button you've already used, are called Quick Keys. They should all be pretty familiar to you, with the exception of the button with a little mouse on it — that's a button you can tap to put your pen in right-click mode.

The keys of interest in editing your input would be the Backspace and Delete keys (see Figure 4-12).

After you've sent text or ink to the Text Preview panel or to your document, you can do one of three things with Quick Keys:

- ✔ Tap the Backspace key to delete text one letter at a time moving backwards to the left of your insertion point in the document.

- ✔ Tap the Delete key to delete text one letter at a time moving forward to the right of the insertion point.

- ✔ Tap and drag (more about how to do this later in this chapter) to select text in the document, then tap either Backspace or Delete to delete it.

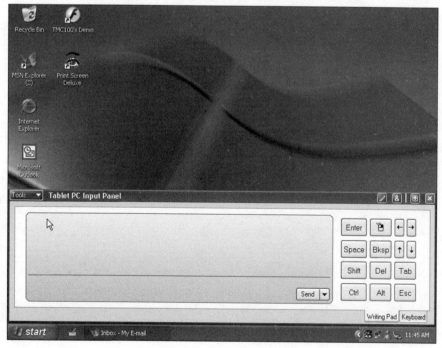

Figure 4-12: These keys are similar to several keys found on a standard keyboard.

If you prefer that Quick Keys be located on the left of your Input Panel, perhaps because you're left-handed, from the Input Panel choose Tools⇨Options; on the Writing Tools tab, select the Quick Keys on Left option and tap OK.

Using Smart Tags to make corrections

When you send handwriting to the Text Preview panel or send a document as text, a Smart Tag will appear when you tap at any point within the text. Tapping the Smart Tag (it looks like a little green corner like the ones you might use to hold photos in a scrapbook) will display a drop-down menu (see Figure 4-13).

You can use this menu in several ways:

- ✔ You can choose one of the optional word choices, in case Tablet PC has (ahem) *misunderstood* what you wrote.

- ✔ You can select the Delete or Rewrite/Respeak command to delete it or start over again.

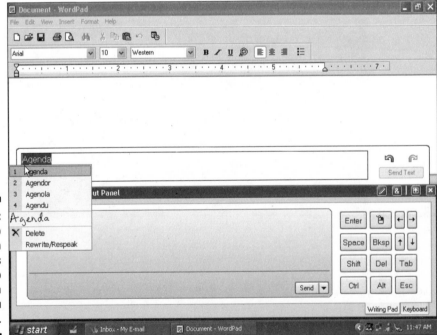

Figure 4-13:
Simply tap any option on this menu to modify a word you entered.

Expanding Your Territory with Write Anywhere

Feeling a little confined by the Writing Pad? A feature of Writing Pad called Write Anywhere enables you to use any part of the screen for a writing pad. For example, if you open Word and turn on Write Anywhere, rather than writing in the Writing Pad and sending it to Word, you can write on the Word window and your writing is automatically converted to text in the Word document.

This is especially helpful if you have a longer set of notes to write, where the Writing Pad might be too confined an area or the delay in sending text to the document is cumbersome.

Windows Journal also offers a larger area where you can write directly in the application; the Write Anywhere feature essentially emulates Journal's functionality in other applications.

Write Anywhere only accepts writing in English. (Sorry, no Japanese or ancient hieroglyphics, please.)

To turn on the Write Anywhere feature and use it, follow these steps:

1. **With the Input Panel open, choose Tools⇨Options.**

   The Options dialog box appears.

2. **Tap the Write Anywhere tab.**

   The Write Anywhere dialog box appears, as shown in Figure 4-14.

Figure 4-14:
Control how the Write Anywhere feature functions from this dialog box.

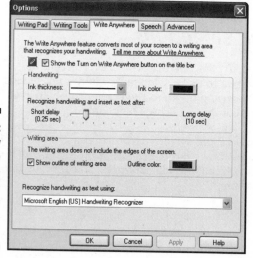

3. **Tap in the check box labeled Show the Turn on Write Anywhere Button on the Title Bar.**

4. **Tap OK.**

   A small pen shape, which is the Turn on Write Anywhere button, appears in the title bar of the Input Panel.

5. **Open an application, such as WordPad or Excel and tap in the document to place your insertion point.**

6. **Move your pen up and down on the page.**

   As you do so, a writing line appears and moves up and down the page as you move your pen.

7. **Write along the line.**

   When you pause for a moment, what you wrote is converted to text and inserted in the document at the insertion point.

Now you can write anywhere you like on the document and what you write goes wherever your insertion point is located. (Is that cool or what?)

You can't select and edit text that's been converted until you turn off the Write Anywhere feature (by tapping the pen icon again).

Look What Your Pen Dragged In . . .

As if it isn't enough that you can use your pen to do mouse clicks and write text, you can also get it to perform the mouse functions of dragging to select things and dragging to move things.

Tap-and-drag selections

Just as you use a mouse to click and drag over text (or cells in a spread-sheet), you can use the pen to make selections. There's not much to know about this, except that you should press the screen gently to avoid damaging it, then drag till what you want to select is highlighted.

If your computer has a pressure-sensitive feature, you can use the Pen and Highlighter Settings in Windows Journal to turn it on. When you do, by press-ing more firmly on your screen you will produce a thicker line. (More about Windows Journal in Chapter 7.)

Drag-and-drop selections

Dragging and dropping to move selections around a document is only slightly more complicated than dragging to select things. That's because it's important that you remove the pen from the screen at a couple of points in the process. Follow these steps to drag and drop with a pen:

1. **Tap and drag to select the text that you want to move.**

   You can select both handwritten and typed text.

2. **Lift the tip of the pen off the screen.**

3. **Move the pen pointer to somewhere within the selection and then press the tip against the screen.**

4. **Drag the selection to another location.**

   As you drag, the arrow cursor turns into an arrow with a box attached to it.

5. **To drop the selection, lift the pen off the screen.**

Chapter 5

When Your Keyboard . . . Isn't

Keyboards are nothing new. There are great big curvy ergonomic keyboards that reside in keyboard drawers the size of an orange crate, and tiny little keyboards that unfold from the size of a deck of cards so you can attach them to your PDA and make input humanly possible.

You've probably even encountered an on-screen keyboard before on your wireless phone or PDA (personal digital assistant) device, and if you have tried to use such a thing to enter more than two words, my condolences.

But the Tablet PC puts its own spin on keyboards: All models offer an on-screen keyboard that may remind you of the one on a PDA, but which is larger and offers full keyboard functionality at the touch of a pen. In addition, depending on the Tablet PC model you own, a regular, old-fashioned plastic-type keyboard may just be lurking somewhere close by.

Checking Out Your Options

To some extent, Tablet PCs aren't exactly a keyboard revolution. The truth is that many Tablet PC models come with a standard keyboard, either built in so that they resemble traditional laptops (such as the Toshiba Portege 3500 or Acer TravelMate C100), or as a detachable feature in *slate* models (also called *slab* because they resemble, well, I guess, a slab of slate), such as the Fujitsu Stylistic ST4000 or Motion M1200.

And all models have the on-screen keyboard. Although the on-screen keyboard (discussed later in this chapter) is a viable option for entering short notes, it may be frustrating to a speed demon. If you have a lot of text to enter — or time is of the essence and you want to exercise your blazing normal typing speed — then eschewing the on-screen keyboard might be a wise thing to do. Sometimes you've just gotta have a standard keyboard attached to your Tablet PC.

Do you own a convertible?

If you own a convertible Tablet PC (also called a *clamshell* style), then you already have a slightly smaller version of a standard keyboard built in (check out the Potege 3500 by Toshiba — www.toshiba.com — to see a really cool convertible).

Your user's manual shows you exactly how to unclip and rotate the computer to change from tablet mode (where the unit folds down to a single tablet panel with the keyboard hidden) to PC mode (in which your Tablet PC looks strikingly like a notebook computer with both screen and keyboard available).

The configuration of built-in keyboards varies slightly from model to model, but most built-ins use a Function key to toggle to additional functions to save keyboard space.

Using a built-in keyboard doesn't limit your options: When you have your computer in PC mode, you have the choice of using either the on-screen keyboard, the pen, or the standard keyboard for input.

Adding a keyboard to your slate-style Tablet PC

If you have a slate-style Tablet PC (one with no keyboard attached), you will probably want to hook it up to a standard keyboard on a somewhat regular basis — especially if you use keyboard entry frequently or are using your Tablet PC as your main computer.

Some Tablet PC models come with a detachable keyboard; others offer a detachable keyboard as an option. In addition, you can always attach any old USB keyboard (such as the one from your desktop computer) if you just like the familiarity of old coffee stains and snack-bar crumbs among the keys.

You can use the USB (Universal Serial Bus) port built into most Tablet PC models to hook up any USB keyboard device to your tablet, from portable folding keyboards to the desktop variety.

In most models, the USB port is hidden under a rubber flap on one edge of your unit and sports a *USB icon* (which looks like a solid circle with three lines coming out of it to the right). Some Tablet PCs have one USB port, others offer two for connecting more than one device at a time, such as keyboard and monitor.

You can get USB adapters for attaching serial devices. Check at any computer supply store or visit your manufacturer's online store to see whether they offer such accessories for your Tablet PC.

When you plug a power supply — or any add-on device — into your Tablet PC, be careful not to hold or place that edge of the device on a desk or other surface or you could disconnect (or worse, damage) the plug or Tablet PC. Instead, rotate the display so the bottom is along an edge of the computer that has no cords connected to it.

You can also use your USB port to connect other peripherals, such as a monitor, printer, or scanner. See Chapter 3 for more about adding USB devices.

Playing Around with the Input Panel

The Input Panel — in particular, the Writing Pad feature — has a starring role in Chapter 4. But Writing Pad is only one feature of the Input Panel: the other features are Speech (covered in Chapter 6) and the Keyboard. Together they make up a powerful input mechanism for your Tablet PC.

The Keyboard and Writing Pad are displayed as two tabs in the Input Panel. Tap the Keyboard tab and a little regulation keyboard is displayed. You can tap on the keys with your pen and that text is inserted in an open document. Tap the Writing Pad and a handwriting input area is displayed.

You can then write input and send it to a document as either text or handwriting. You can use both the Keyboard and Writing Pad to input text, but only the Writing Pad can input handwriting as ink. In this chapter, I focus on the Keyboard tab.

The Speech feature is turned on in the Tools menu of the Input Panel, which displays two buttons you can use whether you have Keyboard or Writing Pad displayed. Learn more about this feature in Chapter 6.

Some Tablet PC models, such as the Acer TravelMate C100, are designed more like a traditional laptop computer and do include a standard keyboard. However, even these models have the Input Panel available for the times when handwriting is preferable or you want to use the unit in tablet mode.

The Input Panel offers some flexibility — you can open and close it, resize it, move it around, or dock it at the bottom of your screen. And that's what this section is all about.

Showing and hiding the panel

The Input Panel made a cameo appearance in earlier chapters, but here's a pocket review: You have two ways to open the Input Panel: by tapping an icon or by using a fascinating feature of Windows XP for Tablet PC — a *gesture* (no, not *that* one).

Here's how the two methods work:

- The Input Panel icon is located on the Windows taskbar, just to the right of the Start button. Tap it with your pen and the panel opens.
- To use the gesture, simply wave your pen back and forth anywhere just above the Tablet PC screen; after a moment — poof! — the panel appears.

The Input Panel always appears on top of other applications ready for you to use when you need it.

True, sometimes that on-screen keyboard is simply blocking your view like a tall man wearing a top hat in a movie theater. Fortunately, you don't have to ask, "Excuse me, would you please take off that hat — and lose a few inches in height while you're at it?"

You can hide the panel quickly — reducing it till it displays only its title bar — and bring it back as needed. The two-part drill looks like this:

- Tap the Show/Hide Pen Input Area button (shown in Figure 5-1) to hide the panel.
- Tap the Show/Hide Pen Input Area button again to redisplay the panel.

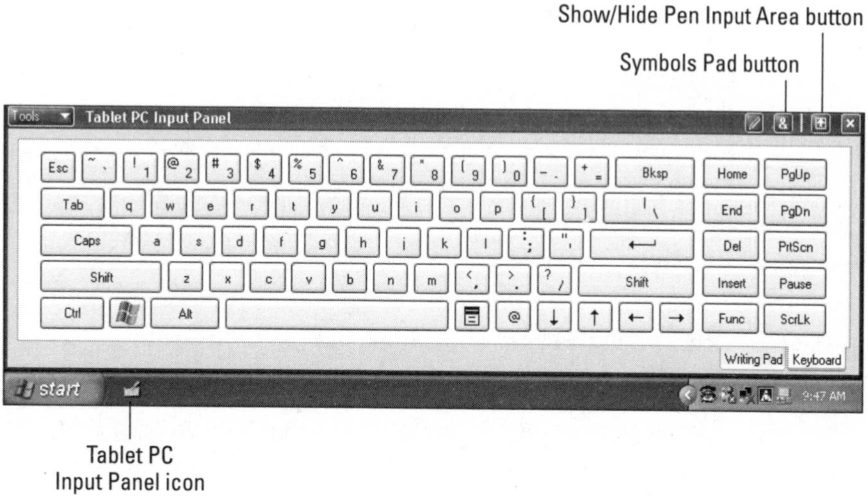
Show/Hide Pen Input Area button
Symbols Pad button
Tools
Tablet PC Input Panel
Writing Pad
Keyboard
start
Tablet PC Input Panel icon

Figure 5-1: The Input Panel Keyboard has a familiar looking configuration, just like your desktop keyboard.

Docking the panel or setting it free

The Input Panel appears at the bottom of your screen by default. You can dock the panel there so that it can't be moved, or undock it and move it around to your heart's content. If you move the panel, when you open it again it appears in the same spot it occupied when you hid it.

To dock and undock the Input Panel, follow these steps:

1. **With the Input Panel displayed, choose Tools➪Dock.**

   The command is checked (as shown in Figure 5-2).

2. **To undock the panel, choose Tools➪Dock again.**

   The command is unchecked; the panel floats free.

TIP: For a quick way to dock the Input Panel, you can also double-tap its title bar.

To move the undocked panel around your screen, you use a similar method to the one you've used many times to move windows around a computer desktop. Simply press on the title bar of the panel with your pen, and drag the panel wherever you want it.

Figure 5-2:
The Tools menu of the Input Panel.

Occasionally, when you press and drag a window with your pen, nothing happens. Frankly, the pen is just less foolproof than your mouse for moving windows around. I can't provide a handy clue that helps explain this phenomenon — the cursor doesn't change when a window is ready to be moved or anything. My advice is to practice, practice, practice.

If you move the panel around your screen and then hide it by tapping the Close button, its title bar floats wherever you placed the panel on your screen (see Figure 5-3).

Figure 5-3:
When you hide the panel, it appears as this single title bar, sitting wherever the panel was on your screen at the time you hid it.

Resizing the panel

Because the Input Panel takes up almost half of your screen (depending on how big a screen your Tablet PC model has), you'll be glad to hear that in addition to hiding the panel, you can resize it so that it's still around, but not so much in the way. How's that for the best of both worlds? Figure 5-4 shows how small the panel can get.

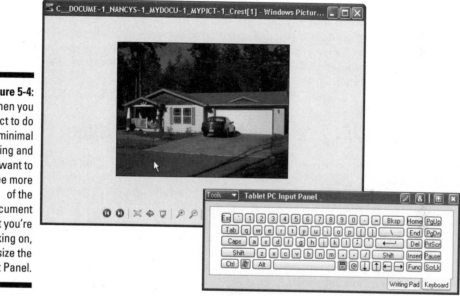

Figure 5-4: When you expect to do minimal typing and you want to see more of the document that you're working on, resize the Input Panel.

To resize the panel, follow these steps:

1. **Choose Tools and check to make sure the Dock command isn't checked.**

   If the command isn't checked, the panel isn't docked, and that's as it needs to be to resize it.

2. **Move your pen over any edge of the Input Panel until the cursor turns into a line with two arrows.**

3. **Tap anywhere on the screen and drag outward or inward.**

   Dragging outward expands the keyboard; dragging inward shrinks it.

You can set up the Input Panel to become smaller automatically when not in use. Choose Tools➪Options, and on the Advanced tab, check the When Input Panel Is Not Docked, Hide the Pen Input Area check box, and then use the slider to select a length of time for the delay.

Tapping to Type

Typing may be something you can do like the wind, or it may be your own personal one-fingered definition of torture. But however you feel about typing on a regular keyboard, you can use your knowledge of the keyboard to tap out text letter by letter on your Tablet PC. You can also use the keyboard to navigate around open documents, and you can use function keys (like F1, which displays help for the application you're working in).

Entering text with on-screen keys

Using the on-screen keyboard is *exactly* the same as typing on a regular keyboard . . . except there's no real keyboard, you use a pen instead of your fingers, and you can't type nearly as fast (details, details . . .).

Okay, so it's pretty different, really. But for an on-the-go way to enter short notes or quick e-mail messages, the on-screen keyboard can be pretty efficient. And because many of you want the Tablet PC for its lightweight portability, giving up a regular keyboard to lose a few pounds of baggage seems a reasonable trade-off.

The first thing to know about using this (ahem) virtual keyboard is that you have to have a document open (say, an Excel spreadsheet or WordPad document). With your insertion point active, whatever you type on the keyboard appears in the document (as shown in Figure 5-5).

When you have an application open and a document displayed on-screen, it's time to hit the keys. Sort of. The equivalent to pressing a key on a regular keyboard is tapping a key on the Input Panel Keyboard with your pen. Tapping a letter inserts the letter, tapping the spacebar inserts a space, tapping the tab key inserts a tab, and so on. When you hold your pen over a key on the keyboard, the key becomes highlighted with a border (shown in Figure 5-6). Tap on the key, and that letter, number, punctuation, or action is inserted in the document.

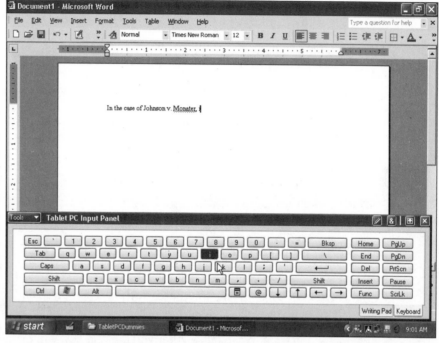

Figure 5-5:
When you
tap a key
on the
keyboard,
it is
highlighted,
and the
letter is
inserted in
the open
document.

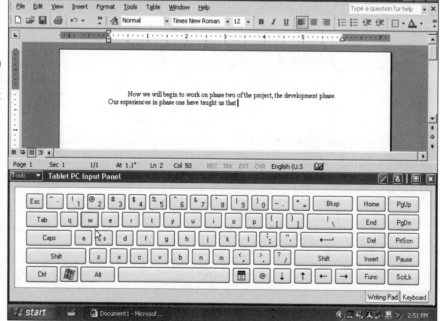

Figure 5-6:
A highlight
around
a key
indicates
that when
you tap
again you
will have
done the
Tablet PC
equivalent
of typing
the key on
a standard
keyboard.

To use function keys (such as Ctrl and Alt) that you often hold down simultaneously with other keys, just tap the first one in the sequence. It stays highlighted as you tap additional function keys. Tablet PC is smart enough to know that Ctrl followed by V is a cut command, Alt followed by Tab is a command to switch from one open application to another, and so on.

Tablet PCs feature a Windows Security tablet button somewhere on the hardware surrounding your computer screen, depending on the model you own. Look for the symbol of a key to identify the button. You can use this instead of Ctrl+Alt+Delete to display the Task Manager dialog box.

In addition to entering text, you can use the Tab, Space, and Enter keys on your keyboard just as you do with a regular keyboard to add space or move to the next line in the document.

Capitalizing your type

When, in the course of typing, you want to use a capital letter or alternative punctuation or symbol, on a traditional keyboard you press Shift and the key together. On a Tablet PC, you tap Shift and all the symbols on the keys switch to uppercase options (as illustrated in Figure 5-7). Then tap the key for the character you want to capitalize. After you tap that key, you're right back in lowercase land.

Figure 5-7:
Note that the number and punctuation keys all show their uppercase options, and all letter keys display uppercase letters.

If you want to capitalize a series of letters, you use a Caps Lock feature just as you would on a standard keyboard. Tap the key labeled Caps on the Input Panel and then capitalize away. When you no longer want to capitalize, just tap Caps again.

When a gesture will do

A neat feature of Tablet PC is gestures. If you've used a PDA handwriting program such as Graffiti, gestures may already be old hat. You can use gestures to perform four standard keyboard operations by using the Writing Panel or Write Anywhere features (see Chapter 4 for more about using both of these).

For example, you can press your pen on your screen in Write Anywhere mode and draw a line to the left to perform a Backspace operation. You can press on your screen and draw a line to the right to enter a Space. Press and draw down and to the left instead of tapping the Enter key. Then press on the screen and draw up and to the right to Tab.

With Caps on, numbers are not automatically switched to their uppercase alternatives (for example a percent sign instead of the numeral 5). You'll need to tap the Shift key to get optional input for numbers, punctuation, and symbols such as forward slash.

Working with the Symbols Pad

There are certain symbols people use all the time. For example number-minded people use dollar signs and percentage symbols, while anybody who writes e-mail probably uses the @ symbol about 3,578 times a day.

Your Tablet PC provides a handy little pad attached to the Input Panel that you can use to quickly and easily insert symbols. Many of these symbols can be found on your regular keyboard keys, but you may have to press Shift to use them. Being able to access them without the Shift function can speed your input.

The Symbols Pad, shown in Figure 5-8, can be displayed by tapping the Symbols Pad button in the title bar of the Input Panel, and it can be hidden by tapping the Symbols Pad button again. When you then tap a symbol key on the pad to insert a symbol, the pad disappears. You have to tap the button again to display it.

If you'd like the pad to always be available, you can tap its title bar and drag it away from the Input Panel. When the Symbols Pad is floating freely, it will stay open until you close it by tapping the Close button.

If you close the freely floating Symbols Pad, then the next time you open it, you'll discover it's gone right back to being docked to the Input Panel.

Figure 5-8: Commonly used symbols can be input easily from this handy little pad.

Editing text

Because the keyboard types text into an open document in an application such as Word, one obvious option for editing text is the editing tools found in that application. However, just as with your desktop computer, you'll often use keys such as Delete and Backspace to modify text.

With your insertion point in existing text, tap the Backspace key to delete one letter at a time to the left. Tap the Delete key to delete one letter at a time to the right of the insertion point.

If you want new text to overwrite existing text, remember that you can tap the Insert key on your on-screen keyboard, or tap it again to have new text you enter be inserted within existing text.

You can use your pen to select text and use the keyboard to edit it. For example, tap in a document and drag your pen to highlight several words. Then, tap the Delete or Backspace key to delete that text (as shown in Figure 5-9).

You can also use shortcut key combinations, such as Ctrl+X to cut text and Ctrl +V to paste it.

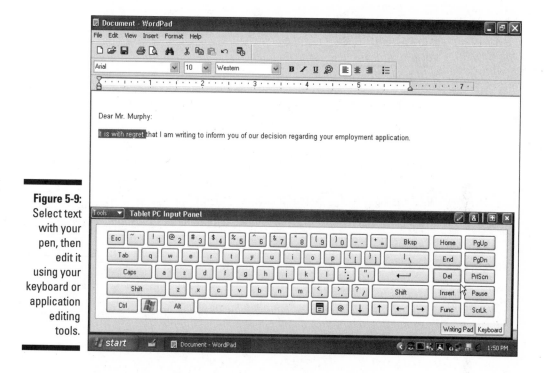

Figure 5-9:
Select text
with your
pen, then
edit it
using your
keyboard or
application
editing
tools.

Moving around in documents

By now you've figured out that using the on-screen keyboard is pretty much
like using any old keyboard, except that it's on-screen and you tap keys with
a pen. So if you guess that the Home, End, Page Up, and Page Down keys all
help you move around the document you're working in, you're right. . . .

Taking shortcuts

You may have noticed a couple of keys in the Input Panel that have little symbols on them. First, there's the Windows logo key that you probably have on
your standard keyboard. Then there's a little key on the other side of the
spacebar that looks like a little menu. Table 5-1 shows how these work.

Table 5-1: Tablet PC Keyboard Shortcut Combinations

Key(s)	Function
Windows logo	Opens Start menu
Windows logo+Tab	Makes next taskbar button active
Windows logo+E	Opens Windows Explorer
Windows logo+F	Opens Windows Search function
Windows logo+M	Minimizes all windows
Windows logo+R	Opens the Run dialog box
Application	Opens a context-sensitive menu (as right-tap does)
Left Arrow	Turns Brightness down

Chapter 6

Talking to Your Tablet PC

• •

• •

Speech recognition is a mixed blessing. It's just as cool as can be — suddenly you're behaving like a starship captain who can just speak commands into thin air and have the computer do your bidding. (You know — you say, "Computer, summarize the profits from merchandising the products of the following mega-movie franchises . . ." and it does!) But on the negative side, speech recognition technology is still in a somewhat clunky, infantile stage of its evolution.

That clunkiness means that the best speech-recognition technology can hear you about as well as you can hear someone speaking to you when both your neighbors are mowing their lawns and your dog is barking. A word such as "meow" might come out as "right now."

I once spoke the words "Don't forget to do a quality check," and the Tablet PC recorded "Dover get to college to." (Actually, some of the attempts speech recognition makes can be pretty funny — and possibly the basis of a new board game.)

But the good news is that speech recognition is improving all the time, and as you use it, both you and the technology will get smarter.

Giving Tablet PC an Earful

The Speech feature of Windows XP for Tablet PC enables you to dictate content for documents such as letters, e-mails, or spreadsheets. You can also speak commands to your computer and software, such as Launch Program or Print.

Speech is probably best used for shorter notes and even entries you might make in form fields. Although you can enter longer content, you'll have to do a certain amount of editing where Speech hasn't recognized your words quite accurately.

Also, if you can't remain in a quiet environment for the longer period of time it may take to write a longer document, your use of speech may be rendered inaccurate by intruding noises such as phones ringing or people speaking to you. You can pause the Speech feature, but it can get irritating to do so too often.

The first step in using the Speech feature is to train it to understand the way you talk.

First, Teach Tablet PC to Listen Up

Imagine that you just made a new friend from a foreign country — I'll call him Hans. Now, Hans speaks English, but with an accent. It may take a few days or weeks to really get the hang of his accent so you can clearly understand him when he says things like "please pass the butter" or "you have something disgusting on your shoe."

Well, in essence, *everyone* who speaks English does so with an accent, and Tablet PC has to get used to your particular accent, as well as to your unique way of pronouncing words. That's why you have to create a *speech profile* before you use this function of the Tablet PC. A speech profile gives the speech-recognition program some speech samples to go by when deciphering what you say.

Training Tablet PC

In order to get Tablet PC familiar with your pronunciation, you need to walk through its Voice Training wizard.

Tablet PCs come with microphones built in; however, you can also attach an external microphone or headset. This option is probably easier (and less funny-looking) than holding your Tablet PC to your mouth and speaking into the front-left or back-right corner of it.

Whether you use Tablet PC's built-in microphone or an external mic, you should have the microphone you want to use connected before proceeding with the wizard.

You can train your Tablet PC for the first time through the Input Panel. When you open the panel and turn on Speech for the first time by choosing Tools⇨Speech, a small pane appears at the top of the Input Panel with an area in the center that tells you that you have to go through speech training before you can use the feature.

To use the Voice Training wizard, follow these steps:

1. **Open the Input Panel and choose Tools⇨Speech.**

   The option to go through the speech training only appears on the Input Panel once. After you train the Tablet PC for the first time, if you or somebody else who uses your Tablet PC wants to create new profiles, just open the control panel and select Speech. Then tap New to create a new profile.

   You're taken through the Training wizard again. The speech-recognition feature can store multiple profiles.

   The wizard begins with an introductory screen that explains how to adjust your microphone.

2. **Tap Next to proceed.**

   The Adjust Volume screen (shown in Figure 6-1) appears.

Figure 6-1:
The first step in under-standing you is for Tablet PC to adjust to your speaking volume by adjusting your microphone.

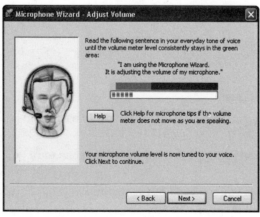

3. **Read the phrase shown there in a normal voice (no shouting!).**

   Your Tablet PC sets the correct microphone level (this controls the recording volume).

   A note that says that the microphone has been tuned to your voice level appears.

4. **Tap Next.**

   The Test Positioning screen appears (see Figure 6-2).

5. **Read the sentence that appears on-screen.**

   Tablet PC checks to see whether your mouth is too close or too far from the microphone for you to be heard clearly. When the check is complete, Tablet PC plays the sentence you just read.

6. **If your voice sounds clear, tap Finish.**

   If it doesn't sound clear, then reread the sentence, speaking more loudly, until the playback sounds clear.

   You've now set up your microphone and are ready to start the actual voice training.

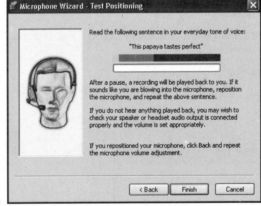

Figure 6-2:
If the playback is fuzzy, you may be too close to the microphone.

7. **Tap Next to continue.**

   The next screen simply explains that you will be asked to read sample text contained on the next several screens.

8. **Start reading and proceed through these screens until you reach the end.**

   As you do, words you read will be highlighted as they are recognized (see Figure 6-3).

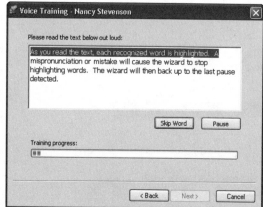

Figure 6-3:
Speak
slowly and
clearly; the
highlights
tell you the
words that
have been
recognized.

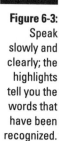

If the highlighting stops, you have to go back to the last highlighted word and read from there forward again.

When you finish reading text on one screen, the wizard continues to a new selection of training text.

If the highlighting stops at any point and you just can't seem to get it to move on no matter how many times you read the next word, tap Skip Word to move forward.

9. **When you've completed the training, tap Finish. You are returned to the Speech dialog box.**

10. **Tap Apply, then OK to close the dialog box.**

Tablet PC now has a profile to help it better recognize your speech.

Going back to school

You can provide additional training to Tablet PC Speech at any time by selecting Voice Training from the Speech Tools menu in the Input Panel. When you do, a list of documents is displayed, such as *Aesop's Fables* or *The Fall of the House of Usher* by Edgar Allan Poe.

Though this is a somewhat tedious task, going through as many of these selections as possible *now* is a good idea. You can always wait until later to make the system most efficient with your pronunciation, but why not go through the agony all at once?

This list of additional readings is also displayed when you first complete a new voice profile.

The additional selections offered when you initiate more training (see Figure 6-4) are slightly more entertaining than the ones in the initial speech-recognition training. In fact, why not just read *The Wonderful Wizard of Oz* selection as a bedtime story one night while you're recording and kill two birds with one reading?

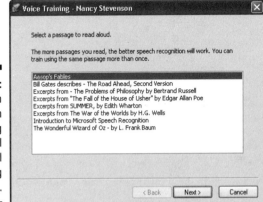

Figure 6-4: You can choose from among several additional training options.

Becoming a Dictator

Tablet PC's speech-recognition program has two capabilities. You can speak content (or dictate) into a document, and you can speak commands, such as "Open" or "Save." In this section, I show you how to dictate content.

Speech is accessed through the Input Panel. Dictation works with programs that the panel works with. For example, Windows Journal won't accept speech dictation because it doesn't accept entries from the Input Panel, but it can handle commands. Word and WordPad can accept speech entry and commands.

Speech voice commands work with all Windows programs.

Knowing what you can (and can't) say

So, you've completed your training and you're ready to try this puppy out for real. All righty, then. Here's what you can say to your computer in dictation mode. You can

- Say words, numbers, or punctuation such as "comma" or "period."

- Use the "Spell" voice command to force Speech to spell out the letters you speak rather than words.

I love this feature! For example, if you use the voice command, you can say the letters C A T and Tablet PC spells the word cat, not the words "see a tea."

This is also a great feature if you want to make sure Tablet PC inserts a numeral (like the number 2) instead of a word (the word "to" or "too"). See "What can you do with voice commands?" later in this chapter.

✔ You cannot spell out something and have it appear as a regular old word (versus individual capital letters). I read the sentence "I went swimming in the sea" to my Tablet PC and it printed "I went swimming in the C." But if I spell out "S-E-A" with the Spell command, I get SEA, not sea.

Go figure. . . .

If you end a sentence by saying "period," the next word will be capitalized automatically.

✔ You can use Speech and your pen or keyboard together. For example, if you want to move to the next line in your document, you can finish your sentence, then tap Enter on your on-screen keyboard with your pen.

You can write an acronym with your pen and then continue speaking the rest of a sentence. If you have a convertible model, you can use your real life keyboard as well.

TIP

Voice recognition do's and don'ts

Before you start speaking to your computer willy-nilly (reading limericks aloud, doing impressions of your favorite comedian, or whatnot), I've got some advice for you:

✔ **Speak clearly and slowly:** Enunciate each word as clearly as possible.

✔ **Step up to the mic:** Speak directly into the microphone, whether into a headset or into the built-in microphone in your Tablet PC (your user manual will show you where your built-in microphone is located).

✔ **Find a quiet environment:** The Speech feature is sensitive to noises around you, such as a radio playing in the background or a dog barking in the next room.

✔ **Stay slow, steady, and even:** Find a volume of speech that seems to work well and keep your voice at that volume at all times.

✔ **Avoid slang:** If you use obscure slang expressions (like "jive mamma") or business-specific acronyms, you might consider avoiding them when using Speech input.

✔ **Be aware of your environment:** I don't know if anybody has written a book of Speech etiquette, but I'm going to suggest rule number one: Don't use Speech in settings that will drive other people crazy. Generally, if people can't escape the sound of your voice (in a meeting, on a plane, in a restaurant, or in a movie theater), leave the program turned off. After all, the speech system probably won't work properly anyway, what with all the people around you talking loudly on their cell phones.

Ready, set, talk

To speak content — whoa, what a concept! — follow these steps:

1. **Open an application, such as Word or WordPad, enabled for working with Windows XP for Tablet PC.**

2. **Tap the Input Panel icon to open it.**

3. **Choose Tools⇨Speech; put a check mark next to Speech to turn it on.**

4. **Tap the Dictation button.**

   The Speech area displays the word Listening (as shown in Figure 6-5).

5. **Begin speaking.**

   If you're at a loss for words, start with "Once upon a time . . ." or simply read these steps.

   If the Input Panel displays the words What Was That? you'll have to repeat what you said, perhaps louder, more slowly, or into the microphone.

6. **Continue reading into your microphone, adding punctuation (such as periods and commas) where appropriate.**

7. **When you're finished, tap the Dictation button again to turn it off.**

Figure 6-5:
If you say
something
Speech
can't
recognize,
the phrase
Listening
will change
to What
Was
That?

Making Corrections (And There Will Be Corrections!)

If you have been reading this chapter from the beginning, you know that I warned you early on that speech-recognition programs aren't quite as *refined* as they someday will be. You will get errors. You could say **Begin speaking** and get **Begins eighteen**. (I did.) You could cough and get the phrase **days in**. (I did.) Or you could have some real fun and try singing to your Tablet PC and get complete garbage. (Nope, "Smoke Gets In Your Eyes" is not on Tablet PC's hit parade.)

In some instances, speech won't come across looking like what you said. That happens for a variety of reasons. You might have spoken too quickly. Speech also takes context into account. If you say random words rather than phrases that have common sentence syntax, you'll have more problems.

When errors occur, you have a few tools at your disposal, via the Smart Tag function. A *Smart Tag* is a context-specific feature that appears when you take certain actions in Windows programs, such as pasting text from the Windows Clipboard in a document or inserting speech with Input Panel. You can tap on a Smart Tag, and a drop-down list offers options to complete the action. With the Speech Smart Tag, you could, for example, choose an alternate word to insert from a list of similar-sounding words.

Use the Smart Tag function access some correction options:

1. **Select a word you have just inserted in your document using Speech.**

   The Smart Tag appears (it looks like a little green corner).

2. **Move your cursor over the Smart Tag and tap the arrow that appears.**

   A menu like the one shown in Figure 6-6 appears. This menu offers some optional words you can select to replace a word. You can also opt to delete the text or Rewrite/Respeak it. If you choose the latter command, whatever you type or say will replace the current word.

3. **After you choose a Smart Tag option, the action is performed and the Smart Tag disappears.**

   A typical example is when you replace a word with an alternate word.

4. **Choose the Replay Dictation choice to hear where you went wrong.**

   It can also help you figure out how to say the word more accurately next time!

You can also simply use the editing tools in the application you have open, or keys on the keyboard such as Delete, Backspace, or Insert to make corrections to text.

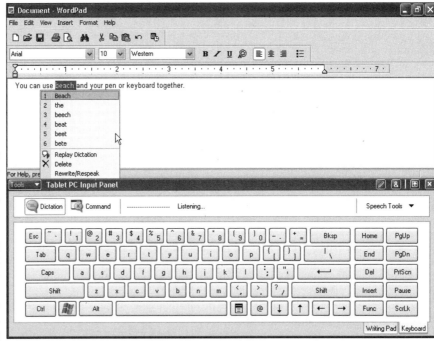

Figure 6-6:
If the word
you really
meant to
input is on
this list, just
tap it and it
will replace
the word
that Speech
input.

Telling Tablet PC the correct pronunciation for specific words

So, here's a challenge: I tried saying "speech" five times and got this input:

- ✔ Beach
- ✔ Each
- ✔ Eighth
- ✔ Saint Pete
- ✔ B. she

Here's hoping you have better luck, but even if you don't run across this problem with the word "speech," you will have a problem with some other word. I promise. What to do? Sometimes you have to teach Tablet PC how you say a specific word so that it can be added to the Speech database, and (hooray!) be recognized every time you say it in the future.

Well, *most* times you say it. . . .

Here's how to use the Speech database:

1. **With Dictation turned off, choose Speech Tools⊅Add Pronunciation for a Word.**

   The dialog box shown in Figure 6-7 appears.

Figure 6-7: Adding to Speech's dictionary will make it convert your speech more accurately.

2. **Enter the word in the Word box.**

   You can even do this with handwriting!

3. **Tap the Record Pronunciation button and speak the word.**

   The word appears in the Dictionary list.

4. **Tap Close.**

You're in Command

The other half of the speech-recognition equation is the ability to speak commands to your computer. This is eminently satisfying, because your computer has ruled your life for so long it's nice to finally get back in charge, even briefly. I find that voice commands work better than speech as a rule — probably because there are only so many set phrases you can speak, and the recognition technology only has to relate your speech to one of them, not the entire language.

Voice commands work with Windows functionality, so they work with all applications, whether they are Tablet PC enhanced or not. The commands available to you enable you to launch programs, select text, activate menus, and so on.

For some rules about using voice recognition in public (whether you're barking orders or dictating content), see the sidebar earlier in this chapter called "Voice recognition do's and don'ts." Be clear, speak slowly, and don't annoy your neighbors.

Let's face it: It's especially dangerous speaking commands in crowded public spaces. For example, phrases such as "Scratch that," when uttered in a commanding voice, could be misconstrued and cause painful repercussions.

What you can say

Commands are specific phrases. In other words . . . you can't *use* other words. If the command to undo your last action is "Undo that" you can't say "Undo last" and expect anything to happen. When you speak a command, it is acted on in the currently active program.

Given this need for specific command phrases, it's helpful that Tablet PC provides you with a context-sensitive list of commands. *Context-sensitive* means that if you have Excel open, you may have one set of commands available, but if you are in Outlook, that same set may not be available to you because those commands aren't relevant to Outlook.

You access a list of these commands in the Input Panel when you have the Speech feature active and the Command feature turned on by choosing Speech Tools⇨What Can I Say. The dialog box shown in Figure 6-8 appears. Any item in gray is unavailable for the open application. You can expand categories of commands by tapping the plus symbol next to them.

You can leave this dialog box open while working in an application so you have a handy reference available.

Making your first verbal command to Tablet PC

Now that you know what you can say, try commanding your Tablet PC to do something and see how this all works.

Some logical computing-type stuff you might want to do is open a program, play around in a document, and close the program. Of course, you can also undo changes, opt to save (or not to save) files you've been working with, and more. Follow these steps to make Tablet PC perform basic file-related tasks:

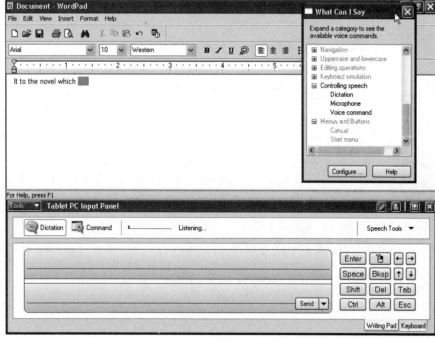

Figure 6-8:
Anything
grayed out
in this dialog
box is not
relevant to
the open
application.

1. **Open the Input Panel and choose Tools⇨Speech to turn the Speech feature on (if it isn't on already).**

2. **Tap the Command button.**

3. **Launch a program.**

   For example, to launch WordPad, say **Launch WordPad**.

   WordPad opens with a blank document displayed.

4. **If you like, you can type text using the Input Panel, even while you're using voice commands.**

   For example, you could type **I am going to speak to my computer now.**

5. **To delete written text, say** Undo that.

   The text you just entered is deleted.

6. **Type something else, if you like.**

   For example, I typed **Using commands is more fun than working.**

7. **To save the file, say** Save.

   The Save dialog box appears.

8. **To cancel saving the file, say** Cancel.

   The dialog box closes.

9. **To close the file, say** Close.

A dialog box appears, asking whether you want to save changes.

10. **If you don't want to, just say** No.

If you want to save this masterpiece, say **Yes**.

11. **Tap the Command button to turn the feature off.**

Cool, huh? (Sorry, no warp drive is available yet, but just *try* not to feel like a starship captain. . . .)

If you're in Windows Journal or another program where you can write with your pen directly in the application, use the Lasso tool to select words before performing actions such as Delete or Copy.

What you can do with voice commands

It may take getting used to: The commands available to you can vary slightly depending on the active application. I broke down Tables 6-1 through 6-10 by function. The tables offer a rundown of the types of commands you can use. Items in brackets *<like this>* are actual text or application names you should insert as applicable.

Table 6-1	Inserting Breaks
Command	*What It Does*
Force num *<number>*	Inserts number as numeral rather than as word
New line	Inserts soft line break
New paragraph	Inserts hard line break
Spell it	Inserts spoken letters rather than words

Table 6-2	Commanding the Input Panel
Command	*What It Does*
Close Input Panel	Closes Input Panel
Hide Text Preview Pane	Closes Text Preview pane
Open Input Panel	Maximizes minimized Input Panel

Command	What It Does
Send text	Sends handwritten entry to Text Preview pane
Send that	Sends text in Text Preview to document
Show Text Preview Pane	Displays Text Preview pane
What Can I Say	Opens What Can I Say command list box

Table 6-3	Starting Applications
Command	**What It Does**
Launch *<application name>*	Opens named application
Open *<application name>*	Opens named application
Start *<application name>*	Opens named application

Table 6-4	Switching and Selecting
Command	**What It Does**
Switch to *<application name>*	Makes named application Selection and Correction
Correct that	Displays correction menu for selected word
Delete *<phrase>*	Deletes spoken phrase
Delete *<phrase>* through *<phrase>*	Deletes text from one phrase you read through another
Scratch that	Deletes selected text
Select *<phrase>*	Selects spoken phrase
Select *<phrase>* through *<phrase>*	Selects text from one phrase you read through another
Select all	Selects all text and objects in document
Select paragraph	Selects paragraph within which cursor is resting
Select sentence	Selects sentence within which insertion point is resting

(continued)

Table 6-4 *(continued)*

Command	What It Does
Select that	Selects word to the right of the insertion point
Select word	Selects word within which insertion point is resting
Unselect that	Unselects selected item

Table 6-5	Navigating
Command	**What It Does**
Go to beginning of line	Moves insertion point to beginning of line
Go to bottom	Moves insertion point to end of document
Go to end of line	Moves insertion point to end of line
Go to top	Moves insertion point to beginning of document
Insert after <*phrase*>	Moves insertion point after the word you specify
Insert before <*phrase*>	Moves insertion point before the word you specify

Table 6-6	Capitalizing and Lowercasing
Command	**What It Does**
All caps <*phrase*>	Capitalizes all letters in selected phrase (But remember: You have to select the text first!)
All caps that	Capitalizes all caps in selected text
Cap it <*phrase*>	Capitalizes selected spoken phrase
Cap that	Capitalizes word to immediate left or right of insertion point
Capitalize	Capitalizes word to immediate left or right of insertion point
No caps <*phrase*>	Uncapitalizes spoken phrase

Command	What It Does
No caps that	Uncapitalizes text to immediate left or ` right of insertion point
Uncapitalize	Uncapitalizes word to immediate left or right of insertion point

Table 6-7	Editing
Command	**What It Does**
Copy that	Copies text to immediate left or right of insertion point
Cut that	Cuts text to the immediate right or left of insertion point
Paste that	Pastes copied text or object at insertion point location
Undo that	Undoes last action or insertion

Table 6-8	Simulating Keyboard Activities
Command	**What It Does**
Backspace	Moves insertion point back one space
Delete	Deletes one letter to the immediate left or right of insertion point
Enter	Inserts hard line break
Move down	Moves insertion point down to next line
Move left	Moves insertion point one space to left
Move right	Moves insertion point one space to right
Move up	Moves insertion point up one line
Next cell	Activates next cell to right
Next line	Inserts hard line break
Page down	Moves document down one half page
Page up	Moves document up one half page

(continued)

Table 6-8 *(continued)*

Command	What It Does
Space	Inserts one space
Spacebar	Inserts one space
Tab	Inserts tab

Table 6-9	Controlling Speech
Command	*What It Does*
Dictation	Turns on Dictation
Microphone	Turns off voice command feature
Voice command	Turns on Command feature and turns off Dictation

Table 6-10	Using Menus and Buttons
Command	*What It Does*
Cancel	Cancels any action and closes open dialog box
Start menu	Opens Windows Start menu

Voice commands can be demanding; for example, the Start command requires that you use a full application name to work. "Start Word" may do nothing, whereas "Start Microsoft Word" will.

Customizing Voice Commands

I can just imagine that about now you are going crazy telling your computer to do things, launching programs, closing programs, and deleting text with your voice willy-nilly just for the fun of it. (This feature always brings out the drill sergeant in people. . . .)

Well, stop for a moment. I have a few more things to say about Speech, then I'll leave you to play with it. First, I want to tell you how to configure which sets of commands Speech will recognize. Then I want to tell you how you can use your keyboard to help you control the speech mode.

Which voice commands do you want?

Voice commands don't offer you too many bells and whistles to customize, but you can tell your Tablet PC which categories of commands you want to be active.

Say, for example, that you don't want editing tools to work through Speech because your second-grader constantly opens your important client report, turns on speech, and says "Delete, Delete, Delete" just for the fun of it. Well, you could send the kid to bed without supper, or you could turn off the editing category of voice commands. (Honestly, I can't think of many other reasons why you'd want to do so, but I figured I should tell you how, just in case.)

To select which categories of voice commands are active, follow these steps:

1. **With the Input Panel open choose Speech Tools⇨Voice Command Configuration.**

   The dialog box in Figure 6-9 appears.

Figure 6-9:
Choose to deactivate any of these five categories from this dialog box.

2. **Tap in any check box to deselect that category.**

3. **If you want to deselect only certain types of commands in a category, select the category and tap Details.**

   The Details dialog box (shown in Figure 6-10) appears.

4. **Tap in any check box to deselect its subset of commands.**

5. **When you're done deselecting categories, tap OK to close the Details dialog box.**

6. **Tap OK to close the Voice Command Configuration dialog box.**

Don't forget your keyboard

When you type a document (*surely* you remember the old-fashioned before-Tablet-PC way to work), you are constantly switching between typing text and using your keyboard, menus, and tool buttons to get the task done.

When you use speech to add content *and* implement computer commands, you'll find the same principle applies: You often switch between the two. For that reason, Tablet PC makes it possible to assign keyboard keys (for any attached non-virtual keyboard) that turn on Dictation or Voice Command.

Dictation and Voice Command can't be on at the same time; activating one deactivates the other.

To set up this handy arrangement, follow a few simple steps:

1. **From the Input Panel, choose Tools⇨Options.**

   The Options dialog box appears.

2. **Tap the Speech tab.**

3. **Near the bottom of the Speech sheet, tap the Keyboard Mode Key Settings link.**

   The Keyboard Mode Key Settings dialog box appears.

4. **Tap the Assign Mode Buttons check box shown in Figure 6-11.**

Figure 6-11:
Just don't
forget which
key you
assigned or
you could
find yourself
dictating
when you
least
expect to.

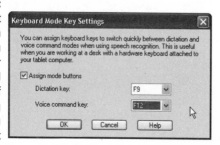

5. **Tap the arrow on the Dictation Key drop-down list; select a key from that list to activate Dictation mode.**

6. **Repeat Step 5 to choose the Voice Command Key.**

7. **Tap OK twice to save your settings.**

Okay, now you can go back to speaking to your computer. Happy talking!

Part III

Exploring Tablet PC's Unique Apps

The 5th Wave   By Rich Tennant

"Chuck's got more experience with Tablet PCs than anyone here. He not only uses handwriting, text, and voice commands, he's also taught one to read lips."

In this part . . .

Tablet PC is driven by Windows XP for Tablet PC, which is a superset of the Windows XP operating system. *Superset* means that there's more to this operating system than there is to regular old Windows XP. Included in this system are features that enable ink and speech functionality, and also some handy applications that take advantage of those features.

In this part, you discover Windows Journal, an application that's designed to work optimally with ink input. Windows Journal allows you to write directly into a document and search and organize your handwriting or convert it to text. You also get to play around with Sticky Notes, a neat little application for adding ink and voice notes to any document; and you may get addicted to a fun little pen input game called Inkball. Finally, because Tablet PC is such a great size computer on which to read electronic books, there's information about using Microsoft Reader and eBooks.

Chapter 7

Thinking Ink with Journal

. . . .

. . . .

*O*nly a few applications are built into Windows XP for Tablet PC specifically for the Tablet PC environment, and Microsoft Windows Journal is one of them. Journal is quite simply handwriting heaven. Here you can write directly in a Journal document — no Input Panel between you and what appears there. And you have more tools for working with handwritten content than you get in Office applications on your Tablet PC.

You may just start keeping a whole library of handwritten notes you can file and search. (Creative writers, researchers, and people who live in meetings, take note!) You can use a Music template to hand write music on preformatted music staffs or a Monthly Calendar template to jot down all your appointments for the month.

But wait. There's more! You can take your handwriting — letters, numbers, and even drawn shapes — and convert them to printed text or perfect geometric objects. You can even send your Journal notes as text e-mails.

Journal Basics

Windows Journal is pretty easy to get into: From the Windows desktop, you simply choose Start➪All Programs➪Windows Journal. When the application opens, you'll see that Journal looks pretty much like a lined paper pad with an area at the top for a title and lines across the page, as shown in Figure 7-1. You can view four toolbars in Journal: Standard, Pen, Format, and View. These are noted in Figure 7-1, though only the Standard and Pen toolbars appear by default.

Journal documents are called *notes.* Just like their word-processed cousins, notes can be many pages long or can be a single page. You can use the scroll-bar along the right side of the Journal screen to move from page to page in a multipage note.

Time to open your first Journal note and find your way around.

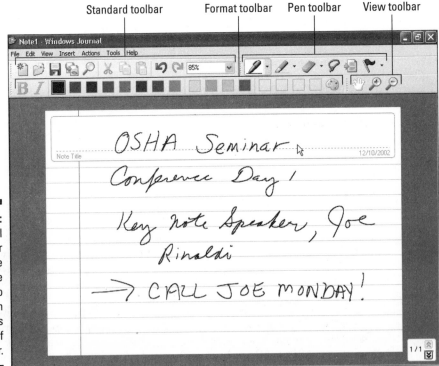

Figure 7-1: Journal will feel familiar to those who are used to writing on legal pads or loose-leaf notepaper.

New and noteworthy

Opening a new note is just about as easy as falling off a log and not nearly as painful.

- ✔ When you open Journal, a new, blank note appears.

- ✔ If you want to open a new note at any time after Journal is opened, you can tap the New Note button on the Standard toolbar (the one that looks like a little paper pad with a sunburst on it on the far left in Figure 7-1), or choose File⇨New Note.

That's it.

Getting fancy with Journal note templates

Perhaps you're not happy with the lined paper look? No problem. Journal comes with built-in templates that provide formats for writing music, to-do lists, calendars, and more. You can open a new Journal note based on any of these templates. Figure 7-2 shows the To Do List template, for example, and Figure 7-3 shows the Graph template.

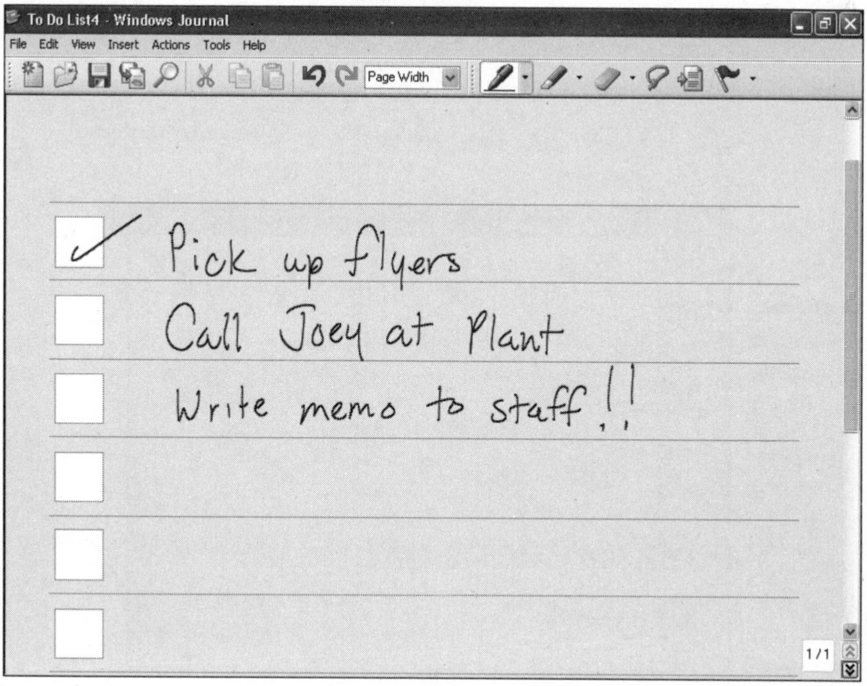

Figure 7-2: Check boxes let you easily check off the tasks you've completed.

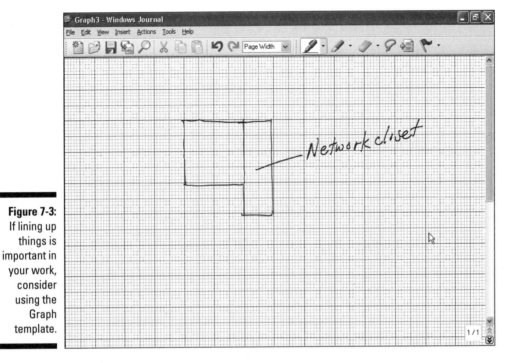

Figure 7-3:
If lining up
things is
important in
your work,
consider
using the
Graph
template.

To open a new note using a template, follow these steps:

1. Choose File⇨New Note from Template.

The Open dialog box, as shown in Figure 7-4, appears.

Figure 7-4:
Because
Journal
has no
templates
preview,
you just
have to
try the
templates
one by one.

2. **Tap a template name.**

3. **Tap Open.**

Setting your own style

Although the ruled stationery appears by default, you can change that setting to use one of the other templates every time you open a new note. Follow these steps to set the default look for your notes:

1. **Choose Tools⇨Options and tap the Note Format tab to display it.**

   See Figure 7-5.

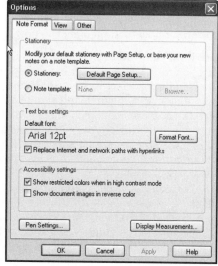

2. **Select Note Template and then tap the Browse button.**

   The Open dialog box (refer to Figure 7-4) appears.

3. **Tap a template name and then tap Open.**

4. **Tap OK again to save the new default setting.**

   Now every time you create a new note, the template you selected here opens.

You can also create your own templates either from notes you create or by modifying the included templates to change such things as the size of the paper, the background color or design, and so on. With a note open that you want to save as a template, just choose File⇨Save As and choose Windows Journal Template for the Save As Type.

Writing between the lines: Adding pages and spaces

Have you ever experienced something like the following?

> It's Wednesday, the third day in a weeklong off-site conference on the future of your department. On Monday, you took notes on your legal pad about the new budgeting process. Today, the speaker from Monday is holding an impromptu question-and-answer session just after lunch to respond to some concerns about how to implement the new process.

> You sit down, pull out your legal pad, and begin to madly scribble things in the margins of the notes you took Monday, drawing arrows from one note to the other, writing asterisks in circles to indicate a new paragraph that should go right *there,* and generally just making a huge mess of things. You get to the office the next week and can make neither head nor tail out of your scribbles, so into the drawer your notes go — and you sit and wait for a memo to arrive with the pronouncement that you're doing the new budget process wrong.

When it comes to editing, the inflexibility of paper can be frustrating. Luckily, Journal Notes aren't carved in stone as their legal-pad brethren (to an extent) are. One of the great features of Journal is that you can take the notes you took in yesterday's meeting, find a spot in the middle, and add anything from a few lines to several pages. You can even rearrange pages in a single note.

To add a new page to a note, simply display the page you want the new page to follow, and choose Insert⇨New Page. The page counter at the bottom right of the page will reflect your page count and location in the document. For example, 2/4 indicates that four pages are in the note and page two is currently displayed.

You can add lines to a page of a Journal Note. The tool you use to do so is called Insert/Remove Space, which could be a tad confusing. You're actually inserting a new writing line on your virtual pad, not a space. To insert a new line on a page, follow these steps:

1. **Tap the Insert/Remove Space button on the Pen toolbar.**

   The button you want is the one that looks like a piece of paper with an arrow pointing at the page.

   Your cursor changes to two horizontal lines with arrows pointing up and down from them. As you move your cursor on the page, a dotted line appears indicating where a new line in the pad would appear if you were to tap and drag with your pen at that spot on the page.

2. **Tap the line above where you want to insert a new line, and drag down with your pen to draw a new writing line.**

   You can see the dotted line that appears while you're dragging to draw the new line, as shown in Figure 7-6.

3. **Release the pen by lifting it from the screen to create the new line.**

   If you want to create multiple lines, you can drag upward by more than one line height on the page.

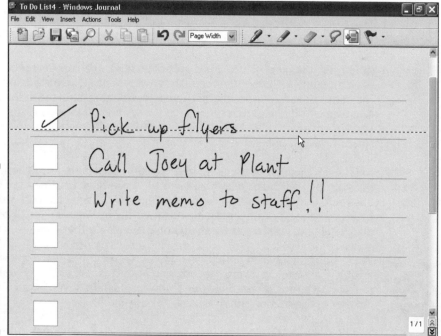

Figure 7-6:
You can drag this dotted line down as far as you like to create multiple new lines in one move.

To delete a space, repeat this process; but instead of placing your pen above the area where you want to add a line and dragging down, place your pen on the line at the bottom of the area you want to delete, tap, and drag upward. This trick works only with blank lines.

When you insert new lines, you may see a dialog box that says that the page is not long enough to accommodate them. You get two options in this dialog box: increase the page length, or add a new page and move anything beneath the new line to that next page. Choose your option and tap OK to implement it.

Getting Stuff into Journal

If you've used only the Input Panel to input handwriting so far, you're in for a treat. Switching from writing in the confined area of the Writing Pad to writing in Journal is like moving from an 8-by-8-foot jail cell to an 1,800-square-foot house — with a view.

Writing and drawing by hand in Journal

In Journal, you have pages and pages of lines to write on (or squares or whatever, depending on the note template you are using). Go ahead and write in the margins; anything you write there is searchable, along with the rest of the document. You can even write upside down and still be able to convert what you wrote to right-side-up text (which I tell you all about later, in the section titled "Converting handwriting to text").

And here's the best part of all: There's really no trick to writing in Journal. Put your pen on the page and write. You can write on the lines, cross over the lines, and write sideways (as shown in Figure 7-7). You can write words, add punctuation, and draw things. In short, writing in Journal is just like writing on a legal pad, and I know that you know how to do that.

There's no spacebar to hit between words — just leave space where you want it. However, be aware that you can move text around after you write it to relocate it or add space between words, which I tell you about later in this chapter in the section titled "Moving ink around."

You do not need to place an insertion point in your document in Journal, so don't tap on the spot where you want text to appear; that little tap results in you drawing a squiggle on the page! If you want to insert something within existing writing, you'll have to move that writing around on the page or insert a new writing line on the pad.

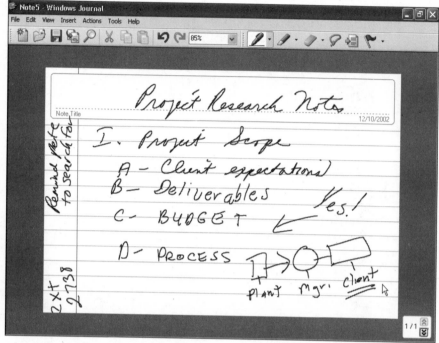

Figure 7-7:
Fill up the
page if you
like, but
remember
that you
have as
many pages
as you need
on this pad.

Changing pen styles

Just to help avoid confusion, you should understand how your Tablet PC pen relates to your Journal Pen tool. You use a Tablet PC pen to write on a Journal note; you can tap a Pen button to put yourself in Pen mode in Windows Journal (versus Eraser or Highlighter mode, for example).

When you write with your physical pen on your tablet screen, whatever Pen style you have set in Windows Journal will be used (for example Very Fine Point or Marker). By default, the pen style used in Journal is Fine Point. However, just as some people like to write with fine line gel pens and others prefer chunky markers, you can use other pen styles in Journal to add variety to your writing and emphasis to what you write (as shown in Figure 7-8).

To change the pen style, follow these steps:

1. **Tap the arrow on the Pen button on the toolbar (you guessed it: It looks like a pen).**

   The Pen drop-down list appears.

2. **To select a new style, tap a style shown on the drop-down list.**

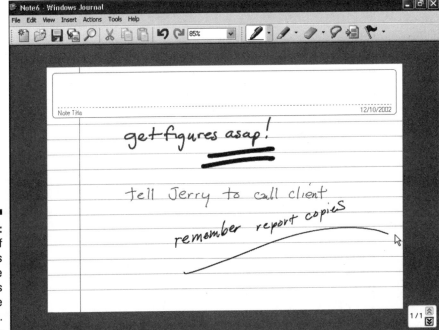

Figure 7-8:
A variety of
pen styles
can make
your notes
more
interesting.

If you want to make further changes to the pen style, do this:

1. **From the Pen drop-down list, tap Pen Settings.**

   The Pen and Highlighter Settings dialog box, shown in Figure 7-9, appears.

2. **Tap a pen style in the Current Pens list to select it.**

3. **Tap the arrow on the Color field and select an ink color from the drop-down palette that appears.**

4. **Tap the arrow on the Thickness field and select a thickness from Extra Fine to a 10.5 mm Marker.**

5. **In the Tip Style drop-down list, you can select either a Point style or a Chisel style.**

   The Chisel style creates a line that is a bit thicker than the Point.

   If you'd like the thickness of your pen line to vary, depending on how hard you press on the screen (sort of like a fountain pen functions), put a check in the Pressure Sensitive check box.

6. **Tap OK to save the new settings.**

Figure 7-9:
You can use
this dialog
box to
change
several pen
settings or
apply a new
pen style.

My advice is to play around with these settings until you find a combination
that appeals to you for your everyday writing. Writing on a screen feels different than writing on paper, but one thing that can make it more familiar is finding a pen style that *feels* comfortable when you write.

Inserting pictures

To paraphrase somebody, a picture is worth a thousand notes. Just because
these notes are handwritten doesn't mean that you may not want to spruce
them up or add visual interest beyond your own hand-drawn masterpieces.

You may add a picture of your company's new product, for example, and
then use Journal to write up a custom spec for a customer, indicating where
you would modify the color, size, or accessories for him. Or you could
insert a picture of an office blueprint and draw arrows and write callouts of
which employee and equipment goes in which room. The possibilities are
endless.

To insert a picture, follow these steps:

1. **With a note open, choose Insert➪Picture.**

   The Insert Picture dialog box appears.

2. **Use the Look In drop-down list to locate the picture file you want to
   insert.**

3. **Tap the file you want to insert and then tap Insert.**

   The file is inserted on the currently open Journal Note.

Drawing text boxes

Journal liberates you from the Input Panel. Well, not completely. The one place where you have to use the panel to insert text is in text boxes.

You've encountered text boxes in word processors and drawing programs. Text boxes are drawing objects into which you can enter text. You can move them around and resize them. You can also reformat the text entered into them.

One good use for text boxes is to input exact text. For example, if somebody spells out their rather complicated company name in a speech and you want to get it just right, don't rely on your handwriting to be converted later. Enter the spelling into a text box where you're sure that it's preserved exactly as written.

To insert a text box into an open note, follow these steps:

1. **Choose Insert⇨Text Box.**

   When you move your cursor over the page, it changes to a crosshair shape.

2. **Tap anywhere on the page with your pen and drag to draw the text box.**

3. **When the text box is the size you need, release by lifting your pen off the screen.**

Now you can open the Input Panel and use the Writing Pad or Keyboard to enter text. Whichever method you use, the input will appear as typed text, not as handwriting (as shown in Figure 7-10).

See Chapter 4 if you'd like a refresher course on using the Input Panel.

Adding flags of many colors

Have you ever used those colored tabs that you stick on the edges of pages so that you can quickly flip to important items? You know, like those ones that say "Sign Here" on contracts. (Can you imagine how filthy rich the person who invented those notes is?)

In Journal, you've got colored tabs; but they're not sticky, and they're called *flags*. Flags can be inserted at any point in a note, and you can use different colors for flags of different types — for example, try a green flag for budget information (as shown in Figure 7-11) and a red flag for potential problems.

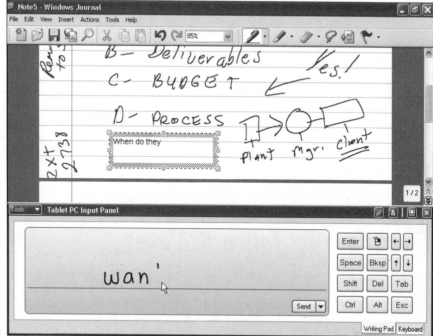

Figure 7-10:
When you tap a text box to select it, the insertion point is active, ready for you to input text with the Input Panel.

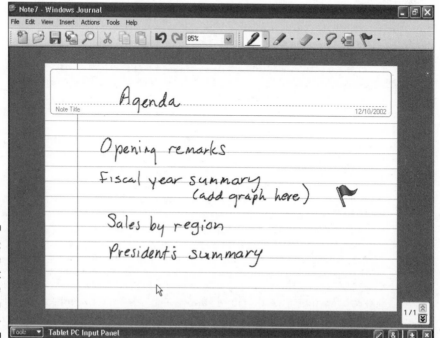

Figure 7-11:
Flags are easy to spot as you move through a note.

To insert a flag, simply tap the Flag button on the Pen toolbar, then tap and drag your pen on the page next to the text you want to flag.

After you insert flags, you can display a list of flagged notes, use the flags to page through your notes, search for flags, and take a look at all your flagged items all in one place. (See "Searching for What You Need," later in this chapter, to find out how to perform these searches.)

Another way to visually flag things is to use the Highlighter button on the Pen toolbar. Just tap the Highlighter button on the toolbar (looks like a marker pen with a yellow tip), and drag your pen over anything on the Note page to highlight it. To deactivate the Highlighter button, tap another tool such as Pen or Eraser.

Fine-Tuning Journal Notes

Not content to write notes and insert flags? Want to see your notes become neat little lines of text and your hand-drawn circles become perfect, symmetrical spheres? Want to use a colored highlighter to mark up text, or cut and paste a sentence from page 3 and put it on page 4? You ask for a lot.

Luckily, Journal delivers.

Converting handwriting to text

The idea behind notes isn't necessarily to enter handwritten notes just to convert them all to pristine text documents. Tablet PC proponents want folks to get used to treating handwritten documents like typewritten documents — storing, editing, and searching the handwritten notes just as they are.

That said, sometimes you want to convert your handwriting to text, and the handwriting recognition program built into Journal is the way to go.

Now, I've mentioned elsewhere in this book (like in Chapter 1 and 4 and one or two other places) that handwriting recognition isn't perfect, but it's not bad. If you write neatly, you've got a shot at converting short documents rather painlessly. If you expect to convert a ten-page handwritten note to text, plan on spending a good bit of time correcting the interpretation of several words. In other words, I wouldn't count on converting notes of more than a page into text documents on a regular basis if I were you.

So, how does it work? Quite simply. You use a Lasso tool to select the handwriting you want to convert; then you use a menu command to convert it. The tricky part comes with the interpretation, which is pretty much in Windows Journal's hands.

Follow these steps to convert handwriting to text:

1. **Tap the Selection button (shaped like a lasso) on the Pen toolbar.**

2. **Tap and drag to select one or more words you want to convert (as shown in Figure 7-12).**

3. **Choose Actions⇨Convert Handwriting to Text.**

   The Text Correction dialog box appears (as shown in Figure 7-13). Questionable words are highlighted, with the first questionable word displayed in the Ink from Note box, and Alternatives listed.

4. **Tap a word from the Alternative list to replace the word; then tap Change.**

   If no word on the list matches, tap the next word in the phrase that is highlighted and see whether you can find a match for it.

5. **After you're done making any changes, tap OK.**

   The Text Correction dialog box, as shown in Figure 7-14, appears, offering you the chance to copy the text to the Clipboard or insert it in the Journal note where it was created.

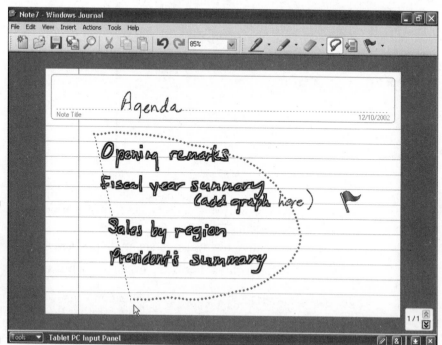

Figure 7-12:
The Selection tool creates a circle around words as you drag it.

Figure 7-13:
The
highlighted
words are
in doubt —
this is
about the
percentage
of words
you can
expect to
review each
time you
convert.

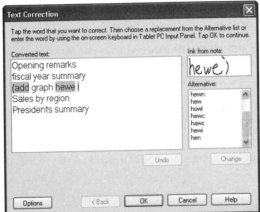

Figure 7-14:
If you want
to take
information
from
Journal and
plop it into,
say, a Word
document,
choose the
Clipboard
option here.

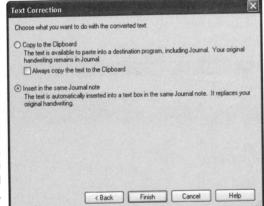

You can use the Input Panel to backspace or delete and edit text to make any final corrections you couldn't make from the options presented in the Text Correction process.

6. **Tap an option; then tap Finish to complete the conversion.**

   The handwritten content has been turned into a text box with text.

If you want to convert an entire note document or a single note page, use Edit➪Select All or Edit➪Select Page commands (rather than the Selection tool) before converting.

Changing shapes

You can change more than just handwritten words to text in Journal. You can also convert hand-drawn lines, circles, or squares into formal drawing shapes. So, if you've drawn a series of boxes to represent phases in a project, with a circle in the middle to represent the client, just convert each drawing to perfectly drawn shapes (as shown in Figure 7-15).

Unfortunately, this conversion is currently limited to circles, squares, and lines, so for triangles or stars, for example, you'll just have to draw neatly.

Follow this procedure to convert hand-drawn shapes:

1. **Tap the Selection tool and tap and drag over the drawn item to select it.**

2. **Choose Action⇨Change Shape To, then choose either Square, Circle/ Ellipse, or Line.**

    The shape is converted to a formal drawing object.

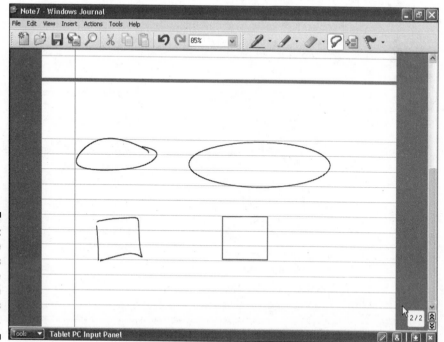

Figure 7-15:
The shape on the left is drawn; the shape on the right is converted.

Erasing things

Dante (you remember him) said that everything, by an impulse of its own nature, tends towards its own perfection. Well, I say perfection is very over-rated. I'm not perfect, and I admit it. If you're not perfect, too, you'll be glad to know that you've got an out if you make a mistake in Journal.

Moving ink around

You may have several reasons to move things around a Journal note. One reason is this: When you cut a word or phrase, it leaves a space. Unlike in a word processor (where the words on either side of a cut word regroup and move together), cutting something (say, a word or a phrase) in Journal leaves you with an empty space where the word or phrase *used* to be. You can move words closer together if this bothers you.

You may also just want to move one piece of writing to another area of the note, so it's located near related information. Or you may want to take pieces of information from various locations and put them in a list on another page.

Whatever your reason, you can easily move things around in a Journal note by either dragging them to a new locale or using the familiar Cut and Paste tools on the Standard toolbar or Edit menu.

Nixing shapes, words, and letters

There are even a variety of ways to get rid of things. You can use

- ✔ **Cross 'em out:** The scratch-out gesture, rubbing your pen tip back and forth over a word or phrase until it's covered with ink. Then, magically, it just disappears.

- ✔ **Erase 'em:** The Eraser button on the Pen toolbar. Tap to select it, then rub your pen over the word or words you want to erase. They disappear.

- ✔ **Select 'n' edit 'em:** The Selection tool to select a word or phrase, along with Edit menu commands to cut or delete.

- ✔ **Use Quick Keys:** The Selection tool to select a word or phrase; then tap Delete on the Input Panel Quick Keys (about which Chapter 4 is a treasure trove of details).

The only trick to using Cut and Paste tools or commands is that you have to select what you want to move with the Selection tool first. After you've cut the selection, tap the location on the page where you want it placed and use the Paste button or command to paste it there.

To move text by using a dragging motion, follow this procedure:

1. **Tap the Selection button on the Pen toolbar.**

2. **Drag around a word, words, or drawing to select it.**

   A *Selection box* (a box with little square handles you can use to resize what's in the box) appears around the selected item, as shown in Figure 7-16.

3. **Move your pen over the edge of the box until your cursor changes into a Move cursor (a set of four-way-pointing arrows).**

4. **Tap and drag the item to the point where you want it to appear.**

5. **Remove your pen from the screen, and the item has been moved.**

6. **Tap outside of the Selection box to unselect the selection.**

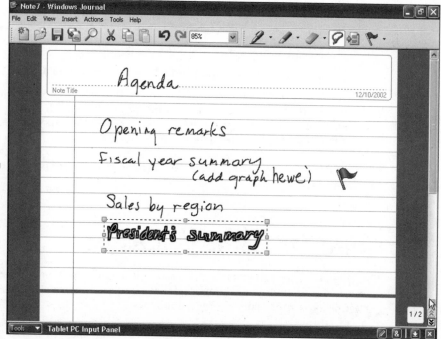

Figure 7-16:
The small boxes around this selection can also be used to resize the handwriting or drawing.

You can tap any of the handles around the Selection box and drag in or out to resize the contents.

Grouping things

If you know that you want to treat certain items in a Journal note as one set, (for example, squares and circles you've drawn to form a diagram or words that go together, such as in a poem), you may want to use the Group feature.

Grouping has a couple of functions. First, it allows you to quickly select and perform actions, such as deleting, copying, or moving a set of items. Second, the Group As One Word command allows you to instruct Journal that when converting letters that have spaces between them, or even drawings, they will translate into text as a single word.

Follow these steps to group items:

1. **Tap the Selection tool.**

2. **Tap near the items you want to select and drag the Selection tool until it encircles all the items.**

3. **Choose Actions⇨Group (or Actions⇨Group As One Word if you want to group words for conversion).**

   The Selection box appears around the items.

4. **Tap outside of the grouped item. Now tap the group again.**

   You'll see that the entire group is selected at one time with a single tap (as opposed to having to turn on the Lasso tool and drag to select several separate items). After you tap a group to select it, you can move, cut, or copy the grouped items more quickly.

To Ungroup, just tap the grouped object to select it and then choose Actions⇨ Ungroup.

Searching for What You Need

You may have searched successfully for truth, enlightenment, or just an honest politician in your time; but if you search for a word in those handwritten notes you took last Thursday, good luck.

A seemingly simple yet powerful feature in Journal enables you to search your handwritten notes and find words and phrases instantly. This adds a functionality to note taking that you've never had. Imagine — in twenty pages of notes, you can actually find the one you need! Now you should know that the Find feature finds only writing, not drawings. Other than that, the Find feature has got a lot of settings to help you pinpoint what you seek.

Do this to search your notes:

1. **Open the note you want to search.**

2. **Choose Edit⇨Find.**

   The Find panel appears just under the toolbars with the Look For, Look In, Find, Previous, Next, and More options displayed.

3. **Tap the More button (at the far right of this panel) to expand it and display advanced search features.**

   For example, you can search by Last Modification Date or specify that the search include close matches (as shown in Figure 7-17).

4. **In the Look For box in the Find panel, enter the word or words you want to find.**

5. **Select the notes you want to search.**

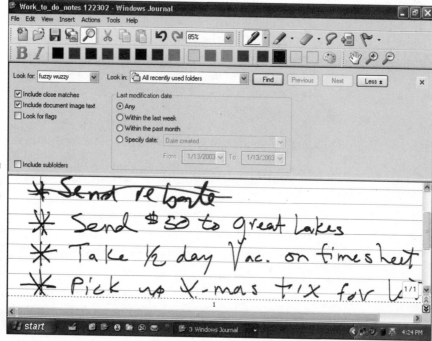

Figure 7-17: Search by specific text or attributes, such as flags or text that is a close match.

You can search the currently open note by one of two methods:

- You can display the Look In list and then choose Current Note.

- You can select a folder containing other notes from the Look In list to search.

6. **Choose the options that are appropriate to your search.**

- Put a check in the Include Close Matches check box to include words that are likely to appear similar to the word you've entered.

  Given the limitations (even today) of handwriting-recognition technology, this technique is probably a good habit to develop.

- If you want to find images of documents that have been converted to become Journal files, choose Include Document Image Text.

- If you want to search for flags, put a check in the Look for Flags check box.

- If you want to limit the search to documents created in a certain time period, use the Last Modification Date selection boxes. If you select the Specify Date option, use the From and To drop-down fields to choose a specific date (or date range).

- If you want to search not only a folder but also its subfolders, select the Include Subfolders check box in the Find panel.

7. **When you've finished making search settings, tap Find to find the next instance of what you're looking for.**

- If an instance of the search word or phrase is found in the currently open document, the word or phrase shows up as selected on the note page (a Selection box appears around it).

- If you have chosen to search notes in folders, a list of matching notes appears beneath the Find panel; tap one of these notes.

  Journal closes the currently displayed note (after asking you whether to save it if you haven't already done so) and opens the note you selected.

- To move through matches within a note, use the Previous and Next buttons in the Find panel.

8. **After you've finished finding matches, tap the Close button to close the Find panel.**

Sending a Journal Note as an E-Mail

I wish I could tell you that Journal lets you e-mail your handwritten content, but it doesn't. What Journal does is convert your handwriting to text; then Journal enables you to send that by e-mail along with a copy of your handwritten content as an attachment that the recipient can open and view with the Windows Picture and Fax Viewer (as shown in Figure 7-18). Still, it's a quick and simple process to send a selection from a note as an e-mail, and we just have to hope for a direct-handwriting-to-e-mail feature in the next version!

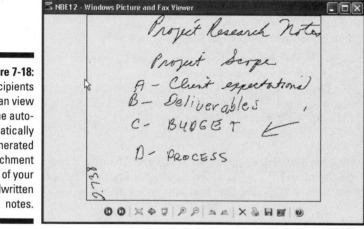

Figure 7-18:
Recipients can view the automatically generated attachment of your handwritten notes.

To send a Journal note in an e-mail message, follow these steps:

1. **Use the Selection tool to select items you want to send as an e-mail. If you want to send an entire page or the entire note, choose Edit⇨Select Page or Select All.**

2. **Choose Actions⇨Convert Selection to E-mail.**

   The Convert to E-mail dialog box (as shown in Figure 7-19) appears.

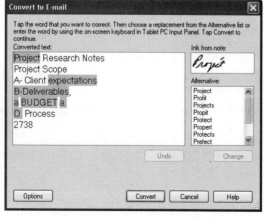

Figure 7-19:
Use this dialog box to make any corrections to your text before completing the conversion.

3. **Choose highlighted words one by one; change them (as needed) to alternative words from the list provided.**

   When you finish making these corrections, you must tap Change to put them into effect.

4. **After you're done correcting text, tap Convert.**

   The Choose Profile dialog box appears.

5. **Select an e-mail program from the list.**

   Outlook is listed there by default. If you want to add another e-mail program, tap New and enter a new e-mail program profile name. Then tap OK and follow the directions in the E-mail Accounts wizard to create a new e-mail account. When you finish the wizard, you return to the Send to Mail Recipient dialog box.

6. **Tap OK.**

   An e-mail form appears (as shown in Figure 7-20) with the note file name as the Subject and the note added as an attachment. The text of the note appears in the e-mail message that has been converted to text.

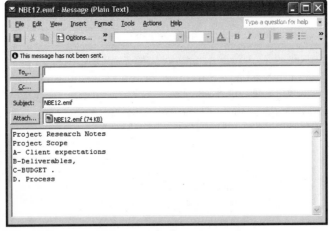

Figure 7-20:
Your note text appears as message text automatically.

7. **Add addressee information, and any other text.**

8. **Tap the Send button or menu command in your e-mail program to send the e-mail.**

If you want to send handwritten e-mails, check out riteMail from *Pen*&Internet. You can find more information about riteMail in Chapter 14.

Chapter 8

Stuck on Sticky Notes

• •

In This Chapter

▶ Setting up your Sticky Note options

▶ Entering written notes

▶ Importing a note

▶ Recording notes

▶ Sticking notes in documents

▶ Deleting notes

• •

For those of you who are too young to remember a time before there were those tiny pads of paper with sticky strips for affixing notes to stuff, let me tell you, those were rough times, indeed. We all had to walk five miles to school in the snow and had to paperclip notes to documents — a chore you are just plain lucky to have avoided.

Because personal computers proliferated on millions of desktops, I'm sure we've all been waiting for the electronic equivalent of those handy adhesive-covered notes. You'll be glad to know it's finally here.

Sticky Notes is a cool little feature of Windows XP for Tablet PC. Using this program, you can create electronic handwritten notes and attach them to your electronic desktop or documents. You can also record audio notes, or use a combination of audio and written content in a single note.

Settle back and prepare to have your note-taking world (gently) shaken.

Creating a Note

Do you want to make a note of that phone number a client gave you in the hallway? Maybe remind yourself to get gas on the way home? Whatever little reminders you want to keep around as you roam with your Tablet PC, Sticky Notes is a great place to enter them.

Write it down

When you open Sticky Notes for the first time (choose Start⇨All Programs⇨ Sticky Notes), voilà — a blank note opens, ready for you to scribble, doodle, or record something. To create a new Sticky Note, you tap the New Note button, as shown in Figure 8-1.

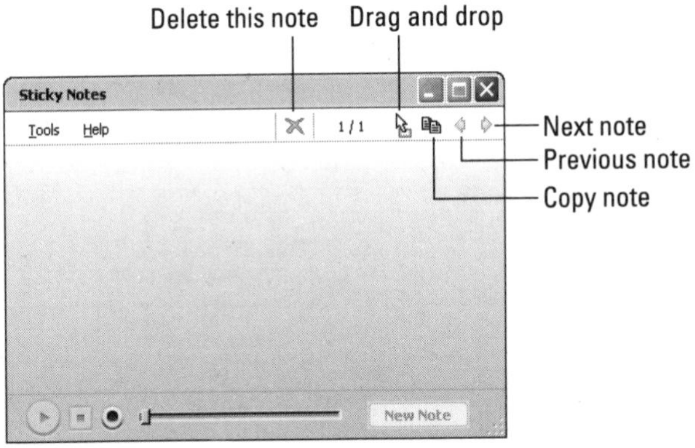

Delete this note   Drag and drop

Figure 8-1: This little pad enables you to write notes to yourself on the fly.

Next note
Previous note
Copy note

The majority of this window is a surface where you can write notes with your pen stylus. Across the top of the Sticky Notes window are a couple of menus (Tools and Help) and a few tool buttons that enable you to delete a note, drag and drop a note, copy a note, or move among a group of notes (called a *stack*).

Across the bottom of the Sticky Notes pad are buttons you use to record a note (which make their entrance a bit later on in this chapter).

To enter a note, simply write in the center area of the Sticky Notes window (see Figure 8-2). You can enter as much text, or as many doodles or drawings, as you like, given the space available.

If you have a longer note, start near the top of the writing area and keep your writing smaller. When you've filled up the Notes area, the only way to add more is to add a new note.

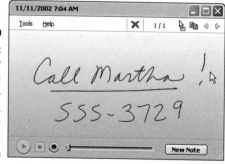

Figure 8-2:
Print or
write in
longhand —
it will look
just the way
you write it.

The Input Panel doesn't work with Sticky Notes. Writing in the Writing Pad or tapping keys on the Keyboard won't have any effect.

A nice gesture

You can use a scratch-out gesture to delete one or more words in your note. When you rub your pen tip across the word you want to delete as if scratching it out, it becomes covered with black lines. You have to get about 60 percent of the word covered in lines (as in Figure 8-3), and then it disappears.

Figure 8-3:
Scratch
your pen
over
anything
you've
written in a
Sticky Note,
and after
a second
it will
disappear.

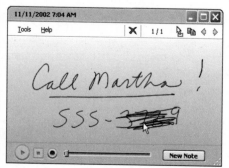

If you delete words as you write, you can then just place your pen where the deleted word was and write something else. However, if you've written a bit and go back to delete a word, you can't move the remaining words closer together, so you'll simply leave a blank space in your note, without gaining any more writing real estate.

The scratch-out gesture is active by default. To turn it off, follow these steps:

1. **Choose Tools⇨Options in the Sticky Notes toolbar.**

2. **Tap Enable Scratch-out Gesture to select or deselect it.**

Just say it

Sometimes there's no substitute for the spoken word. For example, if you need to access a note that contains an address while you're driving to an appointment, playing back a note is certainly preferable to reading it as you drive along. Or you might want to get the exact wording of a phrase that somebody else reads into your Tablet PC (anything from a sweet nothing to the melody of a song, or a legal citation, for example).

You can record notes of up to thirty seconds with Sticky Notes and play them back. You can even add a recording to a written note.

Follow these steps to record a note and play it back:

1. **With Sticky Notes open, tap the Record button shown in Figure 8-4.**

Figure 8-4:
These simple recording buttons should look familiar if you've ever used media player software.

Play   Record

Stop

Recording notes: Do's and don'ts

Here are a few tips about recording notes:

- Locate the microphone built into your Tablet PC (your user manual should show you where it is) or hold a microphone you have plugged into a speaker jack near your mouth and speak clearly into it.

- Speak loudly — the default volume level used to record Sticky Notes seems rather low, so you'll have to speak up if you want to hear it in playback. (If your officemates look at you funny, tell them you're rehearsing lead vocals for a rock band. . . .)

---

2. **Speak your note loudly and clearly.**

   The slider moves across the Sticky Notes window as you speak, reflecting the amount of time left to record.

3. **Tap the Stop button (shown in Figure 8-4) when you're done.**

   If you want to record more with the same note open, you can repeat Steps 1 through 3 until you've used up the thirty seconds allowed.

4. **To play the note back, tap the Play button.**

Managing Notes and Stacks

When you first opened Sticky Notes, you may have noticed a notation in the toolbar area that said 1/1. This indicates you have Note 1 of a total of one notes open. When you've created a few notes, you'll notice that the notation changes; for example, it might read 3/5 to indicate that the third of five notes is displayed. These notes are collectively called a stack. Only one stack of notes can be open at any one time.

You can use the Previous Note and Next Note buttons to move among the stack of notes.

Often you don't want to keep notes around for long — after all, they are typically little on-the-run reminders that come and go and are soon out of date. However, it is possible to store and retrieve notes for the times when that's useful. You do this by exporting and importing them.

Exporting notes

To send a stack of notes to a file (which you can then save on your hard drive or a storage disk, or even send to another Tablet PC user), you export it. Export essentially involves saving the entire stack of notes to a file.

Follow these steps to export a stack of notes:

1. **With Sticky Notes open, choose Tools⇨Export.**

   The Export dialog box (shown in Figure 8-5) appears.

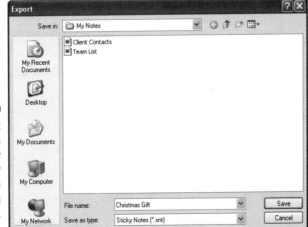

Figure 8-5: This is pretty much your average Save dialog box.

2. **Use the Save In drop-down list to locate the folder in which you want to store the stack.**

   You may want to use the My Notes folder in your My Documents folder for this purpose

3. **Enter a name for the file.**

   As a bonus, you get the `.snt` extension entered for the file type automatically.

4. **Tap Save.**

That's it. However, notice that your stack didn't disappear; it's still the stack displayed in the Sticky Notes window. If you want to clear out your notes and start a new stack, you have to delete the current stack note by note, one by one. (See "Trash It! Deleting Notes," later in this chapter, for details.)

Importing notes

So, you have saved a stack of notes to remind yourself of how to find that long lost gold mine and now you want to retrieve the notes again? Just import them. Import is pretty much the equivalent of opening a file in other applications.

Follow these steps to Import a stack of notes:

1. **With Sticky Notes open, choose Tools⇨Import.**

   The Import dialog box (shown in Figure 8-6) appears.

Figure 8-6:
This should
look similar
to dialog
boxes
you've seen
before.

2. **Choose whether you want the imported stack to merge with any notes you currently have in Sticky Notes.**

   If you don't want to merge with that stack, you can replace those notes altogether by tapping the appropriate choice under Action.

3. **Locate the file you want to import using the Look In drop-down list and tap it.**

4. **Tap Open.**

   Behold! The stack is either added to or replaces any current notes, based on your selection.

Take This Note and Stick It

(Who *says* computers have made people rude and crude?) When they named this feature Sticky Notes, they hinted at one of the most useful features in this little software product: After you create a note *you can stick it* — on your desktop or on a document, in any application. So if you've made a note that lists the names and phone extensions of your new project team, you might stick the note in the Word document that holds the text of the project proposal you're writing. Or, if you want to convert the note to text, copy it into a Journal document and use the tools there to convert your handwriting to text.

Dragging and dropping

Dragging and dropping is the lazy person's way to copy a Sticky Note, and when it comes to working on a computer, I'm all for lazy.

You can drag and drop a note to your desktop or into any open application. To drag and drop, follow these steps:

1. **Display the note.**

2. **Tap the Drag and Drop tool button on the Sticky Notes toolbar.**

3. **Tap the note with your pen and drag it where you like, either to the desktop or into a document in an open application.**

When you drag and drop to your desktop, the note appears as a little icon. You can double-tap the icon to open the note in Windows Picture and Fax Viewer (shown in Figure 8-7).

Using this viewer, you can zoom in and out and print a note just as you'd print a photo or other graphic image. You can even run your note in a full screen slide show view. If you tap the Open Image for Editing tool (shown in Figure 8-7), you can even open the image in Paint, and edit it, adding colors, rotating it, or whatever (see Figure 8-8).

When you drag and drop to an application, the note might change its form depending on the application you put it in. For example, in WordPad it looks much like Figure 8-9. In Windows Journal (which is designed to accommodate handwriting), the note looks as if you wrote the note right into the Journal (as shown in Figure 8-10). Most applications treat the note as a graphic object you've inserted — so you can manipulate it in the same ways you'd manipulate any graphics file.

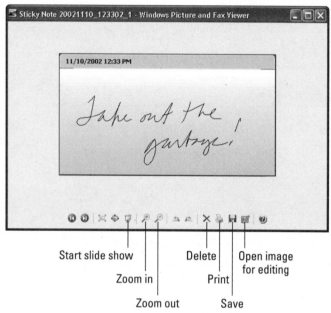

Figure 8-7:
The Windows Picture and Fax Viewer offers some tools that enable you to manipulate a Sticky Note.

Start slide show
Zoom in
Zoom out
Delete
Print
Save
Open image for editing

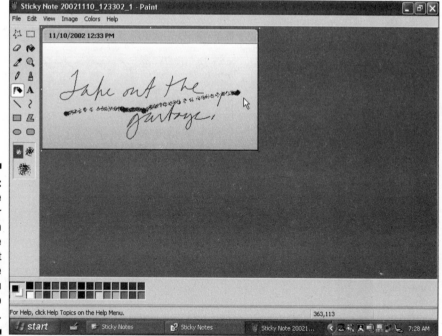

Figure 8-8:
If you'd like to paint your handwritten note purple or turn it upside down, you can do so in Paint.

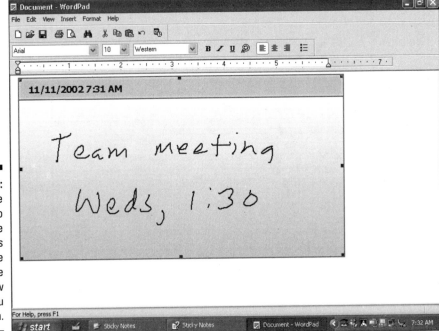

Figure 8-9:
Your note goes into some applications looking like that same little yellow surface you wrote it on.

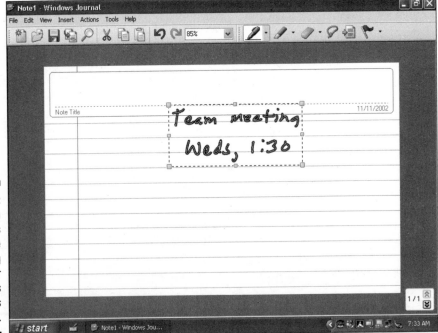

Figure 8-10:
In applications that handle handwriting input, your note goes in as handwriting.

What's in a name?

When you drag a note to the desktop, it is given a really long, obscure name. It took me a while to figure out at least part of the logic for how Sticky Notes names files so I'll save you the trouble. First will be the year, then the month, then the date you recorded it. Then there's a bunch of numbers I haven't a clue about. For example, on November 10, 2002, a note I dragged to my desktop was named Sticky Note 20021110_14315_3. (If you figure out what the 14315_3 represents, please e-mail Bill Gates and thank him for me....)

By the way, after seeing how Sticky Notes names its files, you'll be really glad to hear that you can rename these desktop file icons to names like "Grocery List" and "Mandy's Address." Just right-tap the Sticky Note icon, choose Rename, and type in a name you have a hope of remembering.

To send a handwritten e-mail using a Sticky Note, simply drag and drop the note to your desktop, then right-tap it and choose Send to⇨Mail Recipient. Assuming the recipients of your e-mail have browsers that can view graphics, they will see your handwritten note appear when they double-tap your attachment.

Copying notes

You can also use the Copy button in Sticky Notes to copy a note and use the Paste tool in the destination application or the Paste shortcut combination of Ctrl+V to insert a copy. This works pretty much as dragging and dropping does, giving you slightly different results depending on the destination application (see Figures 8-9 and 8-10).

Audio-only notes won't copy, and though you can drag and drop them, I haven't yet figured out a way you can play them back outside Sticky Notes.

Trash It! Deleting Notes

Sticky Notes are, by nature, somewhat temporary. So, when it's time to get rid of one, you're doing the electronic equivalent of crumpling it up and tossing it away.

You'll be glad to hear it is just that easy: First display the note, and then tap the Delete button. A confirmation dialog box (as shown in Figure 8-11) appears. Tap Yes to delete the note.

Figure 8-11:
If you change your mind and decide to keep the note, tap No in this dialog box to save its life.

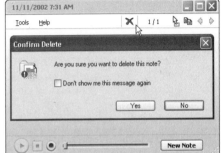

Deleting a slew of notes at the same time

What if you want to delete a stack of notes? You have to do it one by one, but there's a little trick that will make it go quicker. You can turn off the option that displays the confirmation dialog box every time you delete a note by doing this: Choose Tools⇨Options⇨Confirm on Delete. Then you can simply hit delete repeatedly until all the notes in the stack are gone and not have to confirm each deletion.

When you delete a note and get the confirmation dialog box, you can turn off the confirmation feature right there by tapping the Don't Show Me This Message Again check box.

Deleting notes on the desktop or in an application

To delete a note on your desktop, right-tap it and choose Delete from the shortcut menu that appears.

To delete a note you've copied into an application, select it and use the tools built into the application (or the Delete key on your keyboard) to delete it.

Sticky Shortcuts

When working with Sticky Notes, you might find that some handy keyboard shortcuts help you work faster. Table 8-1 shows a variety of keyboard shortcuts that might make your sticky life easier.

Table 8-1	Sticky Note Shortcuts
Keystroke Shortcut	*Function*
Alt+Left Arrow	Go to previous note
Alt+Right Arrow	Go to next note
Alt+Space	Open Sticky Note title bar menu
Alt+T	Open the Tools menu
Alt+H	Open the Help menu
Alt+F4	Close Sticky Note window
Ctrl+P	Play/Pause recording
Ctrl+R	Record note
Ctrl+S	Stop recording
Ctrl+C	Copy note
Ctrl+D	Delete note
Ctrl+N	Insert new note

You can input a function key command on the Input Panel Keyboard by tapping the function key (such as Ctrl), then tapping the next key, such as C. The function key stays selected as you tap the additional key(s) in the series.

Chapter 9

Kicking Back with eBooks and InkBall

I don't know about you, but when I want to relax, two items high on my list are reading a good book and playing a good game.

This chapter is all about relaxing: It covers Microsoft Reader because this reader is included on all Tablet PCs and because the Tablet PC is such a perfect device for reading electronic books.

You'll also discover InkBall, a new game that you play with your pen, that is a unique (and fun) part of Windows XP for Tablet PC.

So prepare to relax. You deserve it.

Welcome to Microsoft Reader

Microsoft Reader is an eBook reader; that is, you can use it to browse through versions of books that have been formatted electronically to be read on your computer screen.

New eBooks are being created all the time and range from reference books, such as dictionaries and encyclopedias (as shown in Figure 9-1), to the latest popular novels and literary classics.

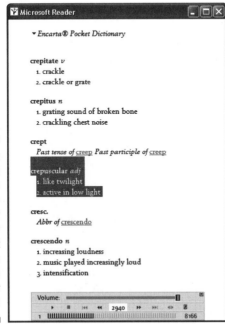

Figure 9-1: Looking up words in the *Encarta Pocket Dictionary* is easy; it will even pronounce them for you!

The Tablet PC is a perfect device for reading eBooks because it's got a good-sized, high-quality color screen (as opposed to a PDA, which is tiny and doesn't have nearly as good a screen quality), and the Tablet PC is portable, so you can read eBooks on a plane, in a cab, or in your living room chair.

Activating Reader

Before you can use Microsoft Reader, you have to activate your software online so that your computer can access certain online content required for downloading eBooks.

After you've activated your copy of Reader, you can access Reader online content from up to a total of eight computers, PDAs, or eBook reader devices, though you have to run the activation process on each one individually.

Follow these steps to activate Microsoft Reader:

1. **Choose Start➪All Programs➪Microsoft Reader to open Microsoft Reader.**

   When you first open the software, you'll be asked to activate it, which you do online; be sure you're logged on to the Internet.

2. **Tap the link that Reader offers you.**

   The Activation screen opens, as shown in Figure 9-2.

   You'll have to have a Microsoft .NET Passport to activate Reader. This program automates logging on to online sites by providing a single sign-in access.

3. **If you have a Passport, tap Sign In.**

   If you don't have a Passport, then tap Get One, follow the steps required to obtain a Passport, and then tap Sign In.

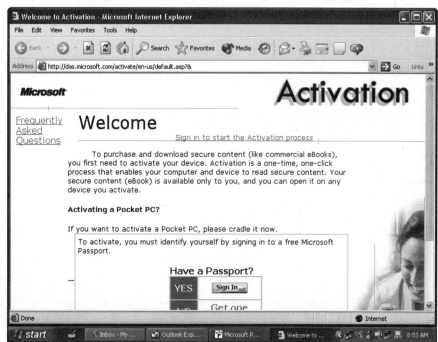

Figure 9-2:
Activating your Reader enables you to browse eBook content online.

4. **If you want to sign in automatically in the future (without having to enter a password) tap the Sign Me In Automatically check box.**

The Passport dialog box appears.

5. **Enter your Passport password and tap OK.**

The Security Warning dialog box appears, asking if you want to install and run Microsoft Reader Activation Client Components.

6. **Tap Yes to proceed.**

The screen shown in Figure 9-3 appears.

7. **Tap Continue to proceed.**

A screen appears, showing the progress of the installation. When installation is complete, the screen disappears and your copy of Reader is activated.

Figure 9-3:
This is the final step in activating your Microsoft Reader software.

Shopping for eBooks!

After the Microsoft Reader software is activated, you're ready to load eBooks into your reader. This usually involves shopping. Now, next to reading, my favorite thing is shopping.

(Well, to be completely honest, next to shopping my favorite thing is chocolate.) This shopping trip involves purchasing eBooks online and simply downloading the content directly to your Tablet PC.

Many companies offer eBooks for sale online. Microsoft provides free eBook downloads, such as the *Encarta Pocket Dictionary* that was available when I wrote this book, to get you started.

Microsoft also offers a catalog of eBooks on its Web site at www.mslit.com, as well as links to booksellers and publishers who offer their own eBooks for sale:

- ✔ Barnes & Noble: www.bn.com
- ✔ Amazon: www.amazon.com
- ✔ Audible: www.audible.com
- ✔ CyberRead: www.cyberread.com

Most booksellers offer a few free eBooks to whet your appetite for the format, though they're not likely to be current bestsellers. Browse around their sites and see what you can find.

To shop for eBooks, follow these steps:

1. **Tap the Shop button on the Microsoft Reader main screen.**

   The Library window appears, as shown in Figure 9-4.

2. **In the Library window, tap the link for Shop with Microsoft Reader (www.microsoft.com/reader/shop.asp).**

   The Microsoft Reader home page appears.

3. **Tap Catalog and Shop in the list on the left.**

   You can shop from the eBook Catalog to buy eBooks from Microsoft; or choose Shop Booksellers; Shop Publishers (as shown in Figure 9-5); or Shop Worldwide.

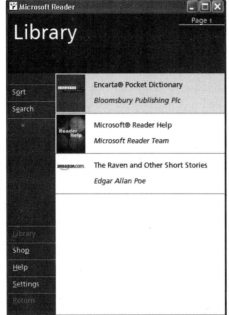

Figure 9-4:
The eBooks
that you
have
downloaded
are listed
in your
Microsoft
Reader
Library.

Figure 9-5:
Links to
publishers,
such as
Smithsonian
Institution
Press, offer
a world of
online
content.

When you find the eBook that you want, you have to go through the shopping process for that particular site (placing the eBook in your shopping cart and entering payment information, for example).

Then you initiate the download process. Your eBook will be downloaded directly to your Microsoft Reader Library, ready for you to open and read.

eBooks cost around $10; you have no paperback or hardcover pricing difference to worry about!

Navigating an eBook

Whether you're juggling your Tablet PC on your knees in your doctor's waiting room or on a towel on the beach, you'll find navigating eBooks to be easy with your pen device.

To open an eBook in Microsoft Reader, just tap its title in the Library (refer to Figure 9-4). The title page of the eBook opens.

To navigate around the eBook, tap the Go To button to display the menu shown in Figure 9-6.

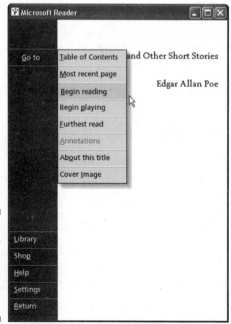

Figure 9-6:
Control your
reading
experience
from this
menu.

From this menu, you can tap items to go to any of the following:

- **Table of Contents** displays a listing of contents; each item in the table of contents is a link that takes you to that area of the eBook.

- **Most Recent Page** takes you back to the last page viewed.

- **Begin Reading** takes you to the title page of the eBook and provides a set of navigation tools for listening to an audio reading of the eBook or navigating among the eBook's pages.

- **Begin Playing** takes you to the start of the eBook with the audio narration activated.

- **Furthest Read** takes you to latest spot in the eBook that you have displayed previously.

- **Annotations** displays any annotations you've added in the eBook.

- **About This Title** displays the copyright information for the eBook (you know, that page at the beginning of a book that nobody reads).

- **Cover Image** takes you to a full-page view of the cover page; to close it and return to the cover page with the menu that appears when you first open an eBook, simply tap the page.

Reading an eBook

When you are reading the contents of an eBook, you see something called a Visual Guide at the bottom of each page, as shown in Figure 9-7. This guide contains a set of tools for moving around your eBook.

To read an eBook, tap the Forward button in the Visual Guide to move forward in the eBook, and tap the Back button to move back one page. Tap the Next Section button to move to the next chapter or story in a collection, and tap the Previous Section button to move back to the preceding chapter or story.

When you're viewing a page of an eBook, you can use a drop-down list to return to the main Reader menu.

To open this drop-down list, tap the downward-pointing arrow next to the eBook title at the top of any eBook page.

You may encounter linked text in an eBook. If you do, you can tap it to be taken to a referenced Web site, as long as your computer is online.

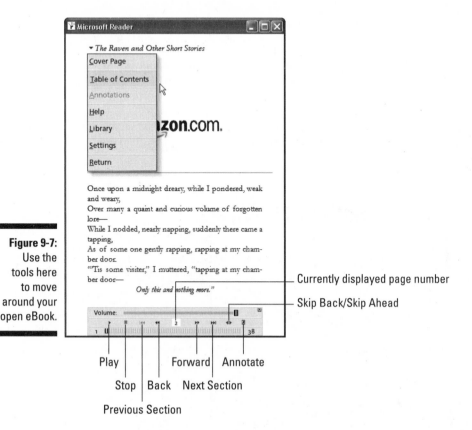

Figure 9-7:
Use the tools here to move around your open eBook.

Currently displayed page number

Skip Back/Skip Ahead

Play

Stop | Back | Next Section

Forward | Annotate

Previous Section

Keeping your place: Annotating

When I read a book, I have to confess that I'm guilty of folding down page corners, keeping my place with an old grocery receipt, and even occasionally highlighting important passages with a thick yellow highlighter.

(Not library books, of course; please don't send the Library Police after me!)

If you're anything like me, you'll be happy to hear that Microsoft Reader allows you to add a variety of notations to an eBook.

If you see a page you'd like to mark so you can easily return there, you can bookmark it by tapping the Annotate button in the Visual Guide.

This action puts a small flag on the margin of the page that looks like a little bar outline with a couple of points on the end (as shown in Figure 9-8).

Wherever you are in the eBook, you can tap this flag and instantly return to that page. Annotation flags are automatically color coded so that each one is a unique color, making it easier to keep track of multiple annotations.

You can also tap and drag with your pen to select text in an eBook; then choose Add Bookmark (from the menu that appears) to insert an annotation flag.

Annotations

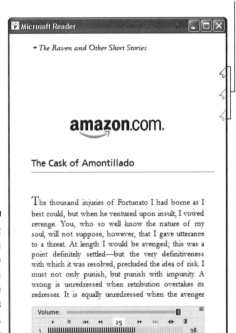

Figure 9-8:
If you
want to
remember a
page, use
these flags
to mark it.

You can display a list of all your annotations in the open eBook; just display the Go To drop-down list and choose Annotations. A list of all annotations you've made in that eBook appears, each with its appropriately colored flag.

To go to a particular annotated page, just tap it in this list.

You can change the color used for any annotation: Just right-tap the flag on the eBook page and choose Change Color. Then choose a different color from the drop-down palette that appears.

You can do other things to mark up your eBook. Tap anywhere in the text of a page and drag to select some text; a menu that enables you to do any of the following then appears:

- **Add Bookmark** places an Annotation flag on the page that is currently displayed.

- **Add Highlight** highlights the selected text in yellow.

- **Add Text Note** opens a window where you can type a text note. When you tap outside of the note, it is attached to the selected text.

  A small note symbol appears in the margin of the page; you can tap the note symbol to read the note.

- **Add Ink Comment** is unique to Tablet PC; it provides you with a toolbar so you can write directly on the eBook page by using your pen (see Figure 9-9), erase ink text, and save an ink comment.

- **Add Drawing** is available only if freeform drawings are in an eBook. If the eBook has freeform drawings, select one by tapping on it and choose this command from the menu to edit or delete the drawing.

Figure 9-9: If you see something you just have to comment on, do it with the tools on this toolbar and your Tablet PC pen.

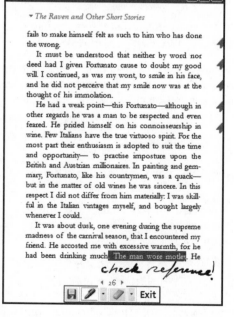

- **View Picture** lets you view any selected graphic in a separate window, where you can magnify or shrink it.

- **Find** looks for selected text elsewhere in the eBook as either an exact or approximate match.

- **Copy Text** copies selected text; you can then use the Paste command in any other program to insert a copy of the text in another document.

- **Play** begins playing the audio narration, starting at the selected text.

- **Lookup** opens the *Encarta Pocket Dictionary* feature and displays a definition for a selected word.

Changing the display

I hate to say it, but I have recently joined the ranks of those who are noticing the page getting a bit blurry when I read. This means that my eyes are getting older (not me, just my eyes . . .).

Whether you have older eyes or younger ones, you may appreciate some control over the Microsoft Reader display to make reading on your screen as comfortable as possible.

To get optimum-quality text display in Microsoft Reader, use a resolution setting higher than 800 x 600 on your Tablet PC display.

You can control the size of the font, the clarity of the type, and the size of the Reader environment. You can also control whether annotation features are turned on or off and control the settings for how the voice narration reads your eBook text.

To modify font settings, follow these steps:

1. **From the main Reader screen or the drop-down list on an eBook page, select Settings.**

   The Font Settings screen, as shown in Figure 9-10, appears. (Note if another Setting screen appears, tap Go To, then select Font Settings from the menu that appears.)

2. **Move the slider to a different selection to make text larger or smaller.**

   The preview text changes to reflect the size choice.

You can select other setting options from the Go To menu and follow the directions to make the simple setting choices offered.

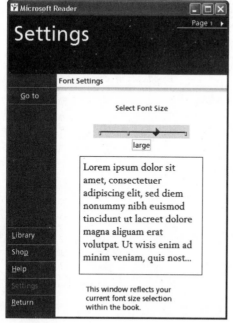

Figure 9-10:
View a
preview of
text at the
size setting
you select
here.

Sorting and searching your library

I suppose there are people who alphabetize their books (librarians come to mind), but I admit that my own bookshelves are pretty chaotic.

You can imagine how delighted I was to find that in Microsoft Reader, you can easily find what you need, as if a little librarian snuck into my Tablet PC overnight.

After you have quite a few eBooks in your Microsoft Reader Library, you can use the Sort feature to sort eBooks by Title, Author, Last Read, Book Size, and Date Acquired. You can also search by Author or Title.

Sorting and searching are very simple. You simply tap the Sort menu (as shown in Figure 9-11) or the Search menu; then tap the option you prefer, such as By Author. That's it!

The current sort order will be unavailable on the Sort list when you display it.

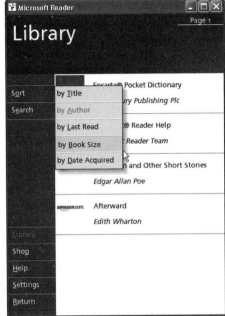

Figure 9-11:
If you want
to clear
out older
eBooks,
why not sort
by Date
Acquired?

Meet Your New Addiction: InkBall

What would a new computer be without a new computer game? InkBall takes advantage of your ability to work with a pen on your computer screen. It's fun, it's challenging, and it's addictive.

Ready to play? To go ahead and open InkBall, choose Start➪All Programs➪ Games➪InkBall.

The rules of the game

InkBall is a simple game to learn. Winning it depends on quick responses and a touch of manual dexterity.

The game board, as shown in Figure 9-12, changes slightly with every game and also changes depending on the difficulty level at which you're playing.

Essentially, InkBall will have a certain number of blank squares where the colored balls can float free, a few solid squares that the balls will bounce off of like the bumpers in a pinball game, and color-coded holes.

The object of the game is to get the blue balls into the blue hole, the green balls into the green hole, the orange balls into the orange hole, and so on. You do this by drawing on-screen with your pen to direct each colored ball into the corresponding hole.

Starting a game

When you open InkBall, it automatically begins a game. You can choose Game⇨New Game at any time to start a new game. When the game begins, the colored balls (sometimes one of each color; sometimes more than one of a single color) are loaded in the little window at the top-left corner of InkBall.

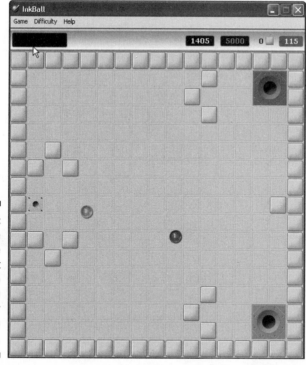

Figure 9-12:
Note the little score counter at the top to remind you of your score to date.

After a moment, the balls pop out of the square in the playing area that has a hole surrounded by four red dots. The balls appear one by one within the game area and begin to move in random patterns.

To play the game, perform any of these actions:

- ✔ Draw a line with your pen to block a ball from going in the wrong-colored hole (as shown in Figure 9-13). When you draw a line, the ball bounces off of it.
- ✔ Draw a line to direct the ball toward the correct color hole.
- ✔ Choose Game➪Pause to pause the play.
- ✔ Choose Game➪Clear Ink to remove lines you've drawn. Though these lines disappear automatically when a ball hits them, some lines may not get hit, and you can use this step to clear them manually.

After you land all the balls in the right-colored holes, the game is over, and your score will be added up and shown at the top of the screen.

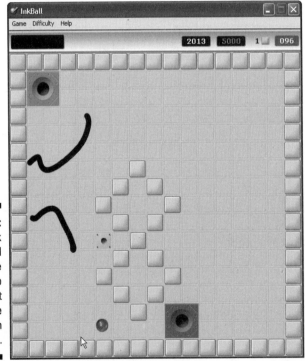

Figure 9-13:
These ink lines will deflect the ball to help you direct it into its hole to win the game.

If a ball goes into a hole that doesn't match its color or if the timer at the top of the game window runs out before all the balls get in their holes, the game is over!

Setting the difficulty level

InkBall is set for Beginners by default. This is the easy stuff, and you may soon master this level and want more challenge.

The different levels present scads of different configurations and complexities. For example, the Expert level game, as shown in Figure 9-14, has six balls in play; the balls all started out as clear, then turned into different colors as I played.

They also changed color periodically, so a blue ball I was trying to push into a blue hole suddenly turned green and I lost the game when it landed in the blue hole.

Note (also in this game) the blocks of solid color; these disappear if they are struck by a ball of the same color, but they deflect a ball of another color.

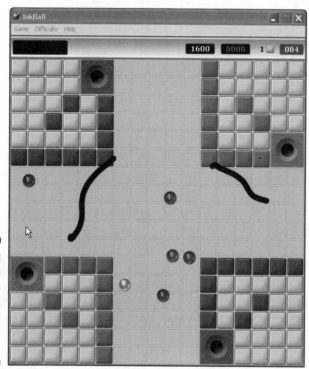

Figure 9-14:
With this many balls in the air, winning a game is hard!

Figure 9-15 shows an Intermediate-level game, where directional blocks with arrows indicate that you can only move balls in a clockwise direction around the screen; if a ball moves into a row of blocks where the arrows are facing towards it, it will bounce off and not be able to pass.

To select a difficulty level, open the Difficulty menu and tap the level you want. A new game begins automatically.

InkBall continues to start a new game at the same difficulty level when you finish each game, and it starts a game at that same level the next time you open InkBall.

Racking up scores

Here are a few things you should know about InkBall to succeed. First, a timer appears in the upper-right-hand corner that runs for each game.

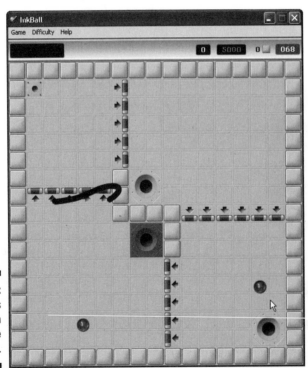

Figure 9-15:
Challenges
vary with
every game
you play.

If you get all the balls into their holes before the time runs out, you get a bonus point for each second left on the timer. Points carry over from game to game until you lose.

Here are few tips about how to win InkBall games:

- You need to stay ahead of the balls, so try to anticipate their movement and draw a line about one inch ahead of their path.
- If your lines aren't appearing where you expect them to, you may need to recalibrate your pen and screen by choosing Start⇨Control Panel⇨ Tablet and Pen Settings.
- Balls are worth different points, depending on their color, so go after them strategically.

  Gray balls are worthless, red balls are 200 points, blue balls are 400 points, green balls are 800 points, and gold balls are a hefty 1,600 points.
- Gray balls can go into any color hole.

You can find lots of variations on the different game levels, so explore them and get better with every game.

Part IV
Office XP, Tablet PC Style

The 5th Wave   By Rich Tennant

"He saw your Tablet PC and wants
to know if he can take a quick
inventory of the tribe's supply hut."

In this part . . .

*I*f you invented a car that ran on soy sauce, its success would depend on people opening soy sauce gas stations all over the place. Well, similarly, when you introduce a new type of computer, the success of that computer actually lies in the software that becomes available for it.

Microsoft understands this, and it therefore provided a kind of interim software plan for the first generation of Tablet PC by providing an Office XP for Tablet PC pack that adds some basic ink and speech functionality to applications such as Word, Excel, PowerPoint, and Outlook.

Using these features is what this part is all about.

Chapter 10

Office XP, Meet Tablet PC

*O*ne of the keys to the Tablet PC's eventual success will be the software that's built to take advantage of its speech and ink capabilities. Of course, you can use any Windows software on Tablet PC, but to really take advantage of what makes Tablet PC what it is, you want to have access to some Tablet PC–specific software. Otherwise, it's like buying a sports car that can go from 0 to 60 miles per hour in 5 seconds but never driving it above 30 mph.

Because the operating system that is the brains of Tablet PC comes from Microsoft, the office suite that is the first to have Tablet PC functionality is — you guessed it — Microsoft Office.

This functionality is somewhat limited, but it does give you a taste of what you will be able to do with Office on your Tablet PC when the next version comes out with integrated handwriting and speech capabilities.

In this chapter, I focus on the ink and speech features you can use with Word, Access, and Excel on your Tablet PC. PowerPoint and Outlook are a bit unique, so they each get their own chapter (Chapters 11 and 12).

Downloading the Office XP Pack for Tablet PC

First, let me explain how this works. The folks at Microsoft released Office XP about a year and a half before Tablet PC came out, and the next version of

Microsoft Office wasn't slated to come out until a while after Tablet PC was released. So the folks at Microsoft were sort of caught in this in-between time when they couldn't give the public a full-blown Office XP for Tablet PC.

If you're reading this book after the post-XP version of Office is finally released, just skip this section!

What did those clever folks in Redmond, WA, do? They came up with an interim plan. They released an update for Office XP that would overlay some ink and speech functionality on the current product and made that update publicly available for download.

As official members of the Office family, Visio and Project also gain limited Tablet PC functionality when you install the Office XP Pack.

With Office XP installed on your Tablet PC, you can go to

```
http://office.microsoft.com/downloads/2002/oxptp.aspx
```

to download the Office XP Pack for Tablet PC, which automatically installs the update (as shown in Figure 10-1). Most Tablet PC manufacturers also offer a link to this download page from their Web sites.

Figure 10-1: Download the Office XP Pack from Microsoft, and it installs automatically.

After you've downloaded and installed the Office XP Pack, an Office XP Pack for Tablet PC Help item will be added to each Office application's Help menu.

Using Voice Commands

Chapter 6 describes using your voice to enter text; that information also works for dictating text with Office products. However, giving voice commands is slightly different, depending on which Office product you're using.

When it comes to how these applications are enabled to take advantage of Tablet PC speech input, it's sort of like George Orwell said in *Animal Farm:* "All animals are equal, but some animals are more equal than others."

First, when you're using Word, all categories of Voice Commands in the following list are available to you:

- ✔ Commanding Tablet PC Input Panel
- ✔ Starting Applications
- ✔ Switch To
- ✔ Selection and Correction
- ✔ Navigation
- ✔ Uppercase and Lowercase
- ✔ Editing Operations
- ✔ Keyboard Simulation
- ✔ Controlling Speech
- ✔ Menus and Buttons

In Excel and Access, Selection and Correction, Navigation, and Uppercase and Lowercase voice command categories are not available to you at all.

In addition, the Menus and Buttons category of Speech commands offers a lot of choices; the ones you can actually use vary by application.

Access

With Access, you can use Access-specific voice commands, such as these:

- ✔ Create Table by Editing Data
- ✔ Create Table by Using Wizard

- Create Tablet in Design View
- Forms
- Indexes
- Lookup
- Primary Key
- Queries
- Reports

Excel

Excel has these Excel-specific commands:

- Data
- Merge and Center
- Currency Style
- Percent Style

Word

Word has these useful word-processing commands:

- Drawing
- Hyperlink
- New Ink Comment
- Normal View
- Outline View
- Print Layout View
- Professional Report
- Save as Web Page
- Spelling and Grammar

✔ Tables and Border Toolbar

✔ Track Changes

✔ (And so on . . .)

Viewing the available commands

To see exactly which commands are available within any application, follow these steps:

1. **Open a document in Word, Excel, or Access.**

2. **Open the Input Panel by tapping the Input Panel icon on the Windows taskbar.**

   The Input Panel appears.

3. **If the Speech feature isn't on, choose Tools⇨Speech in the Input Panel to turn it on.**

   The Speech area of the Input Panel is displayed, which includes a Dictation button, a Commands button, and a Speech Tools menu.

4. **Tap the Command button to turn voice commands on.**

   The Speech features are more context-sensitive when this function is on.

5. **Choose Speech Tools⇨What Can I Say?**

6. **Tap to place your cursor in an open document in an application (Word, Excel, or Access).**

   The What Can I Say dialog box now reflects the available commands for that application (as shown in Figure 10-2).

7. **Now you can look up the command you want to use, tap the Commands button in the Speech area of the Input Panel, speak a command such as "Save" and your computer performs a corresponding action — in this case, it opens the Save dialog box.**

   (Refer to Chapter 6 for more detailed information about working with Speech commands.)

You have to have your insertion point active in an open document when you speak a command to have it take effect (unless it's a Windows command, such as Switch To, to move among applications).

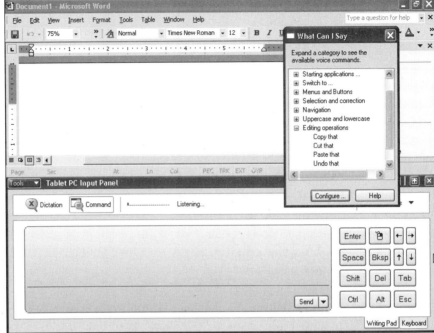

Figure 10-2:
Expand
categories
of
commands
by tapping
the plus sign
next to
them.

Entering Handwriting and Text

Chapter 4 covers the basics of entering text via the Input Panel. Writing or typing text works just the same no matter which Office application you're in.

But what you can enter and where you can enter it are a little different in each Office product. Also, Excel and Word (but not Access) have a neat little feature that enables you to enter handwriting directly in documents.

Working through the Input Panel

Think of the Input Panel as the gateway that your Tablet PC uses to input stuff into documents. The Input Panel enables you to enter information into any Office application via the on-screen Keyboard or Writing Pad.

Here is how the Input Panel interacts with Word, Excel, and Access:

✔ You can use the Input Panel Keyboard to enter text in all three applications.

✔ You can use the Input Panel Writing Pad to enter text in all three applications.

✔ You can use the Input Panel Writing Pad to enter handwritten content only in Word (as shown in Figure 10-3).

In addition, you can use the Write Anywhere feature of the Input Panel (covered in Chapter 4) to write on a document, but what you write will be sent to the document as text in all three applications.

All about Ink Drawing and Writing objects

In addition to accepting voice commands and accepting content from the Input Panel, Word and Excel have also had a little feature, called Ink Drawing and Writing objects, added to them.

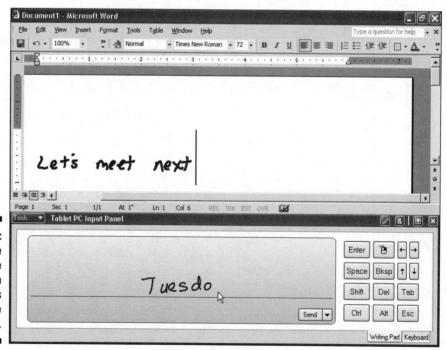

Figure 10-3:
Word is the only Office application that accepts ink from the Writing Pad.

This feature (which I call *IDWOs* because the name's so long) enables you to write or draw in a document. What you write or draw with your pen in the Ink Drawing and Writing area actually becomes a graphic object, which you can move around in your document, resize, and so on.

When you insert an IDWO, an Ink toolbar appears (as shown in Figure 10-4). Here are the tools available to you on the Ink toolbar:

- ✔ **Pen** is used to hand write in the object.
- ✔ **Eraser** erases whole words or drawn objects.
- ✔ **Selection Tool** selects drawn or written items to cut, copy, or paste.
- ✔ **Ink Color** sets the color of the Pen tool.
- ✔ **Ink Style** sets the thickness of the line you draw.

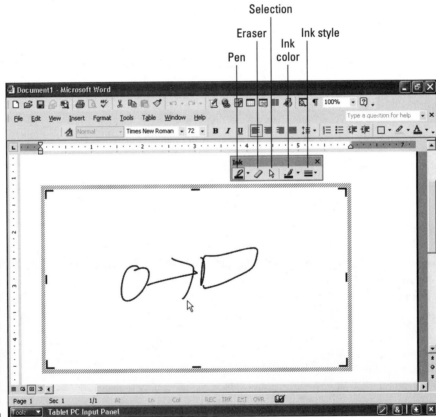

Figure 10-4: The Ink toolbar provides basic tools for working with handwritten input.

Inserting Ink Drawing and Writing objects

To add an IDWO, follow these steps:

1. **Open a document in the application (Word or Excel).**

2. **Tap in the document to place your insertion point.**

3. **Choose Insert⇨Ink Drawing and Writing.**

   A blank object appears, along with the Ink toolbar.

4. **Use the Ink tools to write or draw anything you like.**

5. **After you've finished, tap outside the object to close the toolbar.**

   You can tap the object at any time to reopen it for editing.

Resizing and moving Ink Drawing and Writing objects

As with any object, you can move IDWOs around documents and resize them. However, keep in mind that resizing an IDWO does nothing to resize the hand-written content within it, so there's not a whole lot of point in doing it, except that by doing so you add a bit of white space surrounding the handwritten content. (Figures 10-5 and 10-6 show the difference between an original object and its resized version.)

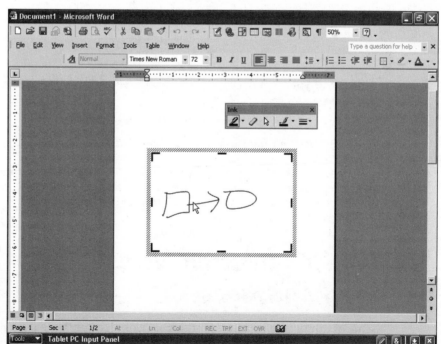

Figure 10-5:
Here's the original object size . . .

Figure 10-6:
. . . and here
it is
enlarged.

To resize an IDWO, follow these steps:

1. **Tap the object to open it.**

2. **Move your pen over any corner until your cursor changes into a corner shape.**

3. **Tap and drag in or out to resize the object.**

4. **Release your mouse when the object is the size you want.**

You move an IDWO the same way you move non-IDWOs: Move your cursor over the edge of the object until it turns into the familiar move cursor (the one with four arrows), tap, drag, and drop the object.

Sending Handwritten Notes as E-Mail Messages

One of the forms of communication that can definitely benefit from the personal touch of handwriting is e-mail. Imagine sending a handwritten e-mail message to your sweetheart to express your affection.

(Or having your children create a drawing and send it off to Grandma's e-mail address on her birthday.)

(Or sending your boss a handwritten note of resignation with a drawing of a jackass to tell him what you think of him . . . well, okay, you can *imagine* that one, but I don't recommend actually doing it.)

But I digress. . . .

You can create a Word or Excel document that includes one or more Ink Writing and Drawing objects and then use a command on the File menu to send your handwritten content in the body of an e-mail message:

1. **Simply create the Ink Drawing and Writing object in Word or Excel.**

2. **Then choose File⇨Send to⇨Mail Recipient.**

   An e-mail form opens, as shown in Figure 10-7, with your handwriting and any other document contents in the message area.

3. **Just address this e-mail form like you ordinarily would and send it on its way!**

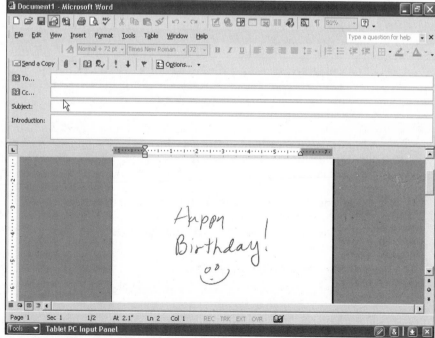

Figure 10-7:
Personalize
e-mail
messages
with
handwritten
content
from Word
or Excel.

You can also insert Ink Drawing and Writing objects directly into e-mail messages in Outlook; find out how to do this in Chapter 12.

Marking Up Documents with Handwritten Ink Comments

Another area where handwriting might soften the blow is when you add comments to a document. How much more personal is it to say, "Rewrite this entire paragraph — it stinks," in handwriting rather than in cold, hard text, right?

Comments are a feature of Word that inserts a little cartoonlike balloon with a line pointing to a spot in your document. You can enter a comment in that balloon.

This feature is great to use for lengthy, complex documents, such as project reports or books, where several writers and/or editors might be involved in reviewing drafts.

Ink Comments are just like comments you insert in a Word document, except that the little balloon where you usually type text is actually an Ink Drawing and Writing object.

You can write words or scribble drawings in it. Ink Comments appear alongside non-ink Comments, and you can view them in the Reviewing Pane when you use the Reviewing feature of Word.

To display the Reviewing toolbar in Word, choose View➪Toolbars➪Reviewing. Tap the Reviewing Pane button (the button on the far right of the Reviewing toolbar that looks like a little note with a bold blue arrow on the top) to display all comments at the bottom of the screen.

Here's how you insert an Ink Comment into a document:

1. **Place your cursor in the document where you want to insert the comment.**

2. **Choose Insert➪Ink Comment.**

   A blank comment appears, as shown in Figure 10-8.

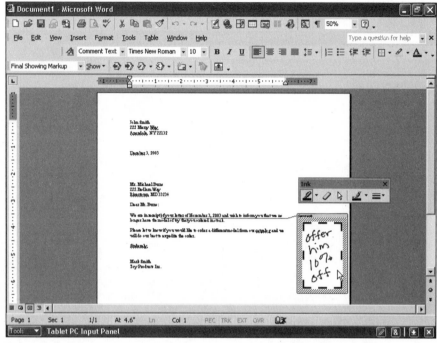

Figure 10-8:
A comment adds a line to show where your insertion point was when you inserted the comment, drawing the reader's attention to that place right away.

3. Write your comment in the balloon that appears on-screen.

Comments are saved when you save the document; no need to save or send them separately.

The Ink toolbar is available while editing comments if you want to use a different ink thickness or color.

You can delete any comment by tapping it and selecting Delete Comment from the shortcut menu that appears.

Chapter 11

Creating Presentations Just Got Easier

- -

In This Chapter

▶ Making choices in task panes with your pen

▶ Handwriting on slides, notes, and the outline

▶ Working on presentations with voice commands

▶ Running a presentation from your Tablet PC

▶ Using ink to add notes during a presentation

▶ Changing the presentation orientation

- -

*O*nce upon a time, people who gave presentations used blackboards or flip charts to write down their key points. They'd cover the pages with exclamation points and little smiley faces and jot notes in the margins. At the end of the presentation, somebody would rip all the flip chart pages down off the wall where the presenter had taped them and gave them to some poor assistant to type up and mail to everybody who had been at the meeting.

Fast-forward to the late twentieth century. Somebody invents computer presentation software (Mr. PowerPoint, I think), and a revolution is started. All presentations now appear on neat computer screens with formal typefaces and crisp columns of bullets. And the presentations can be printed out without any poor soul having to balance 3-foot-by-4-foot sheets of paper on his or her desk to type up notes.

PowerPoint is wonderful, but let's face it: Somewhere along the way, presentations got stodgy and lifeless. Where's the handwritten scrawl of the presenter? How boring is it to create long series of bullet points by just typing them in? Enter Tablet PC. Now you can draw and write on slides, use your pen to navigate your slide show, and even build your presentation by using voice commands. Say hallelujah!

Made for Each Other: PowerPoint and Your Pen

Fred and Ginger, ham and cheese, Mulder and Scully . . . some things were just meant to go together. Tablet PC and any graphics-oriented program, including presentation software, are simply perfect together. That's because the ability to write your input removes the barrier of the awkward mouse that stands between you and your creativity.

As with all Office programs, PowerPoint gains Tablet PC functionality from the Tablet PC Office pack, which is kind of an overlay of functionality on top of the PowerPoint software. That statement means that you need to use the Input Panel to write or speak content into PowerPoint and to use voice commands.

And, of course, you can use your pen just like a mouse to tap things to select or insert design elements on a slide (such as a design template). You can also draw objects with your pen directly on slides just as you draw shapes and lines with a mouse.

PowerPoint XP does have a few other perks: Pen, felt-tip pen, eraser, and highlighter tools are available to draw directly on slides while you're running a presentation. (The non-Tablet PC version of PowerPoint has a single pen tool you can use in presentations, but using it with a mouse to write on a slide is something akin to performing brain surgery with a ballpoint pen.) With the Tablet PC-provided pen tools, you can really go to town with much more legible handwritten comments or drawings. In addition, you can use your pen to navigate through a slide show.

PowerPoint Primer

PowerPoint is essentially a business presentation program that allows you to enter content on slides such as bulleted lists of text, graphs, or graphic objects such as pictures or company logos.

Tapping your way through PowerPoint

Anything PowerPoint-related that you can do on a PC you can also do with Tablet PC. Thus, some PowerPoint tasks you used to do with a mouse click respond to the tap of your Tablet PC pen — such as applying design templates, layouts, animation schemes, and color schemes.

You build slides by entering content in an outline format or by entering it right on individual slides in placeholders (these are sort of like text boxes in Word; when you tap in them they open for you to enter text or insert objects).

You can choose a layout for each slide that determines what types of placeholders will appear (title, title and text, pictures, and so on). You can also apply slide designs; they are preset combinations of background colors, font styles, and graphic elements that make your slides look really nice without requiring you to get a degree in graphic design.

You can use a Slide Sorter view to reorganize slides in a presentation. You can also use features to add animations, slide transitions (special effects that occur when you move from one slide to another in a slide presentation), and even recorded sounds or a narration.

When you've built your slide show, you can play it using PowerPoint, and even annotate your slide content with a Pen tool (PowerPoint's own, but you can also use your Tablet PC pen if you're giving the presentation from a Tablet PC) or take meeting notes.

Got it? Okay, time to see what Tablet PC brings to the PowerPoint mix.

Using Ink in Slides, Outlines, and Notes

You can use three methods to write things in PowerPoint, but right off the bat you have to decide whether you want text to look like text or look like a digital version of your own lovely handwriting. You can write on the Writing Pad tab of the Input Panel and send your writing to PowerPoint as text; or you can use the Write Anywhere feature to write in the PowerPoint environment and have it convert to text automatically. Finally, you can insert a Drawing and Ink object and write or draw and have your handwritten content preserved as a graphic object.

Keep in mind that, no matter how you enter it, content entered in placeholders on slides in PowerPoint is copied to the outline automatically, and content entered in the outline is similarly reflected in slides.

Using the Writing Pad to enter slide contents

What's unique with PowerPoint is that you have three possible areas to enter text: the Outline tab, the Notes pane, and on slides themselves (as shown in Figure 11-1).

Outline tab

Slides tab

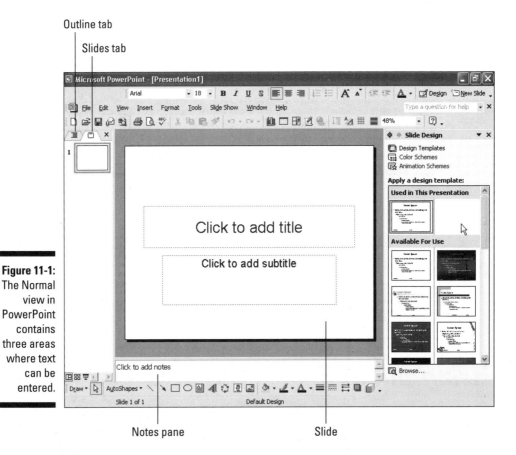

Figure 11-1:
The Normal
view in
PowerPoint
contains
three areas
where text
can be
entered.

Notes pane

Slide

Before you begin writing input, you have to open a placeholder for editing or place your insertion point in the Notes or Outline tab by tapping the location where you want to add content. Only after you perform this action can the Writing Pad know where to put the text you enter.

In PowerPoint, before you can enter text into a title or text placeholder, first you have to tap the text; then anything you enter replaces the placeholder text.

In addition, you can draw text boxes on slides. First, create the text box, and then tap the box to create an insertion point. As with placeholders and the Outline and Notes areas, once the insertion point is active, you can input text with either the Keyboard or Writing Pad area of the Input Panel.

Text boxes differ from placeholders mainly in that whatever you enter into them is not reflected in the presentation outline. So text boxes are typically used to add text that is more of a design element on a slide (for example, the word FREE!!! in large green letters above a product image), rather than text that conveys the concepts and points of the speaker.

You can also enter text or ink objects in an area of PowerPoint called Slide Master (choose View➪Master➪Slide Master). When you use the methods covered in this section to add presentation elements in the Slide Master, they will appear on every slide in your presentation.

Follow these steps to use the Writing Pad in the Input Panel to add text to slides and text boxes:

1. **Choose Start➪All Programs➪Microsoft PowerPoint to open the program with a blank title slide displayed.**

2. **Tap the Input Panel icon on the Windows taskbar to open the Input Panel and display the Writing Pad tab.**

    Your screen should now look like the one shown in Figure 11-2.

3. **Tap in the Title placeholder (the one that says** Click to add title**).**

4. **Write some text (the title of your presentation could go here) in the Writing Pad.**

    After a moment the text appears in the title placeholder.

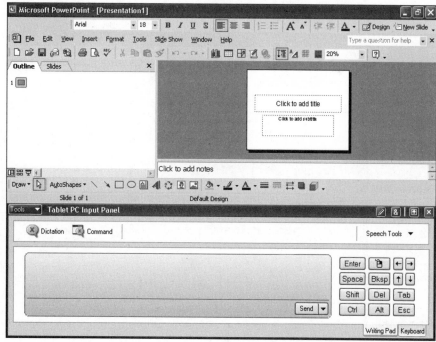

Figure 11-2:
The PowerPoint screen shrinks to allow the Input Panel to be displayed beneath it.

5. **Tap in the subtitle placeholder (the one that says** `Click to add subtitle`**).**

6. **Write a city and date for the presentation in the Writing Pad.**

7. **Tap the Send button in the Input Panel to immediately send the text to the slide.**

   The text appears in the subtitle placeholder.

8. **Tap the Text Box tool on the Drawing toolbar.**

   This tool looks like a little document with an A in the upper-left corner.

9. **Tap above the title placeholder and drag to draw a text box.**

10. **Write a theme (such as Striving for Excellence!) in the Writing Pad (as shown in Figure 11-3) and tap the Send button.**

   The text appears on the slide.

11. **If you want to save this masterpiece, choose File⇨Save and save it as you would any other Word document.**

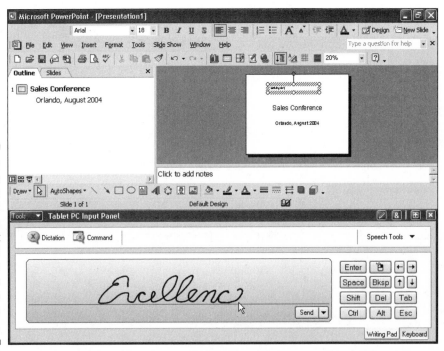

Figure 11-3:
The text box delivers a motivational message that won't be included with the speaker's main points in the outline.

There are two options that appear when you tap the Send button on the Writing Pad of the Input Panel: Send as Text (automatically converts handwriting to text) and Send as Ink (sends your handwriting to a document).

You can't use the Send as Ink option on the Send button when sending handwriting to a slide placeholder, text box, outline, or notes. Content sent to these areas is always converted to text.

Write your outline anywhere

Computer users have personalities, too. Do you hate being confined to the Input Panel? Then you're probably a Write Anywhere type of personality. These W-A types like the freedom that Write Anywhere gives them to write directly on the PowerPoint screen. (What you write still appears wherever your insertion point is resting, such as in the outline or in a slide placeholder.)

One of the biggest benefits of using Write Anywhere to enter text is that you can minimize the Input Panel while you write, allowing PowerPoint to fill much more of the screen. When you're building slides, this capability helps you to see the overall look and balance of design elements, text, and objects on the slides more clearly.

You can make the Write Anywhere function (discussed in Chapter 4) available through the Input Panel options and then activate it by tapping the Write Anywhere button displayed in the Input Panel title bar (it looks like a little pen).

When you enter text in a slide in PowerPoint, that text also appears on the Outline tab — and vice versa. When you enter text in the outline in the following steps, you see the upper-level text for each slide appear in the title placeholder; indented text in the outline appears in the subtitle placeholder on the slide (refer to Figure 11-3).

Follow these steps to use Write Anywhere to enter text into a presentation outline:

1. **Choose File⇨New to open a new PowerPoint presentation with a blank title slide displayed.**

2. **Tap the Input Panel icon on the Windows taskbar to open the Input Panel.**

3. Choose Tools⇨Options.

The Options dialog box appears.

4. Tap the Write Anywhere tab, as shown in Figure 11-4.

Figure 11-4:
In this
dialog box,
you can also
control the
time delay
for sending
hand-
writing to a
document
and the
thickness
and color
of ink.

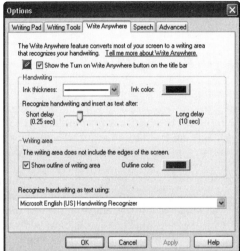

5. Make sure that the Show the Turn on Write Anywhere Button on the Title Bar check box is selected; then tap the Close button.

A button with a symbol of a pen on it now appears on the title bar of the Input Panel. This is the Write Anywhere button.

6. Tap the Write Anywhere button to activate it.

A dialog box appears, explaining how to turn off Write Anywhere.

7. Tap OK to close this dialog box.

8. Make sure that the Outline tab (refer to Figure 11-2 to identify this tab) appears to the right of the Blank Slide icon.

This tab must be in this position to activate your insertion point on the Outline tab.

9. Move your pen around the screen.

As you do so, an entry line appears and moves around (as shown in Figure 11-5). You can write on this entry line anywhere it appears on the screen; what you write appears wherever your insertion point is located on the Outline tab.

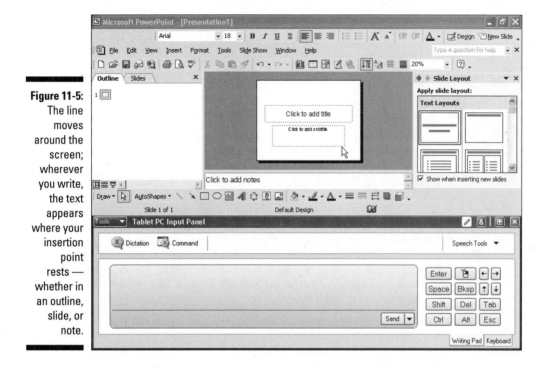

Figure 11-5:
The line moves around the screen; wherever you write, the text appears where your insertion point rests — whether in an outline, slide, or note.

10. **Write some text (such as** Annual Meeting**) on the entry line of Write Anywhere.**

    After a moment, the text appears in the outline and in the slide title placeholder (which matches the upper level of the outline for each slide).

11. **Tap the Enter key on the Input Panel to move to the next line.**

12. **Tap the Tab key to indent the line.**

13. **Enter a date on the Write Anywhere entry line.**

14. **Tap the Write Anywhere button to turn the feature off.**

Adding handwritten objects

Imagine that you're making a presentation to employees about your company's renewed dedication to employee satisfaction. What could be better than to show a sentence, such as "I promise that our employees are #1," on a slide and include the president's signature under that promise?

Or perhaps you want to show handwritten quotes of customer testimonials to give your sales presentation that personal touch.

Whatever your use for handwritten text or hand-drawn graphics, you can take advantage of the Ink and Drawing feature in PowerPoint to add text and drawings as graphic objects.

The Writing Pad and Write Anywhere are the only methods of entering text on the Outline tab and Notes pane; you can insert Ink and Drawing objects only on slides.

Because Ink and Drawing objects are objects, the text within them won't appear in the PowerPoint outline when you add them to a slide.

To insert an Ink and Drawing object on a slide and enter content into it, follow these steps:

1. **With the Normal view displayed in PowerPoint (the one that opens when you open a new presentation), choose Insert➪Ink and Drawing Object.**

   A new object appears on your slide with an Ink toolbar on top of it, as shown in Figure 11-6.

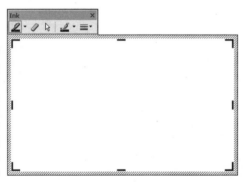

Figure 11-6:
This object can be moved around your slide and resized.

2. **Write your signature in the object.**

   Or write someone else's signature, or the Gettysburg Address, if you like.

   I drew a heart because I'm so sweet and I like to practice drawing things.

3. **Tap the Eraser tool on the Ink toolbar.**

4. **With the pen tip touching the screen lightly, move your pen over a word you wrote; move the pen tip gently back and forth to erase that word.**

5. Tap the arrow on the Pen tool and choose Highlighter➪Pink from the drop-down menu that appears.

6. Move your pen on the screen over the heart to highlight it with a pink color.

7. Tap the arrow on the Line Thickness tool and choose 6 pt.

8. Tap the arrow on the Ink Color button and choose a red color from the drop-down palette that appears (as shown in Figure 11-7).

Figure 11-7:
The few tools on this toolbar let you use different styles of pen, different colors, and different line thicknesses.

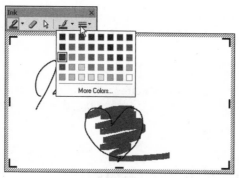

9. Draw a line under a word you wrote in the object with your pen.

10. Tap anywhere outside the object, and it appears alongside other objects in your slide.

The object doesn't appear in your outline.

To edit the Ink and Drawing object again, simply double-tap it. The Ink toolbar reappears, and you can use its tools to make changes or add more content to the object.

Presentations on Command

I'm sure that if you've ever prepared a PowerPoint presentation (especially at the last minute, and especially under pressure), you're quite used to speaking to PowerPoint. However, this is a family book, so I won't go into some of the words a harried presenter might scream at his computer when a presentation deadline is drawing inexorably closer and he's about as prepared as raw sushi.

This section deals with a different and much more productive kind of speech you can use with PowerPoint: the Speech feature of Windows XP for Tablet PC that enables you to use voice commands and enter text by simply saying it.

Chapter 6 covers talking to your Tablet PC, so I won't go into much detail about that here. However, I do want to mention that if you haven't trained your Tablet PC voice-recognition capabilities to understand your voice, 15 minutes before your presentation is due is *not* the time to use this option.

Voice-recognition applications have come a long way, but they still have a way to go before they're going to be as reliable as other forms of data entry (such as keyboards and Pen tools).

The voice commands you can use differ slightly in each application. In fact, speaking content into a presentation requires that you select a destination first. The following section shows what you can do with speech input and PowerPoint.

Entering presentation content

As with entering content by writing with the pen, entering content with speech requires that you select the destination for the content first: a placeholder on a slide, the Outline tab, the Notes pane, or a text box.

After you have chosen the location for the spoken content to appear, follow these steps to use Speech:

1. **With the Input Panel open, choose Tools⇨Speech.**

2. **Tap the Dictation button to begin the listening function for Speech.**

3. **Speak the content clearly and slowly.**

   As you do, it appears in the selected location; if you are speaking too softly or Speech can't understand you, it displays a message in the Input Panel (as shown in Figure 11-8).

You can use the Keyboard tools to invoke actions — such as Enter to move to the next line, or Backspace to delete content — while you work with Speech.

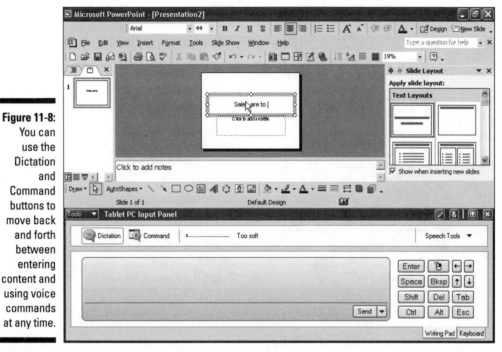

Figure 11-8:
You can use the Dictation and Command buttons to move back and forth between entering content and using voice commands at any time.

You cannot use the Speech feature to enter anything into an Ink and Drawing object — for that, you have to write in the object with your pen.

Editing by voice

You can use any category of voice command in PowerPoint. For example, you can launch or switch to other applications, use commands to navigate (simply say, "Go to Beginning"), convert to uppercase and lowercase letters, and edit (say "Delete" or "Undo That").

The What Can I Say listing, found at Speech Tools➪What Can I Say?, shows you the voice commands that are available (see Figure 11-9).

Check out the list of voice commands in Table 11-1. I find these commands especially useful when I'm using PowerPoint.

Table 11-1	What You Can Say to PowerPoint
Voice Command	*Result*
New Slide	Inserts new slide
New Presentation	Opens new presentation
Spell That	Runs Spell Checker
Clip Art	Opens the Clip Art task pane
Custom Animation	Opens Custom Animation task pane
Increase Font Size	Increases text size by 6-point increments
Decrease Font Size	Decreases text size by 6-point increments
Design	Displays Slide Design task pane
WordArt	Begins WordArt applet

One other very cool thing: When you display a task pane, such as Slide Design, all the choices in that pane become available as menu and button voice commands. So if you display the Layout pane, all the layouts can be applied by voice command; if you display the Custom Animation pane, suddenly those commands are available to you by voice as well. Pretty smart, huh?

It's Showtime: Taking a Presentation on the Road

Tablet PC really shines when it comes to giving your presentation. That's because Tablet PC is light and portable so you don't throw out your back getting it to your presentation site.

It has wireless capability, so you can connect it to wireless display devices, and you can even use the Tablet PC screen to make more intimate presentations, such as a sales presentation to a buyer in her 8' x 8' cubicle. And Windows XP for Tablet PC even adds some on-screen notation and navigation tools available to make the presentation itself go smoothly.

Connecting the Tablet PC to an LCD

Anybody who has ever made a presentation — or attended one — has experienced that tense five minutes before the scheduled start time, when the AV guy from the hotel, the speaker who went before you, and a waiter who happened to walk by at the wrong time with fresh coffee, huddle over the display equipment trying to get some kind of image to project. When an image does appear, it's upside down.

When you get it right-side up, it suddenly gets red and black lines across it.

I can't tell you that those episodes will go away entirely, but the capability to connect without wires is truly a leap forward for presenter-kind. Every Tablet PC model has wireless capability (although some may require an optional wireless card to go wireless). Most are WiFi 802.11b compliant, and some use Bluetooth technology.

Check your user manual if you want to see which you have, though the actually functionality won't vary.

With a wireless connection, you don't have to worry about the connector between your Tablet PC and the display equipment pulling out in the middle of the presentation or whether there's enough cord so that you don't actually have to balance Tablet PC on top of your head in order to connect. You just line up the infrared element of your Tablet PC (as shown in Figure 11-10) with the infrared element on the projector, and they communicate harmoniously. Ahh.

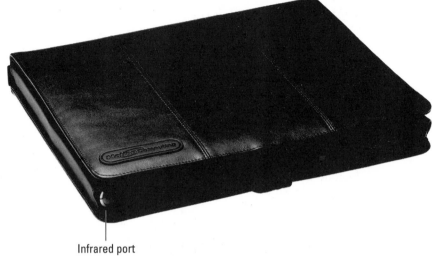

Infrared port

There's a little more to it than that, of course, because the projector and your Tablet PC probably vary slightly in how they set up the wireless connection. Many projectors have a presentation-management feature that walks you through the setup by pushing buttons on the unit or a remote control, for example.

Presentation products, such as Panasonic's PT series (www.panasonic.com), enable you to insert a wireless LAN card in the portable projector and then accept computer transmissions from up to 125 feet away.

If you encounter a nonwireless projection system, you can usually use your Tablet PC USB port to connect.

Navigating through your show

When you run a slide show, you want everything to go as smoothly as possible, right? You don't want to go back two slides when you meant to move forward one. You don't want to appear like a parody of some clown trying to show the slides of his vacation in Atlantic City in his basement. So you need to know the easiest, simplest ways to move around your slide presentation.

Traditionally, the user has a few different ways to navigate through a PowerPoint slide show — click the mouse, press Enter, or press the right-arrow key on the keyboard to move forward one slide. Tablet PC provides a few new methods:

✔ Instead of clicking your mouse button, you can tap the screen with your pen to move forward one slide.

✔ You can use the right and left arrows on the Input Panel to move forward or backward by one slide.

✔ You can use voice commands such as *Enter, Move Right,* and *Next* to move forward one slide, *Move Left* to move back one slide, and *End Show* to end the slide show.

Follow these steps to navigate through a slide show:

1. **Open a PowerPoint presentation that contains at least three slides (or open a blank one and insert two new slides, entering any text you like on each).**

2. **Tap the Slide Show view icon in the bottom-left corner of the PowerPoint screen to begin the show.**

3. **Tap your pen on the screen.**

   The show moves forward one slide.

4. **Display the Input Panel by tapping the Input Panel icon on the Windows taskbar.**

   The Input Panel appears.

5. **Tap the left arrow on the Quick Key pad.**

   You move back one slide.

6. **Choose Tools⇨Speech to activate the Speech function.**

7. **Tap the Command button.**

8. **Say, "Enter."**

   The presentation moves forward one slide.

9. **Say, "End Show."**

   The show ends, and you are returned to PowerPoint's main screen.

Adding ink while you speak

In its last few versions, PowerPoint has had a Pen tool (well, actually a pen-like drawing function that you control with the mouse) that you could use during a slide show to mark on the screen or even write words.

Of course, writing words with your mouse made them look a little bit like they were written by an ancient Egyptian with bad handwriting — hieroglyphics for the penmanship challenged. And all you could do was turn the pen on and off and change the color of ink it wrote in.

Windows XP for Tablet PC, with its pen technology, changes that. You can write on your tablet during a presentation in natural handwriting with your pen, circling things, highlighting them, writing notes in the margins, and so on. Just don't go so crazy that all your audience sees is a big mess of scribbles!

But beyond the much more user-friendly functionality of writing with a pen instead of a mouse, you've also got a few more Pen tools available to you. You can access these on the Slide Show menu that you can display while running a show (as shown in Figure 11-11). By using this menu, you can also erase part or all of what you've written — on the fly.

Follow these steps to use the Pen feature while showing a presentation:

1. **Tap the Slide Show View icon in the bottom-left corner of PowerPoint to begin a slide show.**

   The Slide Show view appears.

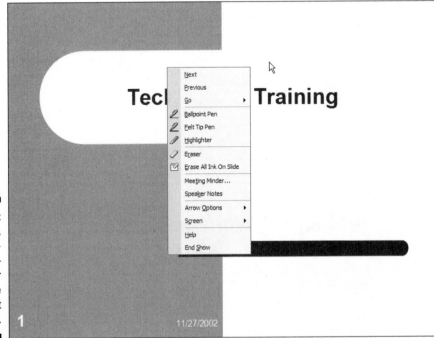

Figure 11-11: Ballpoint, felt tip, high-lighter — pick your pen style and start writing.

2. **Either use the right-tap button on your pen to right-tap the slide area or tap the Slide Show menu icon (which appears at the bottom-left of the screen).**

   The Slide Show menu is displayed.

3. **Choose the Ballpoint pen style.**

   The menu disappears and a small Ink toolbar appears.

4. **Tap the Pen Color button on the toolbar and choose a blue color.**

5. **Use your pen to write some text on the slide (as shown in Figure 11-12).**

6. **Tap the Pointer button on the Ink toolbar.**

   The toolbar disappears.

7. **Either use the right-tap button on your pen to right-tap the slide area or tap the Slide Show menu icon that appears at the bottom-left of the screen to display the Slide Show menu again and choose Highlighter.**

   Again the menu disappears, and the Ink toolbar appears.

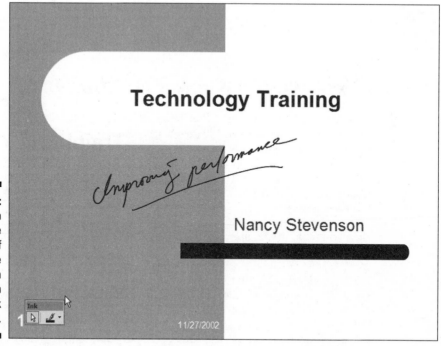

Figure 11-12: You can change the ink color of any of the three pen styles from the Ink toolbar.

8. **Drag your pen across a piece of text to highlight it.**

9. **Display the slide show menu again and choose the Eraser.**

   The menu disappears.

10. **Rub your pen across a portion of your handwriting (created in Step 5) to erase it.**

11. **To end the slide show, right-tap the screen and choose End Show from the Slide Show menu.**

    A dialog box appears, asking if you want to keep the ink you added to your slides.

12. **Tap Yes to save the ink, and it will appear on your slides in Normal view from then on, or tap No to discard the ink — but this discards all of it!**

By using a combination of pens and colors, you can make quite a colorful contribution to your presentation while it's in progress.

You can also enter text in Meeting Minder and Speaker Notes by choosing either of those options from the slide show menu available while you're running a show. For these, however, you have to use the Input Panel to enter text — no handwriting.

Changing the display orientation

On convertible model Tablet PCs, such as the Acer TravelMate C100, you can turn your computer screen 180 degrees, so that you are sitting at the keyboard while somebody sitting across from you is viewing your monitor.

This is a great feature for sales calls, for example, where you're presenting information on your products to a single person or a few people in a more intimate setting.

How you unlatch and spin your display away from you will vary slightly, depending on your unit.

For example, the Toshiba Portege 3500 allows you to swivel the screen in every direction (which is excellent for presentations) *and* lay it flat for writing. You can get a product tour at the Toshiba Web site (www.toshiba.com). Simply click the <u>Portables</u> link and then click the <u>Portege</u> link for detailed information. Or you can get to the Portege product page directly at

```
www.csd.toshiba.com/cgi-bin/
         tais/pc/pc_tabletPcDetail.jsp?comm=CS
```

No matter how your Tablet PC works, always take care with this process, because wrenching the monitor portion of your unit with too much strength, or turning the monitor the wrong way, can damage your unit. In addition, some models require that the top of your clamshell style unit be at a particular angle, or you may damage your keyboard when you turn the monitor.

But these cautions aside, after you try the simple process of converting your monitor to present to others, you'll find that this feature actually *makes* your Tablet PC into a handy little one-on-one presentation device.

Chapter 12

Communicating with Tablet PC

· ·

In This Chapter

▶ Using Tablet PC's wireless capabilities

▶ Using Ink with Outlook

▶ Working in Outlook with voice commands

▶ Sending Journal Notes to Outlook

▶ Using Windows Messaging to chat in real time

· ·

*I*magine this: You are running through a busy airport when suddenly you get an absolutely brilliant idea. You stop, sit down, pull out your Tablet PC, connect it to a wireless network, and send your boss an — e-mail message outlining your idea. When your plane lands in Chicago, you turn on your Tablet PC and discover that your boss has sent a fax to your computer telling you that your brilliant idea was brilliant and that you've been made a Vice President and given a $100,000 raise.

Well, I can't guarantee the brilliant idea and its associated perks, but I can tell you that Tablet PC gives you the ability to communicate while on the go. In fact, one of Tablet PC's most important roles is to connect you to others as you wander around the corridors, airports, and meeting rooms that make up your world.

This chapter focuses on three aspects of that connectivity: using the wireless capability built into most Tablet PCs, working with Outlook using Ink and speech features to write and send e-mail, and using Windows Messaging to chat in real time.

Going Wireless

Although you can connect through a regular phone line or some method of high-speed access to e-mail and fax from your Tablet PC, you may be less familiar with what's involved in making a wireless connection. Because just about every Tablet PC comes with wireless technology built in, this is something you should know about.

Wireless access to the Internet works by using radio frequencies to connect your Tablet PC or other wireless-enabled device to a wireless network. Some companies provide wireless network services to employees, and you can access a wireless network service from a provider, such as T-Mobile, in public places, such as airports and hotels. By using wireless technology, your Tablet PC can connect to a wireless network through a wireless access point and you can send e-mail messages and faxes as well as surf the Internet for documents and data.

Just like any other Internet service provider, wireless providers charge you a monthly fee; T-Mobile's HotSpot service, for example, costs $39.99 per month at the time of this writing. Many ISPs provide a feature in their browser that alerts you when you're within shouting distance of a wireless network.

Your Tablet PC probably came with built-in wireless capabilities, but if it didn't, you can purchase a wireless adapter and insert it into a PCMCIA (PC card) slot on the tablet (as shown in Figure 12-1). With wireless capability in place, you're ready to connect.

Figure 12-1:
This PC card sports a wireless LAN antenna that sends and receives data through a wireless access point.

Exploring wireless standards

A *wireless standard* essentially provides a way of making a connection to a wireless network. The most current wireless communication standard is 802.11. This connection comes in two versions, 802.11a and 802.11b (with more, such as b+ and g coming down the road in future years). You may expect 802.11b to be the newer version, but oddly enough, 802.11a is actually the latest, greatest, higher speed standard.

If you sit down in a public airport or convention center, you're likely to find a wireless network available with the 802.11b standard, which works on a 2.4-gigahertz radio frequency to transmit data. (802.11a transmits in the speedy 5-gigahertz range.)

Controlling wireless connections

If you've ever driven through a rural area while trying to talk to your mom on your wireless phone, you may have had your call dropped and found yourself unable to reconnect until you're closer to a bigger city. Heck, you may have experienced this phenomenon in the heart of the biggest city in the world. Depending on your relationship with your mother, this may be a convenience or an inconvenience.

Wireless connections on your Tablet PC have the same degree of flakiness as wireless phone connections. You're more likely to find a wireless access point in highly populated areas, in public places like airports, convention centers, and other locations. These places are called *hotspots.* Windows XP for Tablet PC is designed to find hotspot connections automatically, but sometimes it needs a little help.

Visit www.80211hotspots.com for a list of hotspots around the world.

The following sections show you how to find a wireless access point.

Setting up your wireless adapter and finding access points

To set yourself up for wireless connections, you have to first have a wireless adapter in the form of a PC Card Check. Now you have to set up the adapter so that it, uh, adapts:

1. **Insert the adapter into the PC card slot on your Tablet PC.**

   The Wireless Configuration wizard appears automatically as soon as you insert the card.

2. **Run through the wizard, making settings appropriate to your location and connection, and tapping Next until you reach the end of the process.**

   A final wizard window appears, letting you know that if you tap the Finish button (aptly named) the installation is complete.

3. **Tap the Finish button.**

   After you've done so, Windows XP starts looking around for access points automatically.

When you complete the adapter installation, Windows pops up the dialog box shown in Figure 12-2. Follow these steps to let Windows start searching for access points.

1. **Tap the name of the network you want to use and then tap Connect.**

   Alternatively, you can choose Programs⇨Control Panel⇨Network Connection, and then tap the Wireless connection option. This technique is especially useful if you want to create your document first and connect when the document is ready; you can come back anytime to this connection window.

2. **When the connection is completed, you're online. Go ahead and browse, e-mail, or whatever.**

   If you see no options in the dialog box in Step 1, that means Windows XP is coming up empty trying to find a wireless access point. Tap the Cancel button, cool down, and read the following section.

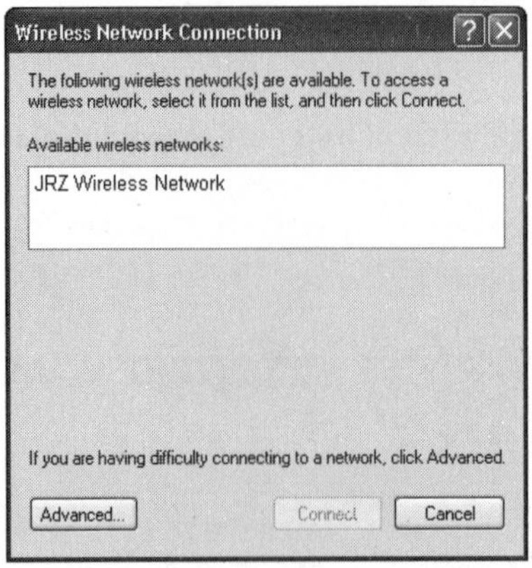

Figure 12-2: Whatever access points are available will be listed here.

Adding access points manually

Tablet PC may not find any access points (see Figure 12-3). If that happens, the next step is to set an access point manually. Follow these steps:

1. **Choose Start⇨Control Panel.**

   The control panel appears, as shown in Figure 12-3.

2. **Double-tap the Network Connections icon in the control panel.**

   Various network connections appear.

3. **Right-tap the Wireless Network Connection item and choose Properties.**

   The Properties dialog box appears.

4. **Tap the Wireless Networks tab.**

5. **Tap on an available network in the list and tap Configure.**

   The Wireless Network Properties dialog box appears.

6. **In the Wireless Network Properties dialog box, enter a wireless network key setting.**

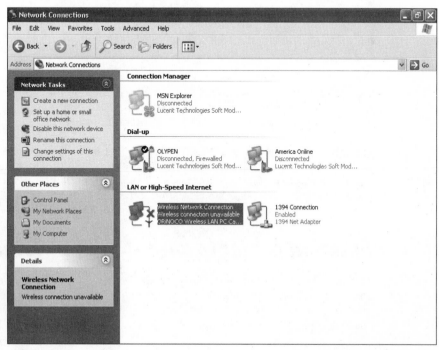

Figure 12-3:
Reach
Network
Connections
from the
Windows XP
control
panel.

You have to get this key setting from your network administrator or the manufacturer of your wireless adapter.

7. Tap OK in the Wireless Network Properties dialog box.

8. Tap OK again in the Wireless Connection dialog box.

Doing so completes the connection process.

If a wireless network doesn't make its network name available, you won't see it listed in the Available Networks list mentioned in the previous steps. In that case, you can add a preferred network (the wireless network that will be used by default), specifying the network name, also referred to as a Service Set Identifier, or SSID. You have to get the SSID from the folks at the network provider to which you pay that monthly fee.

Working with Ink in Outlook

Outlook is a recipient, along with other Microsoft Office applications, of the Ink capabilities that come from installing the Office XP Pack for Tablet PC. (See Chapter 10 for more about this.) These capabilities are

✔ Using the Tablet PC Input Panel to enter text by writing it in the Writing Pad tab or typing it with the on-screen keyboard.

✔ Inserting Ink objects in which you can draw and enter handwritten content.

In Outlook, you can use these Ink features to enter text content in e-mail forms as well as in dialog boxes used to add appointments in the calendar, tasks, and contacts. You can insert Ink objects into e-mails and task and appointment notes areas, but not into contact notes areas.

In addition, you can use the Write Anywhere feature of the Input Panel to write on a document, but what you write will be sent to the document as text, not as handwriting. All these methods are covered in Chapter 4, but in case you skipped that one, here's a refresher course.

Entering contents with the Input Panel

The Input Panel has two parts. Use the Writing Pad, shown in Figure 12-4, to hand write letters or numbers and send them as either Ink or converted text into an item into Outlook. The Keyboard tab is used to enter typewritten content.

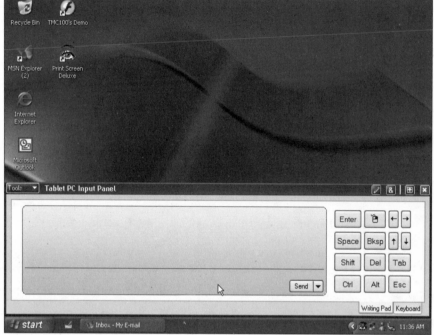

Tools ▼ | Tablet PC Input Panel

Enter
Space Bksp
Shift Del Tab
Ctrl Alt Esc

Send ▼

Writing Pad | Keyboard

start   Inbox - My E-mail   11:36 AM

Figure 12-4:
The Input
Panel
allows you
to add
text to
documents.

Follow these steps to enter text using the Input Panel Keyboard:

1. **Place your insertion point in the appropriate field in a dialog box for a task, contact, or appointment (or in an e-mail form in Outlook).**

2. **Use your pen and the Input Panel to enter data into the task, contact, appointment, or e-mail form.**

   If you want your entry in the Writing Pad to appear in the e-mail form as handwriting rather than text, tap the arrow on the Send button first and select Send as Ink before you write.

You can also use the Quick Keys on either the Keyboard tab or the Writing Pad tab to perform keyboard actions, such as Enter, Space, Backspace, and Tab.

Inserting Ink Drawing and Writing objects

In addition to accepting content from the Input Panel, Outlook gains the ability to insert handwritten content through a feature called Ink Drawing and Writing objects.

What you write or draw with your pen directly in the Ink Drawing and Writing object area actually becomes a graphic object which you can move around your document, resize, and so on.

When you insert an Ink object, an Ink toolbar appears (as shown in Figure 12-5). Here are the tools available to you:

- **Pen** is used to hand write in the object.
- **Eraser** erases whole words or drawn objects.
- **Selection Tool** selects drawn or written items to cut, copy, or paste.
- **Ink Color** sets the color of the Pen tool.
- **Ink Style** sets the thickness of the line you draw.

To add an Ink object to an e-mail message, task, or calendar appointment, follow these steps:

1. Open a new document; the procedure has a familiar Windows feel:

- To open a new e-mail, tap the New button while in your Inbox.

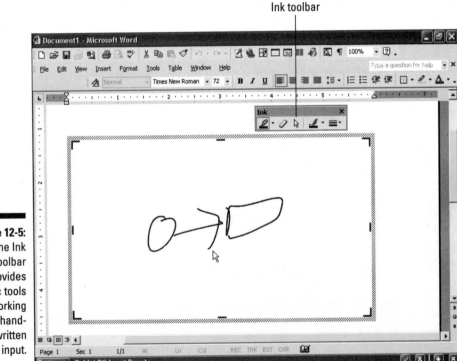

Figure 12-5:
The Ink toolbar provides basic tools for working with hand-written input.

- To open a dialog box for a new task, double-click a task row in the Tasks area.

- To open a dialog box for a new calendar appointment, double-click a date box in the Calendar.

The corresponding form opens.

2. **Place your insertion point in the body of the e-mail (or notes area in the dialog box).**

To do so, tap with your pen tip in the appropriate area.

3. **Choose Insert➪Ink Drawing and Writing.**

A blank object appears along with the Ink toolbar (as shown in Figure 12-6).

4. **Write or draw anything you like in the Ink and Drawing object, using the Ink tools provided.**

5. **When you've finished, tap outside the object to close the Ink toolbar.**

You can tap the object at any time to reopen it for editing.

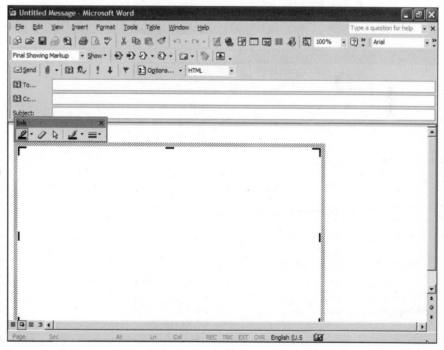

Figure 12-6:
You can insert a handwritten message in an e-mail message by writing in the Ink object.

Adding stuff with Write Anywhere

A feature of Writing Pad called Write Anywhere enables you to use any part of the screen as a writing pad. For example, you open Outlook and open an e-mail; then you turn on Write Anywhere. Rather than writing in the Writing Pad and sending that entry to the e-mail, you can write on the e-mail itself, and your writing is automatically converted to text. This feature is especially helpful if you have a long e-mail to write, where the Writing Pad might be too confined an area or the delay in sending text to the document too cumbersome.

To turn on the Write Anywhere feature and use it, follow these steps:

1. **Tap the Input Panel icon on the Windows taskbar and choose Tools⊃Options.**

   The Options dialog box appears.

2. **Tap the Write Anywhere tab to display it (as shown in Figure 12-7).**

3. **Tap in the check box labeled Show the Turn on Write Anywhere Button on the Title Bar.**

4. **Tap OK.**

   Now a small pen icon appears in the title bar of the Input Panel.

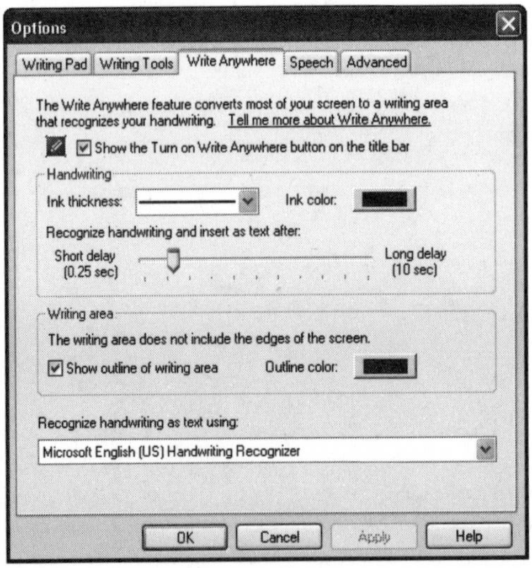

Figure 12-7: Control how the Write Anywhere feature functions from the Options dialog box.

5. **Open Outlook and tap in the body of an e-mail or a dialog box Notes field to place your insertion point.**

6. **Tap the pen icon.**

   A writing line appears in the item you opened in Step 5.

7. **Write along the line.**

   When you pause for a moment, what you wrote is converted to text in the document.

You can move the writing line to any location in the document simply by moving your pen up or down on the screen — but you if you want to edit text that's been converted, you can't select and edit it until you turn off the Write Anywhere feature (by tapping the Pen icon again).

Speaking to Outlook

If you want to talk directly to somebody, pick up an old fashioned telephone. But if you want to talk to Outlook as a method of entering contents in an e-mail or dialog box field, you can do that by using the Tablet PC Speech feature.

Speech allows you to enter text or to speak commands, such as Save and Print. Refer to Chapter 6 for more details about using Speech features, but here's a basic rundown of how you use Speech to enter text in Outlook.

To enter content by dictating with the Speech feature, follow these steps, using (as usual) pen taps to do the needed clicks:

1. **Open Outlook and place your insertion point in an e-mail form or in a task, appointment, or contact dialog box field.**

2. **Click the Input Panel icon to open it.**

   The Input Panel opens.

3. **Choose Tools⇨Speech.**

   A check mark appears next to Speech to indicate it is active; a panel that includes a Commands and a Dictation button appears at the top of the Input Panel.

4. **Click the Dictation button.**

   The Speech area of the Input Panel displays the word Listening, as shown in Figure 12-8. (If you say something that Speech can't recognize, then Listening changes to What Was That?)

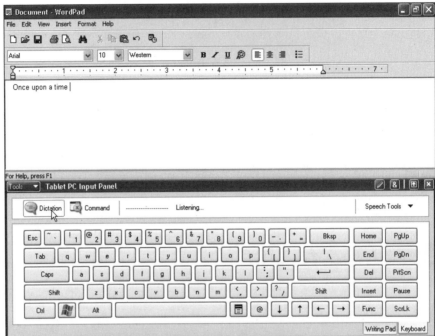

Figure 12-8:
Now it's
listening
to you.

5. **Begin speaking into the microphone.**

   If the Speech area of the Input Panel displays the words `What Was That?`, you have to repeat what you said, perhaps louder, more slowly, or more directly into the microphone.

6. **Continue speaking into your microphone.**

   Add "speaking" punctuation (such as periods and commas) where appropriate, as outlined in Chapter 6.

7. **After you're finished, tap the Dictation button in the Speech area of the Input Panel once again.**

   Doing so turns Speech off.

Sending Journal Notes to Outlook

When you enter handwritten content in Windows Journal, you can convert that content into text, which you can then insert into a message in an e-mail program such as Outlook.

See Chapter 7 for more information about using Windows Journal.

What Journal does is convert your handwriting to text. Journal then enables you to send that text by e-mail along with a copy of your handwritten content as an attachment that the recipient can open and view with the Windows Picture and Fax Viewer (as shown in Figure 12-9). You can use the Input Panel Writing Pad or an Ink object to insert handwriting directly into the e-mail as well.

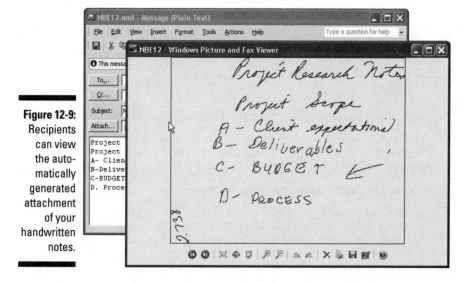

Figure 12-9: Recipients can view the automatically generated attachment of your handwritten notes.

To convert Journal note contents to e-mail, follow these steps (keeping in mind that a pen tap and a mouse click are the same thing to a Tablet PC):

1. **Go to Windows Journal and open a new or saved note.**

2. **Tap the Selection tool and drag over the text you want to convert to e-mail to select it.**

3. **Choose Actions⇨Convert Selection to E-mail.**

   The Convert to E-mail dialog box (as shown in Figure 12-10) appears.

4. **Tap any listed text that you want to correct; then tap an alternative word from the list displayed in the Convert to E-mail dialog box.**

5. **After you're done correcting converted text, tap Convert.**

   The Choose Profile dialog box appears (unless you have Outlook open, in which case an Outlook e-mail immediately appears).

Figure 12-10:
Choose
highlighted
words one
by one and
change
them to
alternative
words from
the list
provided;
then tap
Change.

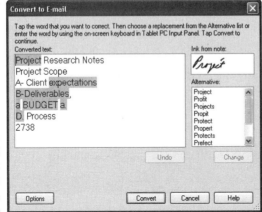

6. **Select an e-mail program from the Profile Names drop-down list.**

   Outlook is listed there by default; if you want to add one, tap New and enter a new profile name. Then follow the wizard that appears and guides you through creating a new e-mail account.

7. **Tap OK in the Choose Profile dialog box.**

   An e-mail form appears (as shown in Figure 12-11) with the note file name as the Subject and the note added as an attachment. The text of the note appears in the e-mail — completely converted from handwriting to text.

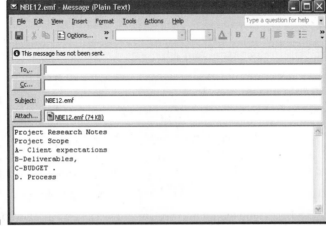

Figure 12-11:
Your note
text auto-
matically
appears as
message
text.

8. **Add addressee information and any other text or handwriting you wish to include.**

9. **Tap Send to send the e-mail.**

One way to send handwritten text in an e-mail is to use the File➪Send to➪ Mail Recipient command in Word to send a Word document (which could contain ink objects) as an e-mail message. See Chapter 10 for more about Tablet PC and Word.

Playing Around with Windows Messenger

Windows Messenger is a feature of Windows XP that you can use to chat with people online or send instant communications (as shown in Figure 12-12) to them in real time (as opposed to e-mail, which may or may not be read as soon as you send it). You can open Messenger by tapping the Messenger icon in the Windows system tray and choosing Open Windows Messenger.

The idea is that Windows Messenger can go out there online and locate any contacts you've created and see if they're online at the same time that you are. If they are, you can use Messenger to initiate a chat, hold a voice conversation, or even hold a little meeting with a *whiteboard* feature (a white version of a blackboard, souped up to be digital).

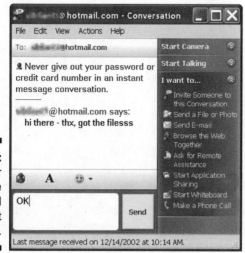

Figure 12-12: Enter your message here and deliver it instantly.

Though no special Tablet PC-oriented functions are available for Windows Messenger, you can use the Tablet PC Input Panel to enter text into Instant Messages or write on the Messenger Whiteboard feature with your pen.

Because Tablet PCs have built-in microphones and speakers, you may also want to take advantage of the Make a Phone Call feature of Messenger (as shown in Figure 12-13). To use this feature, you first have to sign up with a voice service provider, which you can do from the Messenger window. Then you can call anybody you like by tapping out his or her number on the virtual phone pad.

Messenger has a feature called Voice Conversation. You can use this feature to hold a voice conversation between two people with computers that are equipped with speakers and microphones or a connected headset.

Making a phone call from Messenger requires payment to a voice service provider because you're using a phone line. Voice Conversations are held between two computers; therefore, there is no charge!

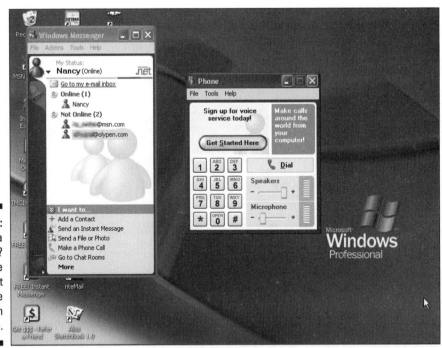

Figure 12-13:
Don't have a cell phone? Just use your Tablet PC to make calls on the go.

Part V
The Part of Tens

In this part . . .

This is the part that divides things into tens: Ten neat things that you can do with a Tablet PC; ten great software products that take advantage of Tablet PC's features; and ten ways that businesses can put Tablet PC to work in their industry's workforce.

Do you want to design a form that lets people fill it out with handwritten content, right on-screen? Do you want to connect your digital camera to a Tablet PC and upload photos and mark them up with your pen? In this part, you learn how to do these things and more. And because pen technology has been around for a few years, you discover that there are software programs ranging from graphics programs to daily planners that work just swell with Tablet PC's ink input. Additionally, you see how everybody from medical staff to salespeople and insurance agents can make Tablet PC part of their working lives to achieve more efficiency.

Chapter 13

Ten Neat Things You Can Do with Your Tablet PC

So far, this book has covered things most people do with Tablet PCs. But this chapter takes you one step farther, into the world of bells, whistles, techno-gew-gaws, and just generally neat things you might want to explore once you've got the Tablet PC basics down.

Some of these activities require that you get additional accessories, software, or peripherals for your Tablet PC. Others can get to work with your Tablet PC right out of the box. So read on — and prepare to be amazed (or at least amused) at what your Tablet PC can do that you didn't know it could.

Working with Ink Forms

Throughout this book I mention the convenience of being able to fill out forms in (cybernetic) Ink. Though handwriting on your computer screen may seem like high-tech gone astray, consider how convenient it is for people who don't know how to use a keyboard. (People of all types fit into this latter category — from Joe on the manufacturing floor to Edna and Bill, who are always at the mall shopping.)

Now Joe, Edna, and Bill (and everyone else) can complete electronic forms, from purchase orders to customer surveys, "out in the field" using handwriting or speech. Using Tablet PC to fill out forms is a very efficient way to go; once data is entered, it can be instantly compiled and sent back to an office for analysis. No need to wait days or weeks for the form's content to be laboriously rekeyed into a database.

If you do market research as part of your job (or you're a really research-driven person by nature), you no longer have to carry multiple paper copies of several versions of a survey with you. For example, you might have versions of a single survey that vary slightly depending on the age group of the survey respondent; you just call up the appropriate version of the form on-screen and you're ready to roll.

In his speeches about Tablet PC, Bill Gates has quoted industry statistics that show how a company can save as much as $150 per form transaction by using ink-enabled forms and transmitting them via a wireless network.

Savings in time and money come from escaping the need to regularly print and distribute new forms — and if you need a new form, you can scan an existing form and modify it in Journal instead of redesigning it from scratch.

Forms-management software such as OmniForm Forms from Scansoft (www.scansoft.com) can convert existing forms into electronic forms. One benefit of electronic forms is that you can update them on the fly, saving the cost of redesign and reprinting. You can stop worrying that out-of-date forms might be used during the transition to a new form. Also, where required, a handwritten signature in an e-form can be used for legal proof of identity (for example on a contract or petition). Ah, progress.

If you have a form you use all the time, try importing it into Windows Journal as an image. When you save it as a template, you can open it and fill it out with a pen (as in Figure 13-1).

A later section in this chapter takes a closer look at importing and annotating documents in Journal.

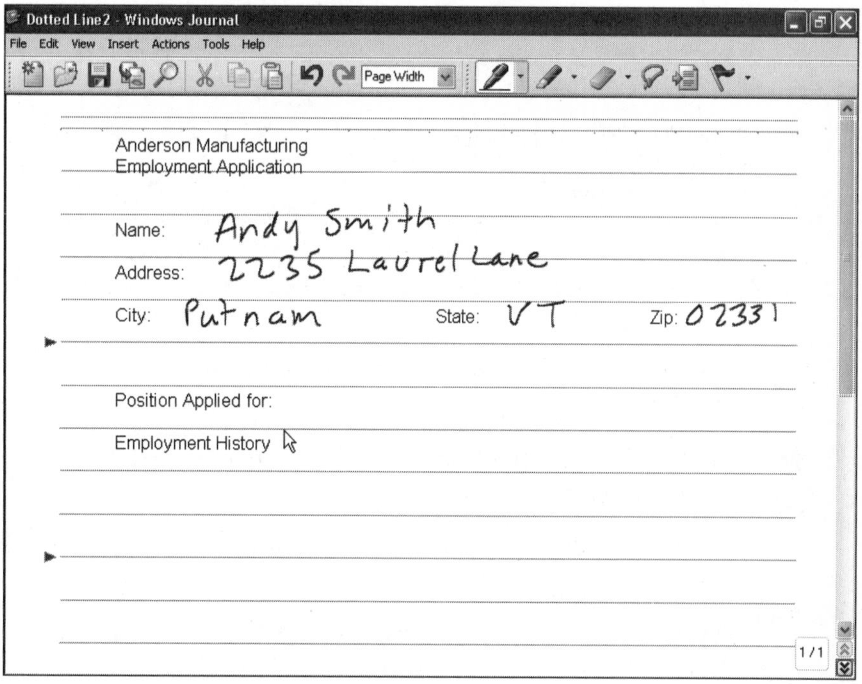

Dotted Line2 - Windows Journal

File Edit View Insert Actions Tools Help

Page Width

Anderson Manufacturing
Employment Application

Name: Andy Smith

Address: 2235 Laurel Lane

City: Putnam   State: VT   Zip: 02331

Position Applied for:

Employment History

1/1

Figure 13-1:
When your
data is
imported
into Journal,
you can
write onto
any form.

Securing Your Tablet PC with a Smart Card

A *smart card* resembles nothing so much as a credit card, except it's not quite as much fun (or nearly as dangerous in shopping malls). Smart cards are used to store sign-in information (such as passwords), as well as personal information and encryption keys that keep what's on your computer safe.

Smart cards have myriad business uses. They can store data such as patient or client records, or serve as a payment mechanism by storing electronic cash that can be used to make payments.

Windows XP for Tablet PC supports smart-card security because it uses public-key encryption, a method of providing secure identification. Several models of Tablet PC come equipped with a smart-card reader; others can have one added on by inserting a PC card.

Get his prints . . .

Another interesting possibility for keeping your Tablet PC secure is a *biometric PC card* such as the one offered by Compaq as an accessory to its Tablet PC TC1000. With this addition, you put your finger on a tiny scanner on the card, and then insert the card into the slot. Your fingerprint is compared with your registered fingerprint. If it matches, you can finish logging on. If it doesn't, you're just not yourself today. . . .

The smart card, once set up, must be inserted into a card reader slot before you can start up the computer. Without the smart card, the boot sequence never completes itself — foiling the attempts of unscrupulous types to take stuff off your computer, and making the computer itself pretty useless to them (serves 'em right).

And it's just about impossible for anybody to retrieve personal information or encryption keys off of a smart card.

If you see a use for smart-card technology in your life, you can buy a PC card to use in your PCMCIA slot. Some available smart-card readers also connect to a USB port.

Using Digital Cameras or Scanners with Tablet PCs

Some Tablet PCs come with an integrated digital camera; others can be connected to a digital camera through a secure Digital or CF Type II slot. With a digital camera connected to your Tablet PC, the possibilities are endless.

Take pictures and mark them up by adding comments in text boxes. You can use a plethora of tools with your pen in a program such as Paint (illustrated in Figure 13-2). When you're done marking up a picture, you can e-mail or fax it instantly. If you have ready access to a decent portable printer, you can even print out your photos on the spot.

Connecting a scanner to your Tablet PC offers even more options. Scan in any document or graphic and use your pen to mark it up or annotate it. Portable scanners offer a lightweight scanning solution for Tablet PC users who travel a great deal.

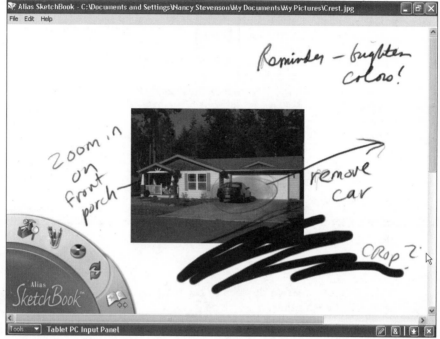

Figure 13-2:
Get creative by adding words, drawings, and effects to your photos using your pen.

Connecting with Your PDA

Eventually, Tablet PC will probably replace your PDA. For now, however, I strongly suspect that if you have a PDA you just about can't live without it. (Doubt me? Try this handy self-test: Imagine losing either your child or your PDA . . . you hesitated, didn't you?)

For you PDA-obsessed people, there's a seriously handy capability: You can wirelessly connect your Tablet PC to your PDA by using infrared connections that comply with standards developed by the IrDA (Infrared Data Association).

With this futuristic connection in place, you can exchange data and files (such as contact records) or documents (such as notes taken in Word for Windows CE) between the two devices.

There's not much to connecting two infrared-capable devices.

Bluetooth versus the radio datasnatchers

If your Tablet PC is enabled with Bluetooth — a wireless technology that circumvents the need for an infrared link — then you can connect your devices by means of a wireless network connection and radio links. Because radio waves can walk through walls (unlike infrared), the two devices don't have to be lined up within a foot of each other but only in general proximity.

Of course, walking through walls comes at a price. Wireless networks have some significant potential for security flaws; by means of a process called wireless sniffing, unscrupulous people could eavesdrop on what you send by radio wave. Encrypting files (essentially using spy-code stuff) can help keep data in transit secure, but that can get expensive fast. Bottom line: Unless you're sending the formula for a top secret product, you probably don't have to worry too much about becoming a wireless-sniffing victim.

Just follow these steps:

1. **Align the two devices so the infrared windows are within a foot or so of each other.**

   The *infrared windows* are tiny, dark red transceivers mounted somewhere near an edge on each of your devices. When they're lined up, a feature of Windows XP called Wireless Link starts up and the Wireless Link icon appears in the taskbar.

2. **Use the features of the infrared software that comes with your Tablet PC to transfer files between the devices.**

If your wireless phone has infrared capabilities, this same technique works with transferring data between the phone and your Tablet PC.

Importing and Annotating Documents in Journal

If you've been working in Windows Journal (all the livelong day . . .) — and enjoying how easy it is to write directly on electronic documents and use features such as the Highlighter and Eraser tools to manipulate electronic ink — then you've got a treat in store: You aren't limited to working with Journal notes: You can work with just about *any* document by importing it into the Journal environment.

Getting into the import business

When you import a document created in another application, the document comes into Journal as a document image. What you do to annotate such an image doesn't change the contents of the original document directly. You are only able to add handwriting to the image, just as you might insert a photo in a note and draw annotations on it.

For example, say you import a proposal that was created in Word XP as a document image, which you save in Journal. If you use the Eraser tool in Journal, you can't erase portions of the image (that is, you can't change any content from the original Word document); you can only add and delete Ink.

But marking up (or adding to) an existing document can be useful. You can even import a form, write in the blank spaces to fill it out, and then print the completed form (or even e-mail it). The ink you've added isn't part of the form, but the end result — especially if it's a hard copy — works the same as any printed form to get the information across.

If you perform a search in Journal, you won't uncover any content from the original document that has been imported as a document image, but you *will* find any content that you added to the document image by using text boxes or handwriting.

Importing documents as document images

There are two ways to import files to Windows Journal:

- ✔ You can choose File➪Import, locate a file, and then open it.

  Looking for more specifics? That's pretty much all there is to it.

  Graphics files won't work with the Import command from Journal. Instead, use the Insert➪Picture process to insert this file format. Note that TIFF files are the exception to this rule — you can import them into Journal as documents.

- ✔ You can use Windows Journal Note Writer.

  When you use Journal Note Writer to import documents, you choose to *print* a document (you know, good old File➪Print) you've already created in an application such as Word, with one important difference: You select Windows Journal Note Writer *itself* as the printer to use. If you're working in the other application, it can be quicker to print to Journal from there than to open Journal and do an import.

You speed demons out there can also drag and drop a document into Windows Journal. Just open a new, blank Journal Note, use Windows Explorer to locate a file, and drag the file into the Journal window. Journal opens the originating application for the document and begins the import procedure.

Follow these steps to import a Word document into Journal:

1. **Open a Word document.**

2. **Choose File⇨Print. The Print dialog box opens.**

3. **Select Journal Note Writer from the Name list.**

4. **Make any other needed adjustments.**

   For example, you can specify whether to print the whole document (or just certain pages) or specify more than one copy of the document.

5. **Tap OK.**

   The document appears in a Journal window, as shown in Figure 13-3.

   The document in Journal is now at your mercy (insert villainous laugh here). You can write on it, use the highlighter, insert pictures and text boxes into it, and otherwise mark up, deface, or modify it.

Now you can use your Journal tools to mark up the document. Figure 13-4 gives you an idea of how this would look.

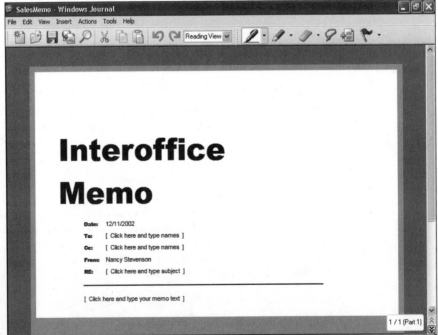

Figure 13-3:
The document is now an image in Journal, ready for you to write on it, highlight it, or add things to it.

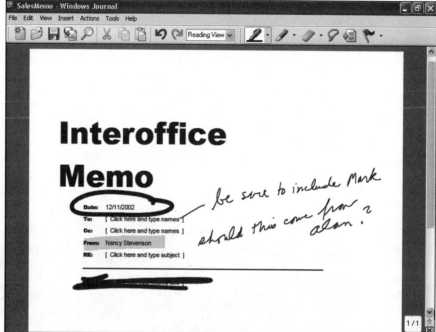

Figure 13-4:
This document image has been annotated to help the reader understand how to fill in a form.

Dressing Up the Tablet PC

They say accessories make a wardrobe, so why should Tablet PC be left out? The accessories available for your Tablet PC will vary depending on your model and its manufacturer — but here are some neat little fashion items you can look for. Most are available directly from manufacturers, but will probably show up at places such as CompUSA and Staples in short order.

✔ **Slipcases** are like little jackets for protecting your Tablet PC (as in Figure 13-5). They're less like that laptop notebook bag you've been carting around (with its pockets and briefcase appearance) than they are slim and trim vinyl or leather sleeves for your Tablet PC. Unless you have a convertible model (or a model such as the Motion 1200 slate that includes its own hard cover), getting such protection for your investment only makes sense.

If your manufacturer doesn't offer a slipcase you fancy, try Targus at www.targus.com for a selection of laptop cases that fit most popular Tablet PC models.

✔ **Screen protectors** are filmlike layers that protect your screen from smudges and strong sunlight. They also help keep down glare so you can read the screen more easily.

 ✓ **Rubber handgrips** can be added to the corners of some models for both improved grip and added protection from bumps and bruises in more rugged environments.

 ✓ **Chargers** for car or airline seatback systems allow you to recharge your battery while on the road.

 Of course, you can also buy additional batteries to keep an extra charge with you when no charger source is available.

 ✓ **Wireless keyboards** come with some slate models but not with others. If you didn't get a keyboard with your Tablet PC, you can buy a USB-connectible keyboard to go along with your Tablet PC.

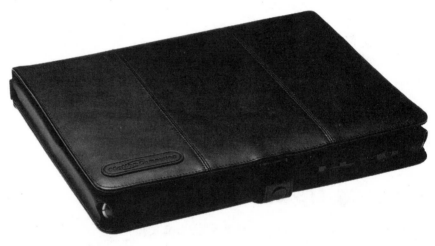

Figure 13-5: The Motion Computing M-Series Leather Executive Portfolio is typical of the slim profile of Tablet PC cases.

Printing Wirelessly

A wireless printer instantly adds magical powers (well, okay, it just adds some more practical functionality) to your Tablet PC without a tangle of cords.

Some models, such as the Canon BJC-55 Bubble Jet are so compact (at 2.1 pounds) that you can take them along on the road pretty easily. Other printers are regular size; you wouldn't want to drag one through an airport terminal without an entourage of porters helping you out.

(Now, I ask you — do you think your boss would approve that little item on your expense report?)

The HP DeskJet 350Cbi, for example, calls itself portable, but weighs in at 12 pounds. Twelve hefty pounds, plus 3 to 4 pounds of Tablet PC — along with its additional battery, power cord, a ream of paper — plus (oh, yes) clothing puts a heavy load on the frequent flyer. On the other hand, those who travel by car can pack one of these beauties in the trunk with little or no problem.

Also consider asking whether the business office of the hotel you're visiting has a wireless or USB printer you can connect your Tablet PC to if you're traveling light.

Wireless printers come in a wide variety of styles, from inkjet to laserjet, photo-quality printers to all-in-one devices that include a scanner, fax, printer, and copier functionality. You'll need software, such as PrintConnect Suite that comes with HP infrared-enabled devices, to complete the connection and print. Prices range from about $175 to $300, though some high-end wireless models can be even pricier (think five or six hundred buckaroos).

Chapter 15 gives you some interesting pointers on how portable printers can be used in conjunction with Tablet PC in a variety of industry settings.

Writing in Other Languages

Windows XP for Tablet PC has been issued in versions for English, German, French, Japanese, Chinese, and Korean. If you or someone you know has a need to use handwriting and speech features in a language other than English, you can set up that capability by using that version of the Windows XP operating system on your Tablet PC instead of the English version.

Not all foreign versions support all Tablet PC features. For example, the Korean and German versions of Windows XP support everything but Speech; the Japanese version, on the other hand, supports all features.

In certain language versions of Windows, the Input Panel has a Character Recognition tab that you can use to enter Asian characters. (The English version doesn't have that feature at this point.)

You can specify the default language you want to use for input. This helps the handwriting recognition feature interpret what you write if you typically use a foreign language. Follow these steps to change your input language:

1. **Choose Start⇨Control Panel.**

2. **Double-tap the Regional and Language icon. The Regional and Languages dialog box opens.**

3. **Tap the Languages tab to display it; then tap the Details button.**

   The Text Services and Input Languages dialog box (shown in Figure 13-6) appears.

Figure 13-6:
You can
choose only
an installed
service for
your default
language.

4. **Tap the arrow in the Default Input Language drop-down list; then select the language you want to use.**

5. **Tap Apply, and then tap OK twice to close all dialog boxes and save the new setting.**

   You must restart your computer to begin working with the new language input.

Making Presentations Using Windows Journal

You've got an outline of the key points for the upcoming sales conference. You want to present it to your team and brainstorm some refinements. Why not use Windows Journal to make your presentation?

Use Journal to make presentations? When you have PowerPoint at your fingertips? You can't be serious, you say!

Well, yes, I am, actually. Sometimes Journal's more sophisticated ink tools make an on-the-fly or interactive presentation easier. For example, you can quickly display a blank page to enter new input — or mark up your existing content with audience comments or feedback — sort of like a very expensive flip chart.

And here's an item from the Way Cool Features Department: You can actually import a PowerPoint slide or presentation into Journal, and then use your Tablet PC pen and Journal's Pen and Highlighter tools to mark it up or make modifications.

In PowerPoint, you have to insert an Ink Drawing and Writing object if you want to actually place handwriting on a slide — or use the PowerPoint on-screen Pen tool — during a presentation. When you use the Input Panel or Write Anywhere, anything you write is always converted to text.

The full-screen view in Journal looks great for a presentation. Also consider taking toolbars off your display (simply choose View➪Toolbars and deselect the displayed toolbars) if you want more screen real estate.

You can use menu commands to modify your pen style (such as marker or fine point). Finally, remember that you don't have to display a lined writing pad; you can choose a blank template (or other notes template) to provide an appropriate background for your presentation (as shown in Figure 13-7).

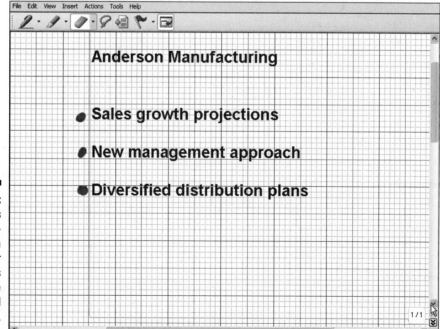

Figure 13-7: This presentation uses a graph paper style notes template to full advantage.

Getting the Most Out of Gestures

In various chapters in this book, I mention a few input gestures — for example, the gesture that opens the Input Panel in Chapter 4, and the Scratch-out gesture that erases handwriting in Journal in Chapter 7. However, several other gestures come in handy when you're editing documents using the Input Panel.

Say you're working on a document in Word. You want to perform keyboard actions such as adding a space or emulating the Enter, Backspace, or Tab key functions. Use the gestures shown in Figure 13-8 for these functions; they're quicker than using the Quick Keypad.

 When you draw a gesture, draw it quickly and make the stroke long. Otherwise your action can be interpreted as a dash or hyphen. Using gestures may take a little getting used to, but once you've got the gesture perfected, it can be very convenient.

You can also use the Scratch-out gesture in the Input Panel Writing Pad, as well as with Write Anywhere activated.

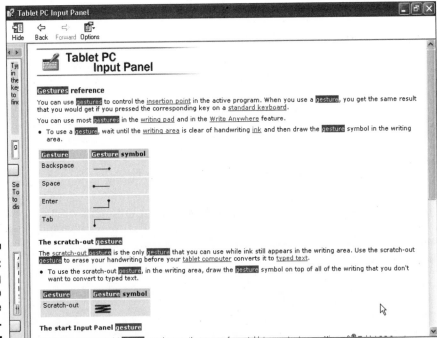

Figure 13-8:
Using
gestures to
activate
functions.

Here you can scratch out single or multiple inkstrokes; but you have to be quick and scratch out before the ink gets sent to the document. Figure 13-9 shows scratched-out inkstrokes.

High-tech-looking, isn't it? Well, no. But it *is* incredibly intuitive.

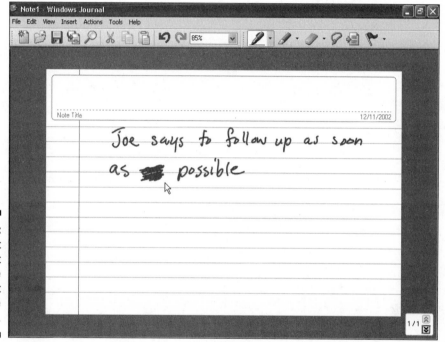

Figure 13-9:
You must scratch out before the ink is sent to the document.

Chapter 14

Top Ten Applications for Your Tablet PC

A Tablet PC can use any software that's Windows XP compatible. But the Tablet PC's success will ultimately depend on the software programs people write that truly take advantage of ink and speech technology.

These are early days for Tablet PC, so a critical mass of applications isn't yet around. But enough applications are available that you can begin to take advantage of your Tablet PC's features today and explore the potential of ink computing.

This chapter looks at a sampling of interesting programs available today. Some products are free; others will cost you some cash.

Several of these products, though available, were still in beta testing at the time of this writing. I provide Web site addresses so that you can find the latest version available.

Many of the companies writing Tablet PC programs today offer a free, downloadable version that may be limited in some way — for example, a program may only be good for 30 days or have limited feature sets — so you can try them out before you buy.

Getting Graphic with Corel Grafigo

Manufacturer: Corel

Web site: www.corel.com/grafigo

Estimated price: Free download

Corel jumped on board the Tablet PC bandwagon right out of the gate with its program Grafigo. That's probably because pen computing is such a natural match for drawing programs, given the ability to draw with your hand rather than a mouse. And the best part? As of this writing, Grafigo is a freely downloadable program.

Grafigo, as shown in Figure 14-1, isn't the most sophisticated drawing program, but it does enable you to sketch out your ideas visually by using a colored pen, a highlighter-type marker, and a symbol library to create flowcharts and drawings.

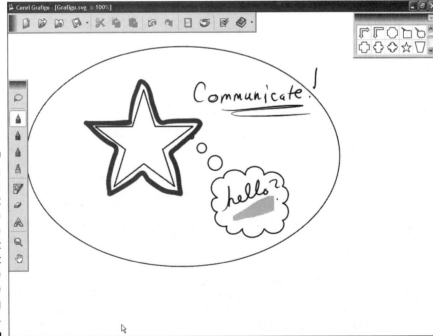

Figure 14-1:
This could be the best program to use to sketch out ideas or just doodle during those long meetings.

If you draw a shape (such as a circle), Grafigo instantly converts it into a smooth drawing object. You can write in Grafigo by using text boxes, and what you write is automatically converted to text; or you can use one of three Pen tools within Grafigo to write on-screen. Leave it as handwriting or use a Windows Journal-like Lasso tool to convert it to text if you like.

You can take images you have on hand and use them as underlays to what you draw or write in Grafigo. You can also use an Onionskin feature to overlay one drawing over another.

 Grafigo documents are saved in the Scalable Vector Graphic (`.svg`) format, so you should be able to open them in SVG-compatible programs, such as Adobe SVG Viewer.

Visualizing Your Work with Visio

Manufacturer: Microsoft

Web site: `www.microsoft.com/office/visio/downloads/default.asp`

Estimated price: $199 Standard Edition

Visio gets onto this list because it's a part of the Microsoft Office family of products. That means that the Microsoft Tablet PC Pack for Office XP does its magic to make Visio ink and speech compatible along with Word, Excel, and PowerPoint.

Visio is a program with a slew of tools for drawing organizational charts, flowcharts, engineering specifications, architectural renderings — you name it. It has built-in symbol palettes (as shown in Figure 14-2) that you use to build your documents. With Ink capability, you can add handwriting to your schematics, annotate drawings, or add highlights all with your pen. As with other Office products, you can also use speech commands to tell Visio to do such things as undoing actions, saving files, or opening files.

Visio also interacts beautifully with other Office products to generate charts from Excel worksheet content or to turn Microsoft Project task lists into graphically depicted timelines.

The current functionality is most useful in marking-up existing drawings because it has no functionality to convert roughly drawn shapes into polished chart elements; but Microsoft is promising greater ink functionality in the next version of Office and Visio.

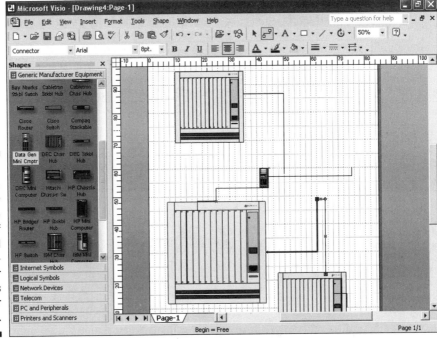

Figure 14-2:
Visio is
a very
handy little
program if
you build
flow-
charts or
schematics
for your
work.

Organize This: Franklin Covey Tablet Planner for Tablet PC

Manufacturer: Franklin Covey

Web site: www.franklincovey.com/tabletplanner/trial.html

Estimated price: $149

Are you the type who runs around with a day planner all day, counting on your notations to get you to the right place at the right time? You may just decide to give your day planner up after you've tried the Franklin Covey Tablet Planner for Tablet PC. You can use your pen to jot down appointments, take notes in a Windows Journal–type environment, and make entries in built-in electronic forms, such as a car mileage log, check register, or expense form.

The planner uses a browserlike environment, allowing you to use Back and Forward buttons to move among the pages you display. You can change views to show a daily, weekly, or monthly calendar (as shown in Figure 14-3).

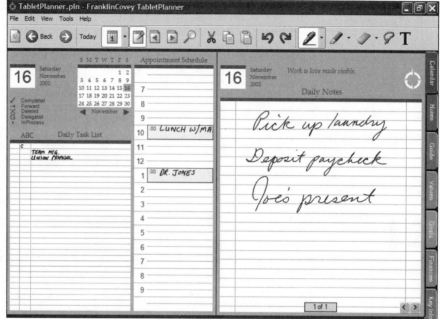

Figure 14-3:
The Daily view shows all the things you have to do, notes, and appointments for each day on one screen.

The variety of forms included is impressive. In the Key Info area, you can find everything from an exercise log to a travel itinerary (as shown in Figure 14-4) and medical record forms. You can look up world time zones and catalog your personal property.

Go to the Contacts tab of the Planner (just tap on the tab from anywhere in the planner, just like a tab in your dog-eared paper day planner), and you can take advantage of contact-management tools. This feature lets you add phone directories from most software that includes contact information, such as Outlook; but the most robust contact-management capabilities seem to be promised for future versions of Tablet Planner. (For example, I found no way to actually make a phone call in the Contacts area, which is a feature most contact-management programs have.)

Other useful tools in the Tablet Planner include capabilities to apply priorities to tasks and appointments, search by keywords, and sort. You can also use your Tablet PC's wireless infrared connection to share contacts and appointments with your desktop computer or PDA.

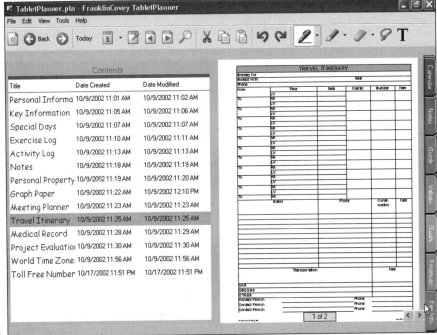

Figure 14-4:
These forms
provide a
useful place
to organize
information
you need to
keep a
record of.

Pulling Things Together with PenOffice Version 1.5

Manufacturer: Parascript, LLC

Web site: www.penoffice.com/piweb/downloads/index.asp

Estimated price: $29.95

PenOffice from Parascript is an application that adds some ease-of-use features when you use your pen in various other software products.

The PenCommander feature enables you to use your pen to automate certain actions, such as inserting text that you write frequently. You can define the command (as shown in Figure 14-5). For example, you could create a command called My Sign and then, instead of entering an entire signature block at the bottom of a letter, you just type **My Sign**, circle it with your pen, and the full text appears. The Inline Gestures feature lets you create your own control gestures for text input.

Figure 14-5:
Add your
signature
to Pen-
Commander;
then simply
write words,
such as
My Sign,
and Pen-
Commander
inserts your
signature
into
documents.

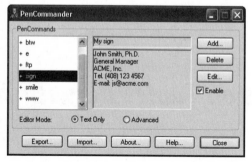

Figure 14-5:
Add your
signature
to Pen-
Commander;
then simply
write words,
such as
My Sign,
and Pen-
Commander
inserts your
signature
into
documents.

You can use a Shape Checker feature to select hand drawings and generate smooth geographic drawing objects, such as squares or triangles. The program also features a Letter Shapes feature that can improve handwriting recognition by enabling you to enter your own letter samples (as shown in Figure 14-6).

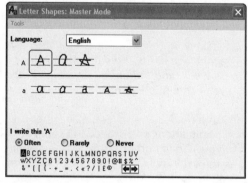

Figure 14-6:
Write your
own letters
to help your
applications
recognize
your
handwriting.

PenOffice includes a robust dictionary and spell checker. And if you *parlez-vous* other languages, it has built-in support for handwriting recognition that works with French, German, and Spanish as well as English.

If you use PenOffice to annotate Word documents, you can only do so if those documents were created in Microsoft Word versions 97 and later.

Another cool little feature is the RiteCalc handwriting calculator. Where other applications have difficulty recognizing input such as equations, this feature makes inputting mathematical information much easier.

Read Magazines on Tablet PC with Zinio

Manufacturer: Zinio

Web site: www.zinio.com

Estimated price: Free downloadable reader; magazine subscription prices vary from around $14 to $50.

Zinio is a reader for electronic magazines, which is projected to be a hot application of the Tablet PC technology. Microsoft itself is getting into this market with a product called ePeriodicals that can be used to prepare complex documents, such as magazines, to be read on the Tablet PC.

You can download digital magazines and then read them on the go. What's great about digital magazines is that you can search for topics and store back issues. You can also send free copies of articles to people. I find the vertical screen orientation for Tablet PC works best, with the most magazinelike appearance.

Currently, Zinio offers a Digital Magazine Stand with publications including *PCWorld, Pocket PC, Business Week,* and *National Geographic Traveler.* You can also find some industry-specific publications.

Zinio's Web site offers the Zinio reader and several magazines for free download. (The choice of digital publications will broaden in time, but one of them is likely to be of interest to you.) To get other publications, you have to subscribe; subscription prices as of the writing of this book ranged from $14.95 for a year of *Game Pro* to $49 for a year of *Rotor & Wing* (a magazine about helicopters — you may need that when you buy that corporate copter to fly yourself to the corporate bungalow in Bermuda).

After you download a magazine, you can use your keyboard or pen to flip pages and jump to articles from the listing of links in the table of contents. By using your pen, you can also highlight anything that interests you or add notes for yourself.

Microsoft Snippet

Manufacturer: Microsoft

Web site:
`www.microsoft.com/windowsxp/tabletpc/downloads/`
`powertoys.asp`

Estimated price: Free download

In my book, this is a must-have for Tablet PC users. Microsoft Snippet sits on your system tray waiting for you to activate it with a tap. When you do, you can use your pen to circle anything in a document you'd like to snip. Whatever you circle (text, objects, ink, or whatever) is snipped as an image, so even if the circle you draw chops through the middle of letters or an image, that's exactly what you'll get.

Some Tablet PC manufacturers have included Microsoft Snippet on their models along with other preinstalled software.

After you have captured snippets, you can e-mail or print them or work with them using the Snippet Explorer feature (shown in Figure 14-7). You can draw on Snippets with your pen, connecting various items with arrows or handwritten text. You can also rearrange Snippets in Snippet Explorer.

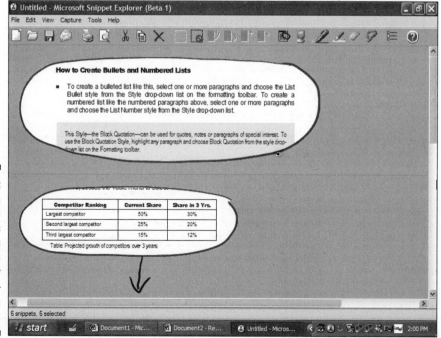

Figure 14-7:
You can build documents of snippets you grab from any program — or even online.

Organizing Docs with ActiveDocs

Manufacturer: Keylogix

Web site: www.activedocs.com/product/try/default.asp

Estimated price: $239 per single-user license

ActiveDocs from Keylogix is document automation software that works with Office XP. This program helps you generate documents (such as contracts, proposals, and form letters), pulling in data from outside data sources easily. ActiveDocs enables you to modify templates without having to become a programmer. It also automates formatting chores to speed up your work.

When you open an Office application, such as Word, ActiveDocs displays the ActiveDocs toolbar. The tools included here are explained in ActiveDocs for Tablet PC Help (as shown in Figure 14-8), which also includes a tutorial to get you up to speed on how to create catalogs, folders, and categories, and the various icons you can use to automate template design.

Figure 14-8:
You can link to data, group similar fields together, and prompt the users of templates to make entries in ink by using these authoring tools.

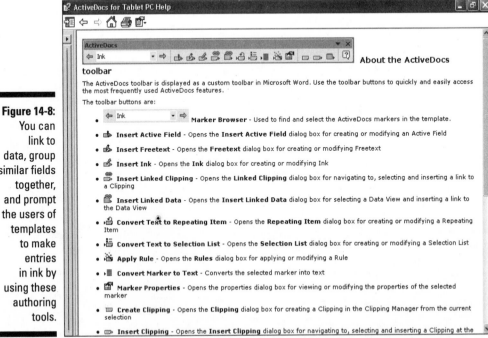

Now I'm not going to kid you: This is not simple software as many of the others in this chapter are. This is serious document template design stuff with linked data fields and sophisticated tools. However, it does offer support for ink-only fields; and when you consider the possibilities of how customer surveys or petitions might be filled out on a Tablet PC (including a handwritten signature), a good form design tool is a handy thing to have around.

Getting E-Mail Right with riteMail

Manufacturer: Parascript, LLC

Web site: www.rite-mail.net (tap Downloads)

Estimated price: $29.95

E-mail is great as far as it goes. But what if you want to sketch a diagram or draw a picture and send it? Sure, you could fax a sketch or send an electronic drawing as an attachment (created in a drawing program that the recipient of your e-mail may or may not have). But if you've always wanted to draw right in your e-mail messages, have I got a treat for you.

riteMail is a handy little program that allows you to take full advantage of the ink environment when writing e-mails. In riteMail, as shown in Figure 14-9, you can write your message by choosing any of six pen thickness settings and by using a variety of colors. You can also use a drawing tool that, with the riteShape feature enabled, automatically converts your roughly drawn shapes, such as squares and circles, into formal drawings.

Recipients of your riteMail messages must have an e-mail program that is HTML capable and JAVA enabled (which basically means it can read graphics, which most major e-mail programs such as Internet Explorer can) because, essentially, you're sending a picture of your handwriting and drawings. Somebody receiving a riteMail e-mail can also open your e-mail in a Web browser as long as it is set to allow Active X controls to run.

When you want to add a personal touch to e-mail messages, being able to send your own handwritten note is definitely a technological leap forward.

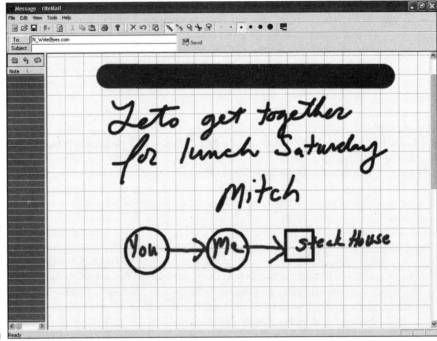

Figure 14-9:
Make your
e-mails
come alive
with
riteMail.

Alias's SketchBook for Creative Types

Manufacturer: Alias/Wavefront

Web site:
www.aliaswavefront.com/en/products/sketchbook/info.shtml

Estimated price: Free limited version; full software coming soon, pricing to be determined

Do you have a burning desire to be a great artist — or at least a great doodler? Alias SketchBook Pro turns your Tablet PC into a digital sketchbook where you can sketch ideas, add comments, and present what you've created all from one powerful little program.

SketchBook sports cool pop-up tool palettes, such as the Color palette shown in Figure 14-10. When you tap a tool palette, the choices appear in a circle of icons. Tools include one set to move or reset an image, another set of pen styles (marker, highlighter, number 2 pencil, and airbrush, for example), a color palette, and tools for saving a sketch or moving among sketches.

You can pull out floating toolbars for colors and pen styles as well as use the pop-up variety. These floating versions of toolbars offer more options and can be moved anywhere on your screen. You can write directly on an Alias SketchBook Pro document by using one of the pen tool settings and your Tablet PC pen. Unfortunately, this program has no feature to convert hand-writing to text or to insert text.

Alias SketchBook Pro provides a simple-to-use tutorial when you first open it that shows you how to use the available tools (as shown in Figure 14-11).

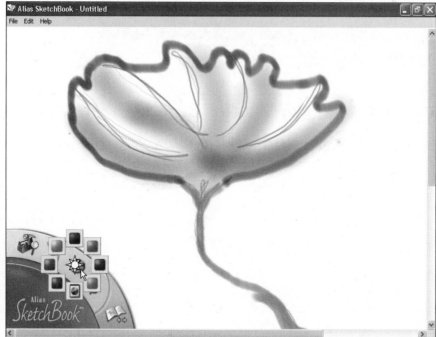

Figure 14-10:
Pop-up palettes are fun to use and offer simple, yet effective, sketching tools.

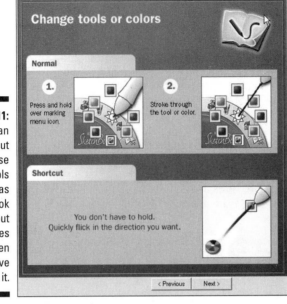

Figure 14-11:
You can figure out how to use all the tools of Alias SketchBook Pro in about five minutes and then just have fun with it.

Power Up Your Tablet PC with PowerToys

Manufacturer: Leszynski Group, distributed by Microsoft

Web site:
www.microsoft.com/windowsxp/pro/downloads/powertoys.asp

Estimated price: Free download

Okay, I saved the best till last. PowerToys are executive timewasters — my kind of program! PowerToys are actually developed by Leszynski Group, but you can get them for free on Microsoft's Web site. (Note that Microsoft doesn't provide any support for these products.) These are kind of like little add-on treats from developers who had nothing better to do.

Here are a few of my favorite PowerToys:

✓ **Tablet Pool** is a pool game that works with your Tablet PC pen. When you hold your pen above your Tablet PC screen, the pen becomes the pool cue, which is cool. You can play alone, with others huddled around your Tablet PC, or on your computer network. (Your boss will hate this game.)

- **Puzzle Game** (as shown in Figure 14-12) is for those addicted to jigsaw puzzles. Use your pen to drag pieces of the puzzle into place. You can change the difficulty level: Level 1 breaks your picture into about four big pieces, Level 5 blows it into dozens of pieces. You tap and drag pieces and spin them around 360 degrees with a push of your pen.

  One really neat feature: You can take your own picture and turn it into a custom electronic jigsaw puzzle by using this fun PowerToy.

- **Writing Recognition Game** (as shown in Figure 14-13) has a double advantage: It's fun to play, and you improve your on-screen handwriting as you rack up points. As letters fall to the ground, you have to write them on your screen before they land. The trick is to write them neatly enough that Tablet PC recognizes them!

- **Tic Tac Toe** is pretty self-explanatory! You can write your Xs and Os with your pen. You can play against the computer (which is, of course, humiliating if it keeps winning this children's game). But this one can be fun in those moments when you need a quick game fix.

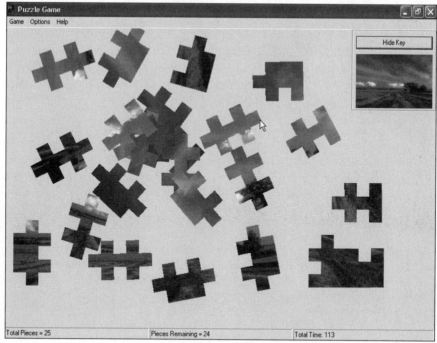

Figure 14-12: Do not try this at work — it will eat up your afternoon faster than a staff meeting.

Figure 14-13:
If you have
to learn
to write
on-screen,
you may as
well have
fun doing it!

Chapter 15

Ten (Or So) Real-World Uses for Your Tablet PC

*T*hough the Tablet PC is a great personal computer on the road, in meetings, or even docked on your desktop, its portability and variety of input methods also make it a natural for use in a wide variety of business settings.

Think about it: The Tablet PC can be used by people who don't even know how to use a computer but do know how to write and fill in forms with a pen or speech. It provides a mechanism for capturing signatures on everything from contracts to surveys and petitions.

The Tablet PC is portable, wireless, and can use smart card technology to read and store data about anything from your medical records to a warehouse inventory.

So this chapter is here to give you some ideas of how Tablet PC might work for your business — and even (if you're a student, or know one) to prepare for the business world by using this handy technology as an educational tool. Take the ideas offered here and tailor them to your industry, your office, your business needs — and your future.

Putting Tablet PC to Work

Tablet format PCs (minus the Windows XP for Tablet PC operating system) have been around for several years now in the form of pen tablets and Web pads. They've been used for everything from inventorying products on a store shelf to tracking the delivery of overnight packages.

The latest incarnation of tablets, Tablet PC, adds the full functionality of a Windows-based computer, an excellent handwriting recognition feature, plus wireless technology to the equation, making it even more useful in vertical applications (that is, specific industries) such as healthcare and retail.

Some Tablet PC models, such as the ProT-10 from ProMark and PSI Electronics' FOX are *ruggedized* — built to withstand some abuse in settings such as construction or property inspections. (The ProT-10, for example, has a shock-mounted hard drive and can operate in colder temperatures.)

These units sport various forms of alloy or rubber casings to protect them from falls of approximately three feet, as well as hard drives mounted in a way that they can withstand a certain amount of shock. They can also withstand colder and hotter temperatures than the non-ruggedized models.

However, this toughness comes at a price: ruggedized models weigh in at around 4.5 pounds, noticeably heftier than their slimmer 3-pound cousins.

Another feature that makes Tablet PC a good tool in the field is that some models can accommodate optional screens that can be read in the glare of daylight. (Daylight-readable screens are, however, still in their infancy; they have a way to go before they consistently fulfill their promise.)

In addition, built-in or add-on smart card readers enable you to tap into large amounts of data such as store inventory or patient records. Smart cards can also provide extra security for your tablet.

Take a look at some ways businesses are taking advantage of all that Tablet PC has to offer.

Healthcare: Take a tablet and call me in the morning

It's no secret that the world today has a serious shortage of healthcare workers — if you want to verify this state of affairs, just go to any emergency room and watch the hours tick by before somebody shows up to treat you.

The truth is that a lot of healthcare workers are probably not showing up in the emergency room because they're buried in paperwork. They have to deal with benefits forms and patient charts, requests for lab results, communications from primary doctors to specialists, and on and on. Much of that paperwork is done by hand.

The contents of some of those handwritten forms then have to be input into a computer, taking more time and risking error. Delays in getting paperwork where it needs to go can cause delays in treatment and billing, which can be costly and even life-threatening.

How can Tablet PC help? Tablet PC provides a way for healthcare workers to take handwritten notes in any setting — in a patient's room or a hospital corridor, for example. No special training on a computer is required because pretty much everybody knows how to write. Here's a list of just a few applications:

- ✓ **Note-taking:** Doctors can dictate patient notes using the Speech feature, or use a stylus pen to annotate X-rays and fill in patient charts.

  Doctors can even make notes during an examination, drawing on a form with diagrams of human anatomy to indicate areas of discomfort or wound locations.

- ✓ **Information gathering:** Patients can enter information about themselves and their symptoms directly into a Tablet PC.

- ✓ **Therapy and recovery:** Tablet PC Speech has even been used in speech language therapy for stroke victims.

  All this input can be converted to text or stored in handwritten form that can be organized, and searched.

- ✓ **Maintaining privacy:** Beyond overcoming mountains of paperwork, one of the big concerns about information in a healthcare setting is privacy. Healthcare facilities must stay in compliance with the Health Insurance Portability and Accountability Act of 1996 (HIPAA), which calls for stringent protection of patient records.

  Where previous tablet formats didn't have strong security, Tablet PC with Windows XP, with privacy and security features such as Encrypted File System and public key infrastructure with virtual private network features and protocols, is in complete compliance.

- ✓ **Medical research:** In addition to routine patient care, Tablet PC has a place in medical research institutions. Clinical trials run by drug companies or research hospitals may involve executives, clinicians, and doctors.

  Clinicians can take notes while making patient rounds, or update records while in patient rooms, and the results can be stored in a central database where they can be easily shared by researchers by tapping into a wireless network.

  Demands in healthcare to document incidents such as errors in patient care (or the emergence of mental-health patient problems) also make Tablet PC a useful tool.

With Tablet PC in hand, patient interviews can happen without the distraction of typing on a keyboard — and incidents can be reported immediately so all facility staff have access to the information right away. If any investigation or official action is required, it can be taken quickly without waiting for handwritten interview notes to be typed up.

Companies are developing healthcare-specific applications that enable workers to access lab results, use smart cards to switch out patient records as they make their rounds, and even examine patients' vital signs. USB peripheral support in Tablet PC means that a PC card can be inserted to add the functionality of a digital camera to take pictures for patient identification and wound care documentation.

External data backup devices can be used for field-based backups, as in a home healthcare setting, and portable color printers can be used for printing patient education materials.

Insurance: Tablet PC as a matter of policy

Insurance is an industry where information is king. Much of that information has to be gathered in unusual environments, such as on the scene after a building fire or in your neighborhood appraising your home for insurance coverage. Tablet PC's support for *surprise undocking* can be a handy feature for such people on the run.

Surprise undocking is a capability that allows a user to remove a Tablet PC from a docking station without having to shut the computer down or close applications.

Here are some other useful ways to use Tablet PC in the insurance field:

✔ **Documentation:** Integrated digital cameras in some Tablet PC models can be used to take pictures for insurance application and claims processes.

For example, the photos of newly insured vehicles can be used to document existing damage, or photos can be used to show damage to vehicles involved in an accident claim.

Instead of having to print out Polaroid photos and staple them to a claim, insurance agents or estimators can take photos with the Tablet PC digital camera, then use their Tablet PC to insert the photo in a form and even circle any damage in photos with their digital pen.

✔ **Speedy claim estimates:** Repair estimates can be requested on the spot using e-mail or by faxing a form from a fax application using a wireless connection. Agents can also use their wireless connection to tap into client records from remote locations.

TIP

In addition to portability and wireless connectivity, ruggedized Tablet PCs can be used in all kinds of weather, making them stalwart companions for people who have to deal with the aftermath of severe weather conditions such as floods, snowstorms, or hurricanes. In addition to dealing better with extreme temperatures, ruggedized models can even deal with humidity levels of up to 95 percent.

Electronic stethoscope for Tablet PC

Stethographics has developed an electronic stethoscope application called STG that can be used with a Tablet PC. This software utilizes the microphone on the Tablet PC to record various sounds from the heart, lungs, and abdomen. The sounds can be played back for other healthcare workers to analyze, and can even be used to identify and perform "wheeze and crackle" counts and analyses.

The software includes samples of normal and abnormal sounds for comparison, and can generate waveform charts of results Doctors and nurses can access information, view sample recordings, and analyze waveform visualizations for common heart sounds with Stethographics.

Now breathe deeply. . . .

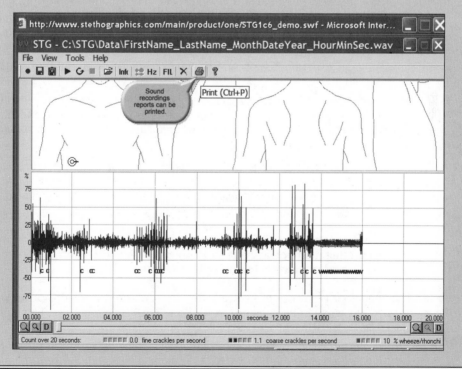

Real Estate: Location, location, location, and Tablet PC

Another industry where people are often out in the world rather than sitting at a desk is real estate. The day of a typical real estate agent involves meeting with sellers at their home or business to sign up listings, taking potential buyers to view buildings, attending property closings, and creating and distributing marketing literature to publicize a listing.

Today the emphasis in real estate is on showing a client that you've got the high tech bells and whistles to get their business and close a sale. Using Tablet PC, real estate professionals can

- **Get facts quickly:** Agents can call up information about property tax, last sale price, and legal property descriptions from city records as they meet with a potential seller.

- **Post and review listings:** Agents can review listings of comparable properties on the market to help the seller determine the sales price, and even write up and post a Multiple Listing Service (MLS) listing for a property, all while sitting with the seller in his or her home.

- **Note taking:** Real estate agents in selling mode can use their Tablet PC to walk through a property and use Speech to dictate notes about features, or write up an offer for a property for a buyer on the spot and fax it to all parties without ever returning to the office.

Using a Tablet PC with digital camera capability, an agent can take property photos for use in a sales flyer. Mobile printers can be used with a Tablet PC to print property flyers when an agent notices that an on-site literature display is running low.

- **Create 3-D online tours:** With increased use of streaming video and 3-D tours of homes available online, an agent can even use the Tablet PC to show a presentation of available homes to buyers, using a pen to highlight features of interest in various listings.

Corporate real estate professionals have unique information needs. Corporations managing multiple facilities and moves between them can perform site inventories without having to duplicate data entry.

Dynamic floor plans can be created with drag-and-drop elements for planning moves. Revisions to floor plans can be made on site by architects and engineers using AutoCAD LT and its Tablet PC enabled features.

WebFront offers Home Appraisals for insurance agents

WebFront Communications of Canada has developed a product called Home Appraisals for the insurance industry. The WebFront application allows insurance professionals such as adjusters to take and convert hand-written notes, as well as fill out automated forms.

For example, the application helps insurance appraisers to be more effective on the job by enabling them to access data from the field, and then convert handwritten notes to text.

Users can receive a form from their home office with client contact information and property location, and then they can fill in the form using their pen with detailed home appraisal information. They can add handwritten sketches, annotate photos, and even capture signatures of clients.

Then, rather than going back to an office and entering the data in a computer, they can transmit the form from the field to the office using an XML format for instant processing by a Microsoft BizTalk server.

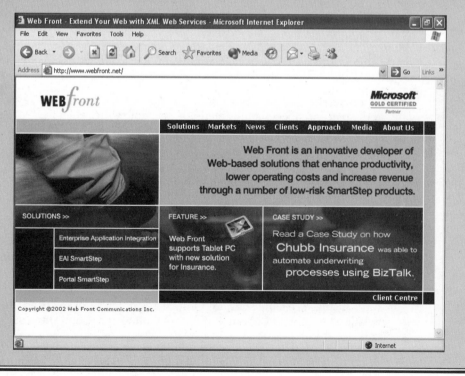

Creating flyers with HP Real Estate Document Assistant

With HP Real Estate Document Assistant 2, real estate professionals can browse, preview, and launch simple templates to generate great looking property flyers, fax cover sheets, and postcards. Using a portable color printer, you can print professional documents — even flyers — from a Tablet PC at a property site. Agents can edit and update the agent profiles that appear in flyers with new information or photos. The program can even be set up to be launched from a toolbar button in Microsoft Word.

Retail: Tablet PC goes shopping

Tablet PC fits right in when it's time to go shopping. Consider the advantages. First, many stores don't have sophisticated offices and equipment available to them because space is at a premium. A store manager may have to fill out forms and write notes while keeping an eye on customer traffic; Tablet PC saves that manager or someone else down the line from having to rekey such data into text format.

In addition, retail personnel may not be familiar with computers or keyboarding, so the pen and Speech input methods available with Tablet PC are ideal for this workforce.

Here are some other applications:

- ✔ **Inventory and merchandising:** Tablet PC can be used by store maintenance crews to take inventory, by field consultants doing a store walk, and by store managers for merchandising (developing in-store displays).

  Because many stores these days are part of a chain, improved information flow from stores to back-end systems is key to timely delivery of products to replenish diminishing supplies and stay on top of customer demand.

- ✔ **Advertising, presentations, and information:** Mall kiosks are an ideal location for Tablet PC, again because of limited space and wireless connectivity.

  Tablet PC can be used to show presentations of products at kiosks where space is at a premium and there's no room to demonstrate or display every product for sale. In addition, retailers can access online catalogs to place custom orders. Using a printer and Tablet PC, stores can even print out coupons or gift certificates on the spot.

✔ **Daily operations:** Maintenance crews in a retail setting can fill out store asset survey forms listing information about shelving, lighting, and special equipment such as a drink machine in a convenience store. They can draw rough measurements with the Tablet PC pen to be used when installing new equipment.

Maintenance personnel can even make notes about power availability, plumbing requirements, and so on, which can go directly to a central database to streamline the ordering of equipment and installation services.

✔ **Customer service:** In any sales setting, such as filling out an order for a special order item for a store customer, typing on a keyboard cuts down on the face-to-face interaction with the customer.

Writing on a Tablet PC, sales clerks can stay more in touch with their customers. Store managers can walk around and interact with customers while doing merchandizing or customer surveys.

✔ **Field sales:** Field reps who visit several stores a month can call up employee records with photos to jot notes about interactions. Because personnel in retail can change frequently with seasonal hiring, this helps managers stay current with who's who.

Construction: Building business with Tablet PC

Next to a hard hat, a Tablet PC may be the best item you can have around a construction site. Because construction workers and materials warehouse supervisors are often not trained on computers, the pen input is a natural fit for this industry's workforce.

Construction sites typically have a small trailer for an office; with space at a premium, having this much high technology in a three-pound portable package is useful.

Fitting a bar-code scanner into a Tablet PC

Bar codes are information lifelines for retail stores. These little sets of lines help you track inventory and buying habits, and automate checkout for customers. For the retail industry, a bar code scanner in the form of a PCMCIA card that can be dropped into a Tablet PC makes the tablet format very attractive. Workers can use the highly portable computer to scan product bar codes on the shelves and instantly send inventory information back to a distribution center to update quantities and automatically generate replenishment orders.

Autodesk and Tablet PC

Autodesk Architectural Studio is a design and communication tool that allows architects to model, present, and collaborate on design projects. The program is used for design purposes by many architects and construction companies. With Architectural Studio, you can sketch out ideas, mark up drawings and floor plans, and instantly communicate changes to remote construction sites or clients. Autodesk On Site View has even been used to help emergency response teams (using Tablet PCs) to work with airport floor plans and schematics to deal with security problems on the scene.

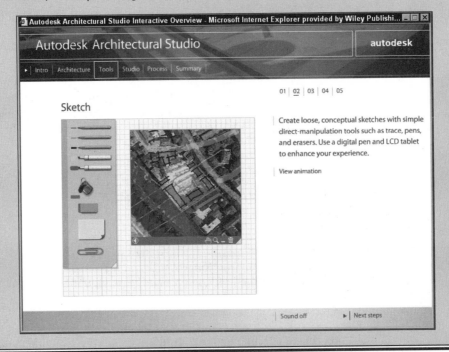

A general contractor with a Tablet PC in hand can go from job to job checking off the progress of various crews, checking on shipments of materials and e-mailing clients with progress reports — even accompanying these reports with photos.

Construction site managers don't escape the being desk bound. They often have to attend meetings with subcontractors, architects, materials suppliers, the home office, and clients. Now, he or she can take meeting notes on the Tablet PC, then distribute them to everyone concerned in minutes. When clients ask for a change in specs or materials, a signature on a change order can be captured on the spot using the Tablet PC stylus pen.

A Tablet PC can be used in materials receiving, project tracking, filling out safety violation or incident reports, and on-site inspections. The capability to convert handwriting to text and transmit it instantly helps to avoid delays between data gathering and data entry. Less delay means quicker billing of clients for materials — and less risk of ordering materials that aren't needed.

Microsoft Project, often used in the construction industry to track project progress, gains ink functionality along with other Office XP products when you install the Office XP Tablet PC Pack.

Legal: Making a case for Tablet PC

Say what you like about lawyers, there's no denying that they're hard working, note-taking people. In fact, attorneys make a ton of handwritten notes that become part of the recordkeeping for cases that may go on for years . . . and years. Transcribing or simply storing these notes becomes cumbersome.

Enter Tablet PC. Using the Ink or Speech features, lawyers can enter notes in electronic format that can be converted to text or simply kept in note form. But, these are notes that can be searched easily for names, dates — whatever. And Tablet PC enables you to search within a single note, or among all notes in a folder at one time.

Besides a need for notes, attorneys have the following needs:

- ✔ **Protecting client confidentiality:** The secure features of Windows XP plus secure wireless communication make transmitting notes or other data from a Tablet PC to another computer or person private.

- ✔ **Increasing productivity without being annoying:** Attorneys are also out of the office a great deal at court or in meetings.

  Wireless connections and the capability to collaborate remotely serve to increase their (highly billable) productivity. The judge may frown on counsel tip-tapping away on a laptop keyboard in court, but probably won't mind you quietly writing on a Tablet PC.

- ✔ **Giving presentations:** Lawyers are big users of graphics to make their point in court, from showing the course of a hit and run driver in a traffic accident to showing charts and graphs of ballistics or DNA findings.

  With Tablet PC, lawyers cannot only run a presentation in a courtroom or at a deposition, for example with PowerPoint, but they can annotate their presentations with ink. They can also annotate a scanned version of an original document without permanently changing it.

NoteTalk gets lawyers talking

Leszynski Group is developing a customized legal document management application called NoteTalk in conjunction with a large international law firm. Using NoteTalk, attorneys can find and work with critical client and case information, and even access documents on file with the court, from the office or the road.

The application enables users to synchronize voice notes with handwritten notes, so information (whether dictated or handwritten by lawyers) can be cataloged by case. The application will make it possible to gather and organize legal documents in a variety of formats.

And because there's a persistent rumor that lawyers like to hear themselves talk, use of voice notes can now expand beyond the capabilities of Windows XP for Tablet PC's Sticky Notes, providing customized extensions for Windows Media Player.

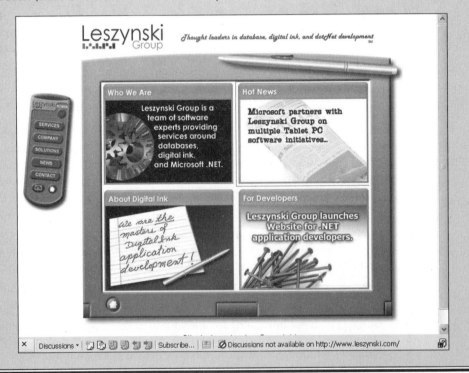

Manufacturing a need for Tablet PC

You may not immediately think of a noisy, dusty shop floor as the home of hi-tech, but consider a typical workday for a shop foreman and see if you can spot how Tablet PC could fit in:

Joe is a shop foreman at an automobile manufacturing plant located on a large corporate campus just outside Detroit. He spends all day going between meetings in the main building and the shop floor ten minutes away. When he jots down a note about a problem on the line, he has to hike back to his office to write up an e-mail about it and get a management decision about the best course of action. Safety auditors from the Union strolling the shop floor have the same problem as Joe — after taking notes, they have to get back to a desktop computer to write up their reports, wasting time and risking data entry error.

Manufacturing is a fast-paced business; delays on the line, materials that arrive late, and safety incidents can change a good day to a bad one in the blink of an eye. Speed of information transmission between the manufacturing facility and corporate headquarters — or even the office at the back of the building — is important. Here's how Tablet PC helps:

- ✔ **Fast communication:** The clipboard of yesterday can be replaced with a Tablet PC to save the time it takes people in manufacturing to communicate data they gather on the floor to management in another location. Their handwritten notes can now be sent out in seconds, speeding up on-the-fly decisions about safety, inventory, productivity, broken equipment, and more.

  Workers can even read manuals as electronic documents stored on Tablet PCs. An extra bonus to this paperless scenario — that the manuals can be updated easily.

- ✔ **Streamlined scheduling:** Production scheduling can be streamlined with up-to-the-minute information about the line input by hand and instantly connected to inventory and work schedules through sophisticated ERP (enterprise resource planning) systems.

The sales force and Tablet PC

Up to now, this chapter has taken a look at vertical industries. Frankly, sales is more of a *horizontal* business use than a vertical one. That is, the sales function spreads across all sorts of vertical industries that have the need to sell their products or services. But this is such a logical use for Tablet PCs, I include it in this group, odd duck though it is.

Sales people share many of the characteristics you've read about in other sections of this chapter. They are on the road a lot, and have limited space to use a computer (such as in a car or a company waiting area). They have a need to retrieve information from the home office, such as pricing charts, product inventory, or online catalogs, as well as to transmit data back, such as a rush sales order that can't wait until they make it back to the office.

Tablet PC meets all those needs, enabling salespeople to access their company network or a Web site to get product data. They can fill out order forms with their stylus pens, and e-mail an order instantly to headquarters. They can even capture customer signatures for orders on the Tablet PC. When an order is placed, they can track the order online as they travel.

Speaking of traveling, a perfect use for Tablet PC is to download maps and directions off the Internet, and make travel arrangements. ESRI has released a Tablet PC compatible version of their GIS mapping software that helps sales people find customer locations. Salespeople can also jot appointments and travel plans into their online planner with their Tablet PC pen.

Keeping up

One use of Tablet PC that will appeal to busy salespeople is that it enables them to download and read magazines on the comfortable and legible screen. With the need to stay competitive and keep up with industry trends, combined with travel downtime sitting on a plane or train, reading electronic magazines is a natural fit. Receive your e-magazines before the paper ones hit the newsstand, and read them anytime — online or off.

You can even use products such as Microsoft Snippet to clip parts of articles and send them to customers, or e-mail entire articles.

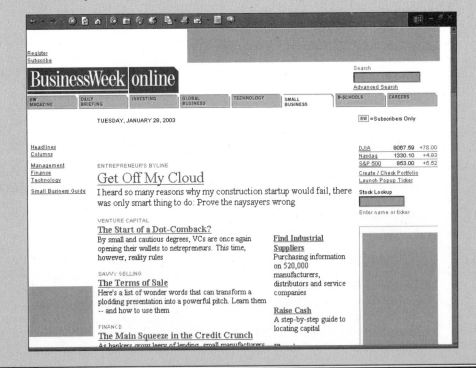

Here are some other ideas for using Tablet PC in the sales field:

- **Presentations:** The convertible model Tablet PCs are great for giving one-on-one customer presentations; you can just spin the screen around and still have the keyboard in front of you to run a presentation.

  Navigating a presentation with voice commands means that even a user with no external keyboard can move around a presentation while the customer views it.

- **Maintaining contact with customers:** Customer relationship management is another aspect of sales that Tablet PC can be helpful with.

  Products such as Franklin Covey Tablet Planner for Tablet PC help keep contact information in one place, and the personal touch of handwritten e-mails can make customers take notice of these unique sales communications.

Use handwriting to prioritize, work with action codes, add notes, and sort your to-do list using the Franklin Covey planning system.

Education: Learning with your Tablet

Quick — think of a setting where lots of people who don't even have an office to sit in need to get information from other people and document that information so they can study it later on. Can't think of an answer? Okay, add a keg of beer. (Aha. I knew you'd see the light. . . .)

College may be the perfect environment for Tablet PC, in part because of a technology-savvy user group. When e-textbooks become more prevalent, the little Tablet PC can replace a stack of heavy books students have to carry from class to class.

Tablet PC can be used in a classroom setting where thirty people clacking away on keyboards would be distracting (to say the least). And if students are equipped with Tablet PCs, then schools can save the cost of a computer lab, which often offers limited hours and less-than-state-of-the-art computers.

In some colleges, students are required to have a computer and even a laptop, so Tablet PC offers a similarly priced replacement. Students collaborating on team projects can stay in communication across campus or from their homes on school breaks.

Here are some other academic uses for Tablet PC:

- **Lesson planning and presentations:** Professors can use the Tablet PC to store course notes and bring them to class.

  They can make their own notes on course content when interesting questions or topics come up in discussion without having to balance a keyboard model laptop.

- **Grading:** Professors can also use Tablet PC in their grading process. They can mark up student papers with ink and e-mail the graded paper back, even adding a voice Sticky Note to an electronically submitted assignment.

  They can post grades to student records using a school's wireless network. In addition, planning tools help to keep track of assignments and due dates, as well as enabling a teacher to take class attendance by checking off an on-screen form with a pen.

- **Distance learning:** Distance learning gives people in geographically diverse settings access to online course material for remote learning. By using online meeting software (such as NetMeeting) with Tablet PC's pen functionality, remote students can participate in live discussions — and even use Ink to add notes and annotations to a virtual whiteboard in real time.

  Such a personal interaction makes distance learning a much more user-friendly experience.

MIT tests Tablet PC with robotics design

MIT recently worked with Microsoft on an experiment called iCampus. During a week-long conference on robotics, students worked together on a design project using Tablet PCs. In an effort to examine how technology can integrate with the educational environment, students found that ink and wireless capabilities improved the way they worked together and cut down on the need for face-to-face meeting time to complete the project. Now MIT is looking at ways to create project-based courses that can use the Tablet PC for both collaboration and personal computing.

Index

Notes

Notes

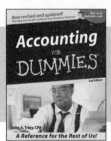

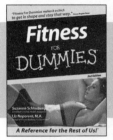

FOR DUMMIES®

A world of resources to help you grow

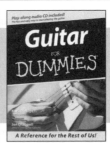

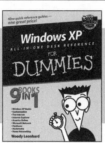
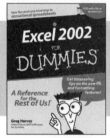

FOR DUMMIES®

Helping you expand your horizons and realize your potential

INTERNET

0-7645-0894-6

0-7645-1659-0

0-7645-1642-6

Also available:

America Online 7.0 For Dummies
(0-7645-1624-8)

Genealogy Online For Dummies
(0-7645-0807-5)

The Internet All-in-One Desk Reference For Dummies
(0-7645-1659-0)

Internet Explorer 6 For Dummies
(0-7645-1344-3)

The Internet For Dummies Quick Reference
(0-7645-1645-0)

Internet Privacy For Dummies
(0-7645-0846-6)

Researching Online For Dummies
(0-7645-0546-7)

Starting an Online Business For Dummies
(0-7645-1655-8)

DIGITAL MEDIA

0-7645-1664-7

0-7645-1675-2

0-7645-0806-7

Also available:

CD and DVD Recording For Dummies
(0-7645-1627-2)

Digital Photography All-in-One Desk Reference For Dummies
(0-7645-1800-3)

Digital Photography For Dummies Quick Reference
(0-7645-0750-8)

Home Recording for Musicians For Dummies
(0-7645-1634-5)

MP3 For Dummies
(0-7645-0858-X)

Paint Shop Pro "X" For Dummies
(0-7645-2440-2)

Photo Retouching & Restoration For Dummies
(0-7645-1662-0)

Scanners For Dummies
(0-7645-0783-4)

GRAPHICS

0-7645-0817-2

0-7645-1651-5

0-7645-0895-4

Also available:

Adobe Acrobat 5 PDF For Dummies
(0-7645-1652-3)

Fireworks 4 For Dummies
(0-7645-0804-0)

Illustrator 10 For Dummies
(0-7645-3636-2)

QuarkXPress 5 For Dummies
(0-7645-0643-9)

Visio 2000 For Dummies
(0-7645-0635-8)

FOR DUMMIES®

The advice and explanations you need to succeed

SELF-HELP, SPIRITUALITY & RELIGION

Sex FOR DUMMIES
Dr. Ruth K. Westheimer
A Reference for the Rest of Us!

0-7645-5302-X

Parenting FOR DUMMIES
A Reference for the Rest of Us!

0-7645-5418-2

Religion FOR DUMMIES
The God Squad
A Reference for the Rest of Us!

0-7645-5264-3

Also available:

The Bible For Dummies
(0-7645-5296-1)

Buddhism For Dummies
(0-7645-5359-3)

Christian Prayer For Dummies
(0-7645-5500-6)

Dating For Dummies
(0-7645-5072-1)

Judaism For Dummies
(0-7645-5299-6)

Potty Training For Dummies
(0-7645-5417-4)

Pregnancy For Dummies
(0-7645-5074-8)

Rekindling Romance For Dummies
(0-7645-5303-8)

Spirituality For Dummies
(0-7645-5298-8)

Weddings For Dummies
(0-7645-5055-1)

PETS

Puppies FOR DUMMIES
Sarah Hodgson
A Reference for the Rest of Us!

0-7645-5255-4

Dog Training FOR DUMMIES
Jack Volhard
Wendy Volhard
A Reference for the Rest of Us!

0-7645-5286-4

Cats FOR DUMMIES
A Reference for the Rest of Us!

0-7645-5275-9

Also available:

Labrador Retrievers For Dummies
(0-7645-5281-3)

Aquariums For Dummies
(0-7645-5156-6)

Birds For Dummies
(0-7645-5139-6)

Dogs For Dummies
(0-7645-5274-0)

Ferrets For Dummies
(0-7645-5259-7)

German Shepherds For Dummies
(0-7645-5280-5)

Golden Retrievers For Dummies
(0-7645-5267-8)

Horses For Dummies
(0-7645-5138-8)

Jack Russell Terriers For Dummies
(0-7645-5268-6)

Puppies Raising & Training Diary For Dummies
(0-7645-0876-8)

EDUCATION & TEST PREPARATION

Spanish FOR DUMMIES
Speak Spanish — the fun and easy way!
A Reference for the Rest of Us!
Susana Wald

0-7645-5194-9

Algebra FOR DUMMIES
Mary Jane Sterling
A Reference for the Rest of Us!

0-7645-5325-9

The ACT FOR DUMMIES
A Reference for the Rest of Us!
Suzee Vlk

0-7645-5210-4

Also available:

Chemistry For Dummies
(0-7645-5430-1)

English Grammar For Dummies
(0-7645-5322-4)

French For Dummies
(0-7645-5193-0)

The GMAT For Dummies
(0-7645-5251-1)

Inglés Para Dummies
(0-7645-5427-1)

Italian For Dummies
(0-7645-5196-5)

Research Papers For Dummies
(0-7645-5426-3)

The SAT I For Dummies
(0-7645-5472-7)

U.S. History For Dummies
(0-7645-5249-X)

World History For Dummies
(0-7645-5242-2)

Available wherever books are sold. Go to www.dummies.com or call 1-877-762-2974 to order direct.

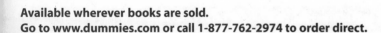